Exploring Race, Ethnicity, Gender, and Sexuality in Four Spanish Plays

Exploring Race, Ethnicity, Gender, and Sexuality in Four Spanish Plays

A Crisis of Identity

Beth Bernstein

LEXINGTON BOOKS
Lanham • Boulder • New York • London

Published by Lexington Books
An imprint of The Rowman & Littlefield Publishing Group, Inc.
4501 Forbes Boulevard, Suite 200, Lanham, Maryland 20706
www.rowman.com

6 Tinworth Street, London SE11 5AL, United Kingdom

Copyright © 2021 by The Rowman and Littlefield Publishing Group, Inc.

All rights reserved. No part of this book may be reproduced in any form or by any electronic or mechanical means, including information storage and retrieval systems, without written permission from the publisher, except by a reviewer who may quote passages in a review.

British Library Cataloguing in Publication Information Available

Library of Congress Cataloging-in-Publication Data

Names: Bernstein, Beth, 1974- author.
Title: Exploring race, ethnicity, gender, and sexuality in four Spanish plays : a crisis of identity / Beth Bernstein.
Description: Lanham : Lexington Books, [2021] | Includes bibliographical references and index. | Summary: "A Crisis of Identity explores the construction of identity and society's influence in four Spanish plays and discusses parallels to these works in popular culture. Through close reading and analysis covering race, ethnicity, gender, and sexuality, the author uncovers what lies behind the mask of each play's characters"—Provided by publisher.
Identifiers: LCCN 2021018631 (print) | LCCN 2021018632 (ebook) | ISBN 9781793620545 (cloth) | ISBN 9781793620552 (epub) | ISBN 9781793620569 (pbk)
Subjects: LCSH: Spanish drama—History and criticism. | Identity (Philosophical concept) in literature. | Cervantes Saavedra, Miguel de, 1547–1616. Retablo de las maravillas. | Vélez de Guevara, Luis, 1579–1644. Virtudes vencen señales. | García Lorca, Federico, 1898–1936. Público. | Pedrero, Paloma, 1957- Llamada de Lauren.
Classification: LCC PQ6102 .B47 2021 (print) | LCC PQ6102 (ebook) | DDC 862.009/353—dc23
LC record available at https://lccn.loc.gov/2021018631
LC ebook record available at https://lccn.loc.gov/2021018632

Contents

Acknowledgments   vii

Introduction   1

1   Marvelous Illusions: The Issue of *pureza de sangre* and Ethnic Identity in *El retablo de las maravillas*   11

2   A "Monstrous" Problem: Examining Issues of Race in *Virtudes vencen señales*   53

3   Struggling with the Mask of Conformity: Desire and Sexual Identity in *El público*   89

4   Living Beyond the Binary: Questioning Socially Accepted Gender Roles in *La llamada de Lauren*   119

Conclusion: Shifting Identities in Four Spanish Plays and Parallels in Modern Popular Culture   147

Works Cited   157

Index   167

About the Author   175

Acknowledgments

I am very lucky to have had so many supportive people in my life during the time I wrote this book. My husband, Aaron Bernstein, has been amazingly helpful and encouraging. He always had awesome ideas, provided fantastic tech support, and fueled me with excellent mochas and laughter during this whole journey. I would like to thank my outstanding mentor, Michael Kidd, whose incredible guidance has helped me tremendously in writing this book. My thanks also goes out to Susana Rivera, a wonderful professor whose encouraging words helped me to develop my ideas at the beginning of this project. I am grateful for my parents, Ira and Gerri Epstein, who have been with me every step of the way during this process. My mother is an English teacher with an amazing eye for clear language, and I appreciated all her astute editing suggestions. I am thankful for my screenwriter sister, Jan Schwaid, who read my work and made fantastic editing suggestions. I appreciate the awesome support and mentoring from Ana Isabel Simon Alegre who believed in me and without whom I would have never embarked on this scholarly voyage. I could not ask for better or more supportive colleagues in the Department of World Languages and Literatures at Texas State University. I am grateful to my friend and colleague, María de las Nieves Pujalte, whose valuable insight helped guide my writing. I am indebted to Lucy Harney, the wonderful chair of my department. She supported me in my scholarly endeavors by encouraging me on my path to publishing and making it possible for me to attend conferences and expand my horizons. I also greatly appreciate Moira Di Mauro-Jackson's wonderful advice, and the encouragement of Esther Horn and Kayla Hill during this process. Thank you to Antonio Gragera whose expertise on translations was invaluable. I can't thank Candice Hastings and Aimee Roundtree enough for creating online writing groups for faculty at Texas State. Their helpful suggestions and encouragement during the pandemic kept me connected to my awesome university community and gave me the push I needed to keep me motivated to write. I appreciate the expert guidance of Holly Buchanan who has been an outstanding, patient, and understanding editor. Thank you to my creative, funny kids, Ari and Shayna, who keep me young at heart and hopeful for the future. I am also grateful for the following family members, friends, and colleagues whose support and encouragement meant the world to me: Carol and Marvin Bernstein, Aaron Epstein, Laura Bernstein, Yuri Porras, Nicole Villalpando, Marcos Romero, Sharon Keefe Ugalde, Eliani Basile, Wyatt Ince, David Navarro, Anthony Cárdenas, Beth Smith, Catherine Jaffe, and Valentina Glajar.

Introduction

Who hasn't struggled with the idea of conformity? Should we show the world who we really are? Should we conform in order to meet the ideals of society? What *is* normal? Normalcy confines us to a strict set of rules, but many dare to confront these rules and attempt to change them. Freedom from these rules gives us greater liberty to be ourselves. At times, society molds our personal identities, but many people have questioned the identities that society imposes upon them.

In this book, I discuss the construction of identity and society's influence on identity in four Spanish theatrical works. In the theatrical works from the seventeenth century, I focus on issues of race and ethnicity. I discuss rebellion against heteronormativity, as portrayed in the plays from the twentieth century. The Spanish theatrical works *El retablo de las maravillas (The Marvelous Puppet Show)* by Miguel de Cervantes Saavedra (1615); *Virtudes vencen señales (Virtues overcome Signs)* by Vélez de Guevara (1620); *El público (The Audience)* by Federico García Lorca (1929); and *La llamada de Lauren (Lauren's Call)* by Paloma Pedrero (1985) all deal with the shifting identities of the characters. In each theatrical work, characters struggle with different aspects of identity, such as ethnicity, gender, sexual orientation, and race. As they reach to define themselves, internal and external pressures help them to interpret what is acceptable behavior, and some who rebel find that their differences are not generally accepted by society. The characters in some of the plays must wear masks and create false identities in order to face society, and, therefore, a fear of true identity is a motivating factor for these characters. Some deny their real identity while others create facades to mask their authentic selves.

Through close reading and analysis of these plays, I explore the central problem of the main characters in each play. In *El retablo de las maravillas*, the characters are so obsessed with the possibility of being Jewish that they accept a false reality in order to escape an imagined identity. In *Virtudes vencen señales*, Filipo, a black prince, denies his ethnicity and identity and exclaims that he is white and noble on the inside although he believes that he is black and "monstrous" on the outside. In *El público*, the main character's mask of conformity crumbles, and his queer identity is revealed. Performance and reality blend, and gender identity is called into question in *La llamada de Lauren* as the character Pedro becomes the woman he had never allowed himself to be. The central characters in these plays battle with self-definition. In this book, I will be exploring the many aspects of racial, ethnic, sexual, and gender identity through the analysis of characters portrayed in Spanish drama. To analyze these plays, I will use quotes from these works, along with quotes from other sources, and include my own English translations of all quotes which appear in Spanish. When translating quotes from the two seventeenth-century plays, I did not try to write the quotes in verse, but rather I focused on translating the message and meaning of each quote.

Society places a heavy burden upon all who function within its strict boundaries, and variations from what is seen as normal are not generally accepted. This book will explore the idea of a flexible or fluid identity which is not bound by the narrow, black-and-white laws of society. Having an ambiguous identity causes the characters much psychological pain since societal pressure strives to shape and mold their internal identity against their will. This book will offer a close reading of the psychological struggle of the "abnormal" character who is driven by society to cover all differences with a mask which will eventually devour and kill the character's true identity.

The twentieth-century theatrical works and the Golden Age dramas hold a mirror up to Spanish society and expose its ugly narrow-mindedness. The playwrights of these works allow us to see the character that is marginalized by society as a person instead of an anonymous outcast. Although the seventeenth- and twentieth-century plays were written in different time periods, we see continuity in the way the characters with alternative identities are treated by society. In both periods, censorship and oppression are condoned by the governing powers. In his book *A Concise History of Spain,* Henry Kamen discusses the foundation of the Spanish Inquisition in 1478:

> The tribunal set itself a task which was more recognizably racialist than religious: to purify peninsular Catholicism by eliminating from the Church and its clergy all descendants of Jewish or Moorish blood. The task was carried out with an efficiency that has left a permanent mark on Spanish history. Even in modern times distrust of Jews and Arabs has played a significant role in Spanish politics. (57)

Throughout many centuries, Spaniards were obsessed with blood purity, and anti-Semitism was accepted as a part of life. This attitude continued during the sixteenth and seventeenth centuries when Spain was ruled by the absolute monarchs Philip II (1556–1598), Philip III (1598–1621) and Philip IV (1621–1665). During these years, political decline and poverty only hardened many Spaniards' hatred towards Jews and other marginalized groups since they were used as scapegoats for all problems in society (Kamen, 83, 85, 88).

The situation of marginalized people did not improve a great deal in the twentieth century. In 1931, the Second Republic sparked optimism among Spain's intellectuals, and they hoped for new freedom from censorship. This hope was dashed, however, when violence erupted, and General Francisco Franco seized power and was named leader of Spain in 1937. During Franco's dictatorship, he imposed a rigid censorship which made it impossible for people with alternative identities to express themselves. Even after Franco's death in 1975, Spanish society had difficulty letting go of old views and accepting people who were different. Marginalized groups were treated as outcasts in the seventeenth and twentieth centuries, a fact that is reflected in the drama of these time periods.

There are several studies about the representation of identity in peninsular plays, and some critics choose to focus on one playwright's work, while others compare different theatrical works.[1] I use a modern lens to link these particular theatrical works, in light of the fact that they all deal with the challenges of identity and society in various ways.

The seventeenth and the twentieth century are the zenith periods of Spanish theater, and therefore, I chose theatrical works from both these periods to best show reactions to the authoritarianism that challenges individuality. In the seventeenth and the twentieth century, the theatrical works specifically show people attempting to overcome oppression that was brought upon them by identities not accepted by society. In the seventeenth century, people in Spanish society were dealing with the repercussions of the inquisition, and blood purity and lineage were extremely important. I chose two works from the seventeenth century or the Golden Age of Spain because people were constantly dealing with discrimination due to ethnicity and a perceived connection to a Jewish heritage. During this period, there were many famous writers who were prolific and openly wrote about society's prejudices. Works from seventeenth-century Spain are especially important in terms of identity.

Oppression is also a main issue in twentieth-century Spain since this period is incredibly significant because of the dictatorship of Miguel Primo de Rivera and the rise of Franco. The Francoist regime oppressed people who did not fit into the accepted social norms. After Franco's death, there was the eventual rebellion against Francoist ideals of homogenous Spanish Society, and we see this rebellion reflected in Spanish theater written after Franco's death.

Using an eclectic approach supported by contemporary theories of race, gender, and sexuality, I analyze the four plays in terms of identity, and I show how society imposes the construction of identity. By employing this approach to critically analyze the literature, I use several theories and critical articles that discuss important elements of the individual plays. The following theorists aid in the exploration of the theatrical works and help to gain a more profound understanding of the plays. Lionel Abel's theory of metatheatre is useful to address the "play within a play" aspect of both *El retablo de las maravillas* and *La llamada de Lauren*. Although these plays are from two different centuries and deal with wildly different aspects of identity, they both share the intriguing theme of metatheatricality. Sander Gilman's theories of "The Other" and self-hatred help to define motivation and identity in the characters of the theatrical works that deal with race and ethnicity. The theories of Bertolt Brecht, Sigmund Freud, Richard Hornby, and Mikhail Bakhtin aid in the analysis of the tricky, rule-bending twentieth century plays that have an edgy, performative nature and deal with themes of sexuality that are often shocking and thought-provoking. This diverse theoretical approach facilitates a deep analysis of the complex situations of the characters in these plays.

According to Lionel Abel, Metatheatre is a philosophical commentary on the theatricality of life where illusion and reality are often blurred (60–61). One can apply the ideas of metatheatre to *El retablo de las maravillas* since the main characters Chirinos and Chanfalla are fully aware that their theatrical performance has the ability to manipulate the villagers' concepts of reality and identity. These "puppet masters" are themselves theatrical entities who can rewrite the other characters' visions of reality.

The village characters in the play *El retablo de las maravillas* are led to believe that the inability to see Chanfalla and Chirino's "puppet show" indicates their Jewish heritage. In *Jewish Self-Hatred*, Sander Gilman clarifies and defines the idea of self-hatred:

> Self-hatred arises when the mirages of stereotypes are confused with realities within the world, when the desire for acceptance forces the acknowledgment of one's difference. (4)

During the imaginary performance, these characters are in denial of their supposed Jewishness, which leads to self-hatred. None of the villagers dares to accept his "difference" for fear of being marginalized by society. Thus, their feelings of shame and hatred are internalized as they externally deny their Jewish origins. Acceptance is the main issue here for the foolish country folk, and all must prove that they are not the Other to continue to live within the boundaries of their small world.

In *Virtudes vencen señales*, the white king of Albania was shocked, frightened, and unnerved when his wife gives birth to a black son. The king was unable to predict that his son would be black, and this allows him to reject his own son as a foreigner who must be imprisoned. In *Difference and Pathology: Stereotypes of Sexuality, Race, and Madness*, Sander Gilman explains why people fear "The Other":

> When, however, the sense of order and control undergoes stress, when doubt is cast on the self's ability to control the internalized world that it has created for itself, an anxiety appears. . . . We project that anxiety onto the Other, externalizing our loss of control. The Other is thus stereotyped, labeled with a set of signs paralleling (or mirroring) our loss of control. . . . Difference is that which threatens order and control; it is the polar opposite to our group. (20–21)

Therefore, the royal father's fear of Filipo stems from a loss of control. He feels that the order of the kingdom is threatened by the existence of the dark prince, and he washes his hands of the whole situation by giving up his only son and condemning him to an isolated life in a tower. The character Filipo represents Gilman's idea of the Other.

Lorca explores his own psyche using incongruous, dream-like images; thus, he uses a surrealist approach in his play, *El público*. According to Bertolt Brecht, the new theater of the twentieth century shakes the public out of its tranquil state in order to make it aware of social issues. The public is supposed to react and learn from the actions in the theater, and through the theater, the audience develops a consciousness, which in turn produces a change in society. Although we are not sure if Lorca is consciously employing Brechtian concepts of theater, the surrealist premise of his play coincides with Brecht's ideas. We see an overlap between the two approaches to theater in that Lorca's surrealist images also cause the alienation effect which is essential in Brechtian theater. We are not familiar with the odd juxtaposition of images in Lorca's play, and therefore, Lorca's work prompts us to react and ponder society's treatment of people with alternative identities. Lorca experiments with the use of shocking and alienating images in his play *El público* to convey a message about sexual identity. In my study of this play, I will also use the theory of Freud and the surrealist manifestos to analyze Lorca's theatrical work.

I will also use Abel's concepts of Metatheater to analyze the idea that illusion and reality merge in *La llamada de Lauren* when the couple marries amidst Carnival revelry. It is not clear if Pedro's marriage to Rosa was merely a performance or if it was a real union of two people in love. I will use Richard Hornby's ideas on metadrama in order to explore the aspect of role-playing in Pedrero's play. In *Drama, Metadrama, and Perception*,

Hornby agrees with some of the ideas of performance theory.[2] Performance theory calls into question the fine line between performance and reality and makes us ponder the notion that everything might be a performance; thus, we are duped into accepting an imagined reality. Hornby explains Pedro's use of metatheatrical games as a way of escaping reality and exploring his fantasies. Outside pressures limit Pedro's behavior, but Pedro uses role-play as a way to alleviate tensions caused by his prohibited, hidden identity.

In *Rabelais and His World*, Mikhail Bakhtin also explains that one can use Carnival as a vehicle to escape reality. According to Bakhtin, the Carnival festivities allow a temporary shift in social structure which liberates people from their socially accepted roles (10–11). Therefore, it is acceptable for Pedro to explore his desires and dress as a woman during the time of Carnival.

These theorists assist in my literary analysis of the four plays that focus on the common theme of identity and the conflict of a crisis of identity. Therefore, they help to construct a more profound and three-dimensional understanding of the characters and their motivations as portrayed in these works.

A BRIEF OVERVIEW OF EACH THEATRICAL WORK

El retablo de las maravillas

In the play *El retablo de las maravillas* by Miguel de Cervantes Saavedra, the rustic characters are made to question their own *pureza de sangre* when Chanfalla explains that one must be of pure Christian lineage in order to see the magical puppet show.[3] Anyone who has "alguna raza de confeso" (belongs to the Jewish race) (220), will not be able to see the performance, and for these gullible characters, the *Retablo de las maravillas* proves to be a test of Christianity. Of course, no one can see the images of the *Retablo*, but everyone emphatically proclaims the delightful and exciting nature of the play. An admission by any character that he cannot view the actions of the drama is taken as a confession of Jewish heritage; therefore, all must participate in the illusion to avoid being exiled and labeled as the Other. Ironically, none of the villagers has anything to fear in terms of their Christian identity since it is well known that most Spaniards from rural areas were *cristianos viejos*. In his play, Cervantes criticizes the hateful attitude of the general public towards *conversos* and Jews.[4] Cervantes also criticizes the self-hatred and hypocrisy exhibited by many Spaniards who deny any Jewish heritage but probably are of *converso* origin. *El retablo de las maravillas* is the most subversive of the two Golden Age plays since the playwright criticizes an accepted social order. I will examine this play by discussing the important elements, such as symbols and characters, which appear throughout the work.

The topic of identity is as interesting and controversial now as it was in the seventeenth century. People are still labeled as "other" and excluded from the dominant reference group.

Sacha Baron Cohen, a popular Jewish comedian from England, who majored in history at Cambridge University, certainly has fun playing with issues concerning ethnicity, gender, sexuality, and race. Through his alter egos, he manages to touch upon various stereotypes concerning identity. His most famous character, Borat, is an anti-Semitic, homophobic, misogynistic reporter from Kazakhstan. This character is the star of two movies, and he first appeared on the HBO comedy, "Da Ali G Show" where he famously encouraged people to shamelessly demonstrate their acceptance of antisemitism. Baron Cohen is a comic genius and could even be called a modern-day picaresque hero. Cohen uses his character as a tool to critique antisemitism and unacceptable ideas in society. Sacha Baron Cohen's comedy and *El retablo de las maravillas* both serve as scathing social commentary, meant to highlight and criticize the injustice of ethnic prejudices in society.

Virtudes vencen señales

In the play *Virtudes vencen señales* by Vélez de Guevara, Prince Filipo is labeled as the Other because he is seen as different and, therefore, potentially dangerous. Filipo's parents are both white, but he is born black because as he was conceived, his father, King of Albania, was looking at a magnificent tapestry hung above the bed. The image on the tapestry was the portrait of a beautiful black queen. This magnificent artistic image had the power to impregnate the queen with a black son. When Filipo is born, his color shocks and disturbs his father who takes it as a bad omen. They announce that their son has died at birth, and they lock him away in a tower.

Filipo's father Lisandro rejects the physical appearance of Filipo and even calls his own son a monster. When Filipo sees his reflection for the first time, he is frightened of his blackness and refuses to accept his own appearance. Filipo echoes his father's sentiments and calls himself a "monstruo." The Prince voices his extreme self-hatred, and he expresses disbelief and horror upon seeing his black reflection. Later, he denies his black identity and claims that his soul is white while his body is black. As the Other, Filipo ignites a feeling of fear and repulsion in himself and others. His difference excludes him from society at first, but he later proves his noble and virtuous nature which will allow him to become the king of Albania. He denies his ethnicity and identity and exclaims that he is white and noble on the inside, although he recognizes that he is black and, therefore, vehemently rejects his appearance.

This play is not as subversive as *El retablo de las maravillas* since Vélez de Guevara rejects the idea of racial equality because he emphasizes that Filipo is truly white. In the end, the social order for seventeenth-century Spain is left a bit askew because a black man will assume power over white men. Despite Filipo's blackness, he is still allowed to be the future king of Albania since he professes that his soul is white thus denying his racial identity. A linear analysis is very conducive to this theatrical work because the main character develops his racial identity as the play progresses.

El público

In modern society, differing sexual identities that are not heteronormative are becoming more accepted, but there is still a struggle to define what society deems "normal" in terms of sexuality. In the play *El público*, Federico García Lorca struggles with the idea of sexual identity and social conformity. He addresses the taboo subject of alternative sexuality which could never be tolerated by the ultra-conservative, Spanish Catholic society of the 1930s. In *El público*, the characters are torn between showing their true feelings and conforming to a society that accepts only heteronormative relationships. In this play, the main character, the Director, struggles with the decision either to reveal his sexual orientation or disguise it in order to be accepted by society. This personal battle is reflected in his choice to direct the "open-air theater" or the "theater beneath the sand." The open-air theater is socially acceptable to the public, yet it stifles the Director's authentic identity. The theater beneath the sand allows the Director and the other characters to reveal their innermost feelings without hiding their alternative sexual identities. At first, the director is adamant about directing the open-air theater, but eventually other characters in the play convince him to become involved with the unconventional theater beneath the sand. However, because of societal pressure to hide his true sexuality, the Director finally retreats into the world of false appearances, and he chooses to dedicate himself to the open-air theater.

Since the spacio-temporal plane of *El público* is surrealistic and disjointed, I will not take a linear approach to analyzing it. Instead, I will break it down and examine the many symbols, characters, and other important elements that appear throughout the work.

La llamada de Lauren

The play *La llamada de Lauren* by Paloma Pedrero also deals with the repression of sexual identity and the desire to fit into society. In this play, we follow the psychological journey of the character Pedro who until now has repressed his desires to dress as a woman and assume a new identity. We also see how

Rosa, Pedro's wife, is affected by Pedro's revealed secret. Rosa must undergo a psychological journey as well. Both *La llamada de Lauren* and *El público* address the theme of sexual identity and the struggle against conformity within a rigid society. These twentieth-century plays focus more on sexual identity than on questions of race and ethnicity. Many are reaching for acceptance and equality for all who live non-heteronormative lifestyles, and, therefore, these issues are made the focus of contemporary theatrical works. I will examine *La llamada de Lauren* in a linear fashion because we can thus see how the development of the characters evolves during the action of the play.

In *La llamada de Lauren*, Pedro feels the need to be a woman at times, and he has felt this longing ever since he was a boy. The fact that Pedro is a person who wears clothing that is thought of as feminine attire does not automatically make him gay; in fact, he proclaims that he loves his wife. In *Vested Interests*, Marjorie Garber acknowledges the confusion between cross-dressing and alternative sexuality by acknowledging that most people cannot fathom that a male who cross-dresses could be heterosexual (129–130). Many people think that cross-dressing and sexual orientation are linked although this is not the case for non-heteronormative straight men who wear feminine clothing and are sexually attracted to women.

In conclusion, society's influence will always help to mold identity. This is clear in Golden Age drama. In the twentieth-century Spanish drama, there are those who will rebel against the accepted norms, and the struggle against conformity and heteronormativity is always difficult. Sexual identity cannot be easily described since it is made up of many factors and cannot be labeled as black or white. Gender identity and sexual identity are different concepts and exclusive of each other, and they do not have to follow the heteronormative rules. In this book, I will be exploring the many aspects of racial, ethnic, sexual, and gender identity through the analysis of characters and their crises of identity as portrayed in Spanish drama.

NOTES

1. See Stoll for an in-depth study of gender and identity in theatrical works by Tirso de Molina. Sloane explores the subject of identity in four plays by Calderón. Seator focuses on the idea of identity in the works of Alfonso Sastre, and Evers analyzes Spanish theatrical works and discusses identity in Spain after Franco. See Friedman and Smith for an analysis of identity in plays about Pedro de Urdemalas. For a comparison of works by two female dramatists from the seventeenth century, see Wilkins.

2. For a comprehensive explanation of performance theory, see Carlson. See Pellegrini for more information on performance, psychoanalysis, and race. Judith

Butler, a key figure of performance theory, suggests that performance is at the root of all our actions, and that gender is a social construct. See Butler's *Gender Trouble* and *Bodies That Matter* for a treatment of the problem of identity and performance. See Thacker for an exploration of the metatheatrical techniques employed by Spanish playwrights of the Golden Age.

3. In his book *Inquisition and Society in Spain*, Kamen describes *pureza de sangre* or *limpieza de sangre* as "purity of blood; freedom from any taint of semitic blood" (302).

4. The term *cristiano viejo* is a label applied to any Spaniard who claims to have no traceable Jewish lineage (Gerber 127). Kamen defines "*converso*," a term that describes "Christianized Jews and their descendants" (302). Although Kamen states that the term "*converso*" "could also be applied to converted Muslims," (302) it is more commonly used for those of Jewish origin. Gerber discusses the idea of the *converso* in Spain and explains, ". . . for most of the population, the conviction began to spread that Jewish ancestry or "race," not professed religious belief, defined who was a Jew" (127).

Chapter 1

Marvelous Illusions

The Issue of pureza de sangre *and Ethnic Identity in* El retablo de las maravillas

The discrimination against the Sephardic Jews of Spain lasted from long before the Inquisition and expulsion of 1492 and lingered for centuries.[1] After Jews were forced to either leave Spain or convert, the *conversos* were treated cruelly even though they had professed their devotion to Christianity. It is clear that the religion of these *conversos* had nothing to do with the perception that they were Jewish through their ancestry or their perceived "race." Although the conversion of a member of someone's family had taken place many years ago, the person was still viewed by Spanish society as a Jew who had been tainted by the blood of an ancestor; thus, society deemed it fair to discriminate against and oppress a person of Jewish origin. Gerber explains the converted Jew's difficult position in society:

> Thousands of them had only the dimmest memories of their prior religion by this time, yet in the eyes of so-called Old Christians they bore the stigma of their origins. (127)

A line was drawn between Old Christians and New Christians, and there was no escaping the label of *converso* even if many generations separated people from their practicing Jewish kin. The *conversos* were in limbo since they could be the most devout Christians and follow the Catholic religion to the utmost, but they were never seen as true Christians because of their lineage. They were helpless to improve their situation in Spanish society. In 1451, "Purity of Blood" or *limpieza de sangre* statutes were introduced to legalize and uphold the oppression of *conversos*. Pope Nicholas V did not approve these ordinances since they went against his belief that all Catholics were equal, and one's religion, not ethnicity, was the determining factor of a true Christian (Gerber 127). Even though the Pope frowned upon them, the *limpieza de sangre* laws were approved in 1451. According to Gerber:

> "Blood purity" statutes would not only prevail but increasingly cast an ever-wider net throughout Spain and Portugal in the sixteenth century. By 1555, *limpieza de sangre* was an official requirement for entry to public office; thereafter, all descendants of Jews were barred from holding positions of authority in the army, university, the Church, and the municipality. In order to discredit Spaniards of questionable or ambiguous ancestry, elaborate books of genealogy were compiled. For the next several generations, until the odious statutes were wiped off the books in the eighteenth century, Catholic descendants of medieval converts were stigmatized unless they were able to devise or purchase false genealogies. (127–128)

Life was not easy in seventeenth-century Spain if one was shown or even suspected to be of "tainted" heritage. Much importance was placed on a person's lineage, and if someone was known to be of Jewish or Moorish origin, they were not seen as equal to "pure" Christians in the eyes of Spanish society.

Many people have speculated about Miguel de Cervantes Saavedra's lineage, and there is no completely conclusive evidence that Cervantes was indeed of Jewish origin.[2] Lokos discusses aspects of Cervantes' life that support the claim that he was a *converso*:

> The frequently cited reasons adduced as proof for the inclusion of Cervantes in the brotherhood of *conversos*, such as his marriage into a patently *converso* family in Esquivias, his frequent changes of residence, his failed attempts to go to Indias, and the association of his father and great-grandfather with the medical profession, have been amply documented and discussed by biographers. Moreover, to say *médico* in the Spain of the time was practically the equivalent of saying *converso*, as many literary texts of the period indicate. (117)

One thing is clear, though: Cervantes' questionable status as an Old Christian definitely hampered the author when he sought employment. In 1569, Cervantes was accused of injuring a man named Antonio de Sigura in a duel on the grounds of the Royal Court (McCrory 47). An arrest warrant was issued that called for Cervantes' right hand to be publicly hacked off after which he was to be banished from Madrid (McKendrick 37). This harsh punishment spurred Cervantes to flee to Italy and seek work. In Rome, he approached the prelate Giulio Acquaviva for a job as a chamberlain, but before he could be granted this job, he needed to produce documents proving his purity of blood. Lokos comments on these documents:

Clearly, Cervantes felt the need to defend himself due to significant difficulties he must have experienced in Italy. . . . It is essential to note that the *expedientes de limpieza (blood purity documents)* in the period were not executed at the petition of a particular person, while in this case, the document is drawn up at the request of Cervantes's father. Moreover, the language of the report indicates that it was created to serve the Cervantes family's needs in this particular situation. Notably missing from the proceedings are the prosecuting attorney *(el fiscal)* and any degree of judicial participation. . . . At best, the document could be said to possess a purely notarial content, but from a judicial standpoint, it must be considered to be entirely invalid and inconsequential. (118–119)

It is interesting that the one document that should prove Cervantes' *pureza de sangre* does more to prove the opposite. Far from showing Cervantes's "pure" Christian bloodline, this document actually makes one suspect that Cervantes was of *converso* origin since nothing in the document gives any concrete evidence of his Catholic lineage. By the same token, we do not have any real proof of Cervantes' status as a *converso*, so in terms of knowing the truth about Cervantes' lineage, we are neither here nor there. One thing we may conclude, though, from Cervantes' entremés (interlude or short theatrical work) *El retablo de las maravillas*, is that the writer was highly critical of the issue of *pureza de sangre*, and he deemed the Spanish society of the seventeenth-century foolish for its obsession with lineage.[3]

RETABLO AND ITS ROOTS

Between 1590 and 1615, Cervantes probably wrote the interlude *El retablo de las maravillas (The Marvelous Puppet Show),* along with seven other short plays and eight full-length plays (Reed 1). His theatrical works received a frosty reception by the theatrical companies, who rejected all his scripts. In 1615, ten years after the publication of the first part of *Don Quijote de la Mancha,* Cervantes's collection of theatrical works, *Ocho comedias, y ocho entremeses nuevos, nunca representados (Eight Comedies, and Eight New Interludes, Never Performed),* was published. In the prologue to this volume of plays, which is reprinted in Spadaccini's edition of Cervantes's *entremeses,* Cervantes explains his situation:

> Algunos años ha que volví yo a mi antigua ociosidad, y pensando que aún duraban los siglos donde corrían mis alabanzas, volví a componer algunas comedias; pero no hallé pájaros en los nidos de antaño; quiero decir que no hallé autor que me las pidiese, puesto que sabían que las tenía, y así las arrinconé en un cofre y las consagré y condené al perpetuo silencio. . . . Torné a pasar los ojos por

mis comedias y por algunos entremeses míos que con ellas estaban arrinconados, y vi no ser tan malas ni tan malos que no mereciesen salir de las tinieblas del ingenio de aquel autor a la luz de otros autores menos escrupulosos y más entendidos. (93–94)

Some years ago, I went back to my old idle pastime, and since people were still singing my praises during these years, I returned to compose some comedies; but I didn't find birds in the nests of yesteryear; I mean I did not find an author that asked for them although they knew I had them, and so I stowed them away in a chest and enshrined them and condemned them to perpetual silence. . . . I turned my eyes to my comedies and some interludes that were stowed with them, and I saw that they were not so bad, and they deserved to get out of the darkness of that author's ingenuity and into the light of other less scrupulous and more knowledgeable authors.

By publishing these works, Cervantes removes *El retablo de las maravillas* and his other plays from the prison of "perpetual silence" and makes them available to all readers.

The purpose of the *entremés* is to entertain the audience during the intermission of the performance of a longer theatrical work. Reed comments:

The interlude was performed most often between the first and second acts of the *comedia* by the same company representing the main play. As such, the short farce was restricted to brief, simple actions with very little of what we now call character development or serious themes, in order not to complicate the audience's shift in attention back to the full-length play at the conclusion of the interlude. Cervantes's *entremeses*, however, differ substantially from the accepted, performed drama of seventeenth-century Spain, incorporating profound ideas and complex structures which may have made them too unsuitable to function in the interlude's traditionally subordinate position within the dramatic performance. (3)

Given the fact that *El retablo de las maravillas* is complex and serves to criticize the attitude of Spanish society, theatrical companies rejected it, most likely because they were looking for interludes that would act as mindless entertainment for audiences that were looking only to be amused during the intermission of a longer play.

The basic premise of *El retablo de las maravillas* is similar to those of folktales written in several countries throughout the ages. This short play reinterprets the popular deception story in which tricksters present a "magical" object to a gullible audience. The tricksters claim that the object can be seen only by people who possess certain attributes, but since the object does not exist, the people involved in the scheme must pretend that they are able to see the object in order to avoid humiliation. Other versions of this folktale include *enxemplo* 32, "De lo que contesció a un rey con burladores que fizieron un paño, (Of what Occurred with Tricksters Who Made a Cloak for a King)" in *El Conde Lucanor* by Don Juan Manuel (1335); the German fable, *The Invisible Painting* (*Das unsichtbare Gemälde*) (1883); the story in chapter 27 of *Til Eulenspiegel* (1480); and, of course, Hans Christian Andersen's *The Emperor's New Clothes* (1837).[4] Molho describes the important elements involved in these deception stories:

> Nuestro cuento, que es una mistificación, comporta cuatro elementos necesarios: un mistificador (I), la mistificación en sí (II), la víctima o el mistificado (III), y, en fin, el desmistificador (IV); con la particularidad de que el elemento II se escinde en dos componentes, que son el objeto maravilloso (IIa) y los criterios de exclusión (IIb). (48)

> Our story, which is a mystification tale, involves four necessary elements: a mystifier (I), the mystification itself (II), the victim or the mystified (III), and, finally, the demystifier (IV); with the special feature that element II is split into two components, which are the wonderous object (IIa) and the criteria of exclusion (IIb).

Although each story varies with respect to the details involved in the different characteristics that Molho describes, these elements unify these folktales of trickery.[5] The hoax, or *mistificación*, might involve an imaginary painting, cloak, or puppet show. Although the swindlers use different types of nonexistent elements, their goal is the same: to cheat their unsuspecting victims, or *mistificados*, out of their money and shame them into lying and claiming that they see imaginary objects.[6]

THE MAIN DILEMMA IN *EL RETABLO*

El retablo de las maravillas contains all these elements typical of a tale involving a hoax. Chirinos and Chanfalla, the *mistificadores*, along with the musician Rabelín, devise a scheme to fleece a group of simple rural folk by using the townspeople's pride in their pure Christian heritage as the basis for the swindlers' trickery. Chanfalla explains that they will present, for a fee of course, a magical puppet show that will be visible only to those who possess certain "honorable" qualities:

Gobernador: ¿Y qué quiere decir *Retablo de las Maravillas*?
Chanfalla: Por las maravillosas cosas que en él se enseñan y muestran, viene a ser llamado Retablo de las Maravillas; el cual fabricó y compuso el sabio Tontonelo debajo de tales paralelos, rumbos, astros y estrellas, con tales puntos, caracteres y observaciones, que ninguno puede ver las cosas que en él se muestran, que tenga alguna raza de confeso, o no sea habido y procreado de sus padres de legítimo matrimonio; y el que fuere contagiado destas dos tan usadas enfermedades, despídase de ver las cosas, jamás vistas ni oídas, de mi retablo. (220)

Governor: And what does Marvelous Puppet Show mean?
Chanfalla: It is called The Marvelous Puppet Show because of the wonderful things it shows and teaches; it was created and written by the wise Foolini using such parallels, courses, stars and celestial bodies, with such items, symbols and observations, that none can see the things that are shown in it if one has any trace of Jewish blood, or is not from and has not been born of parents in a legitimate marriage; and whomever was infected with these two common diseases has no chance of viewing the things in my puppet show that have never been seen or heard before.

The tricksters feed the simpletons fantastical lines of mumbo jumbo about a wizard named Tontonelo who created the discerning spectacle. The oxymoronic nature of the name *el sabio Tontonelo (sabio means wise, and tonto means foolish)* should have clued in the silly villagers, but they fall for the bait, hook, line, and sinker; and they are anxious to prove their untainted Christian lineage. Of course, no one sees the imaginary puppet show, but everyone must emphatically claim to see all the scenes of a play that is not real. The townspeople accept the idea that being of Jewish or *converso* heritage is a sickness (as described by Chanfalla, who is merely catering to common prejudices), thus exposing their ugly anti-Semitic attitudes and bigotry, which were widely accepted and even encouraged in Spanish society of the seventeenth century.

Another limitation on viewing the *retablo* is that one cannot be an illegitimate child. Illegitimacy is also a question of identity and lineage. If there is an uncertainty about who one's father is, then there is a question regarding the lineage of that person. This unknown heritage can lead to speculation about the "purity" of one's blood. An illegitimate child is a potentially illegitimate Christian because the father could be of *converso* origin, and, at any rate, in the eyes of the church, the union of the parents is not a valid one.

The ironic nature of the play is evident when the very name of the "creator" of the *retablo, el sabio Tontonelo*, denotes stupidity—perhaps the stupidity of believing that one can recognize someone's lineage through a magical vision test. The villagers are so eager to prove themselves to be "pure" Christians that they have faith that the nonexistent *retablo* will sort them in terms of their identities. The only thing that the *retablo* proves is that these inane villagers are ignorant enough to spend their money on a phony purity test, ironically presented by tricksters who, as I explain later in the chapter, are probably of *converso* origin. Cervantes, thus, uses irony in his *entremés* as a vehicle to express his opinion and critique the unnecessary obsession with *pureza de sangre* and, therefore, indirectly criticize anti-Semitism.

The characters in *El retablo de las maravillas* struggle to define themselves as their ethnic identities are called into question. They are motivated by external societal and internal psychological pressures to display acceptable behavior. Internally, the characters recognize the possibility that they might be of *converso* origin when they fail to see the magical spectacle. They vehemently deny this newfound loathsome identity when they see their neighbors reacting energetically to the nonexistent play. Since the individual characters believe that they are alone in their "blindness" to the *retablo*, internally they feel isolated from what they perceive as the Old Christian community. Therefore, the villagers feel external pressure to act as if they see the play and, thus, affirm their *pureza de sangre*. Eventually, the townspeople even trick themselves into believing in the existence of the fantastic puppet show. The villagers' bombastic reactions to the imaginary scenes of the magical spectacle serve to mask their "new" ethnic identities. I will analyze the characters' responses to their new identities and discuss their motivations for disguising their imagined Jewish origins. I will study elements, such as symbolic images and the portrayal of the rustic characters, in order to discuss the issue of ethnic identity in seventeenth-century Spain.

The play's most important elements include the imaginary scenes of the nonexistent metatheatrical show. Some parts of the spectacle include biblical figures, and all are linked symbolically to the issue of *pureza de sangre*. The scenes are not organized in any logical chronological manner; therefore, *El retablo de las maravillas* does not lend itself well to a linear interpretation. I will examine the characters who willingly participate in the illusion of the "magical" *retablo* in order to avoid being branded as Other.

The *rústicos* in *El retablo de las maravillas* become frustrated and confused as they strive to suppress their doubts about their Old Christian lineage. Most of the images described by Chirinos and Chanfalla are frightening to the villagers. The rustic characters act terrified of the imaginary scenes, and they exaggerate their reactions in order to prove to their neighbors that they do indeed see the magical spectacle. In fact, since the *retablo* does not really exist, the *rústicos* become melodramatic actors in a play of their own creation. They become actors in order to hide the "impure blood" that they believe they possess. If the townspeople in the play were to admit that they saw nothing, it would be taken as an admission of Jewish heritage. Their reputations would be ruined, and they would be labeled as outcasts of society. The reality is that the majority of Spaniards from rural areas were in fact, *cristianos viejos,* which means that their fears of "tainted blood" were largely unfounded. Gerber explains:

> In the sixteenth and seventeenth centuries, for example, the safest claim was ancestry from peasant stock, for urban origins, evidence of literacy, or any connection with the liberal professions, particularly medicine, immediately tainted one. In that vein, merchants and men of affairs were automatically considered to be descended from *conversos.* (128)

Therefore, the villagers' ridiculous obsession with lineage compels them to create and accept a false reality in order to avoid an imagined and improbable identity.

Critical Approaches to *El retablo de las maravillas*

Numerous critics have studied the many facets of *El retablo de las maravillas*. Some critics focus on a particular theory in order to analyze the play, while others discuss societal values reflected in Cervantes' theater.[7] Several writers examine one character's importance or one particular aspect of the play.[8] One critic chooses to touch generally upon many aspects of this interlude, and others compare the *entremés* to different literary works.[9] The critics' analyses, along with my own opinions and interpretations, have inspired me to delve into the significance of the play and form my own conclusions about the issue of ethnic identity in this theatrical work.

In order to realize fully my in-depth study of *El retablo de las maravillas*, I use several theories and critical studies to form a unique analysis that focuses on the psychological motivation of the rustic characters whose fear of an imaginary Jewish identity drives them to certain madness. Sander Gilman's theory of Jewish self-hatred aids in understanding the extreme actions of these characters. An application of Gilman's theory reveals that the townspeople hate themselves because of the illusion of Jewish identity that the tricksters have bestowed upon them. Spanish society of the seventeenth century dictates that anyone of Jewish heritage be labeled as Other and become an outcast of society. The rustic characters go to any lengths to avoid being recognized as Other, and, consequently, they reject the identity that would cause them to be ostracized by their own neighbors. Thus, they reject themselves and hate their newfound ethnicity.

Additionally, Lionel Abel's theory of metatheater assists in analyzing the theatrical import of the characters' actions and examines their emphatic rejection and denial of a suggested *converso* heritage. The townspeople are aware that they must become actors in order to appear to be of pure lineage; therefore, they are conscious of their own theatricality. The characters' ridiculous reactions to the nonexistent *retablo* create a metatheatrical spectacle within the play itself. Therefore, the interlude is metatheatrical on two levels: the imaginary puppet show and the characters' reactions to that show both form plays within the main frame of *El retablo de las maravillas*. The metatheatrical nature of the play emphasizes that the perception of an imagined Jewish lineage motivates the characters to become actors to mask their newfound impure identity.

The theories of both Gilman and Abel are tools that assist in analyzing the actions of characters created by a playwright who is deeply critical of the injustice perpetuated by a Spanish society that places a very high value on blood purity.

THE PUPPETEERS

The characters in *El retablo de las maravillas* all play an important role with regard to the issue of ethnic identity, and the portrayal of the spectacle's puppet masters evokes the idea that these swindlers might actually be part of the ethnic group that the villagers despise. The characters in this interlude by Cervantes, like those in other deception stories, are divided into three categories: the swindlers or the enchanters, the victims, and the one who breaks the spell. The characters Chanfalla and Chirinos, along with the musician Rabelín, form the group of tricksters who present a "magical" spectacle. There are some interesting historical facts about the name "Chirinos," as Gracia Guillén explains:

> A pesar de la confusión que ha venido envolviendo a este problema, hoy parece posible afirmar que los Chirino fueron una importante y muy conocida familia de marranos españoles. Su fundador se dice que habría sido un médico judío converso, padre del también médico Alonso Chirino (1340?), conocido además como Alonso Chirino de Cuenca o Alonso de Guadalajara. Fue médico de Juan II de Castilla y en 1428 actuó como representante de Cuenca en las Cortes. (14)

> Despite the confusion that has been surrounding this problem, today it seems possible to state that the Chirino family was an important, well-known family of Spanish crypto-Jews. Its founder is said to have been a converted Jewish doctor, father of another doctor, Alonso Chirino (1340?), also known as Alonso Chirino de Cuenca or Alonso de Guadalajara. He was the doctor of Juan II of Castille, and in 1428, he was a representative of Cuenca in the parliament.

The fact that "Chirino" is the name of a *converso* Spanish family adds to the ironic, farcical nature of the magical puppet show. The character Chirinos presents the fantastic *retablo*, but given the probable *converso* origin suggested by her name, according to the rules of the spectacle regarding "impure blood," she should not be able to see the play.

Chirinos and Chanfalla are the puppeteers who know exactly which strings to pull to get their puppets—the audience—to react and, literally, to dance. Chirinos and Chanfalla pick their audience carefully, and they choose to bamboozle a group of people who have a false sense of self-importance. The governing class of a small town is perfect prey for the swindlers since these townspeople esteem their reputation and consider themselves leaders and of a higher class than the majority of the villagers. Although they are the "privileged," higher-class people of the village, they are exposed as stupid, egotistical buffoons. Ramos de Castro discusses the reasons why these particular characters value their reputations so highly:

> En efecto, el pueblo poco tiene que perder, pero las autoridades, es decir, las clases superiores, las clases dirigentes, sí tienen mucho que perder; la llamada gente de calidad puede perder su condición social-sus privilegios diríamos hoy. (181–82)

> Indeed, the villagers have little to lose, but the authorities, that is, the upper classes, the ruling classes, have much to lose; the so-called quality people can lose their social status—their privileges, as one would say today.

Although it is laughable, these rustics deem themselves refined, honorable leaders of society and believe that their reputations must not be tarnished. Therefore, they have much to lose if they do not protect their reputations as "pure Christians" and act as if they see the magical spectacle presented by Chirinos and Chanfalla. Not only would they lose the respect of their peers and the other lower-class townspeople, but they would also become outcasts of society.

The tricksters understand how they must act towards these village leaders, and Chanfalla advises his accomplice on how to talk to them:

> Salgámosles al encuentro, y date un filo a la lengua en la piedra de la adulación; pero no despuntes de aguda. (218)

> Let's meet them, and sharpen your tongue on the stone of flattery; but do not sharpen it too much.

Chanfalla knows that flattery will condition the higher-class members of the town to accept the prerequisites for seeing the show since the compliments stroke the egos of the *vulgo* and inflate their self-image. Chanfalla does warn, however, against overdoing the flattery for fear of seeming as though they are mocking the villagers. They want their comments to the town's leaders to seem sincere and to lead them to believe that they are the perfect candidates for viewing the magical show. After meeting the character *el Gobernador*, Chirinos praises him highly:

> Honrados días viva vuestra merced, que así nos honra. En fin, la encina da bellotas; el pero, peras; la parra, uvas, y el honrado, honra, sin poder hacer otra cosa. (219)

> May you live many honorable days, for thus do you honor us. In short, the oak gives acorns; the pear tree, pears; the vine, grapes, and the honorable, honor, unable to do otherwise.

Chirinos' comment serves to boost the governor's ego and strengthen his belief that he is a highborn, honorable nobleman:

> Aunque rústicos y no pertenecientes al estamento noble, los labradores se creían "honrados" por ser cristianos viejos, es decir, de sangre o genealogía no conversa. (Spadaccini 219)

> Although they are rustic folk, and not belonging to the noble class, the farmers thought they were "honorable" for being old Christians, that is, one does not talk of blood or genealogy.

Of course, the governor thinks that he is no less than a pure-blood Christian, and, therefore, an honorable nobleman. He soaks up Chirinos' flattery, which makes him feel haughty about his "pure" lineage, but he does not realize that Chirinos' praise is nonsensical and empty. If honorable people gave out honor as a fruit tree bears fruit, then no one would have the problem of lacking honor, and nobody would worry about being of *converso* origin. This statement also implies that the governor has no control over his honorable status since he blindly bestows honor upon anyone, pure Christian or not, much like a tree gives fruit. Molho describes the governor's honorable nature as "Honra vegetativa, en suma, que fructifica a ciegas, sin poder hacer otra cosa" (Vegetative honor, in short, that bears fruit blindly, without being able to do otherwise) (177). Therefore, the governor is not actively an honorable person, only passively so. Chirinos achieves the desired affect with her flattery because, as an effect of having his ego inflated, the governor is more determined to show what an honorable, pure Christian he is. In fact, thanks to the empty praises of Chirinos and Chanfalla, all are ready to prove their *pureza de sangre*.

Cervantes' goal is to show Spanish society's foolish preoccupation with *pureza de sangre,* and Chirinos and Chanfalla's hoax highlights this obsession. Ramos de Castro offers one interpretation of the swindlers:

> Chanfalla y Chirinos son, sencillamente, la "conciencia" de la sociedad que Cervantes va a fustigar. Conciencia por cuanto van a poner en evidencia los males, mejor dicho "ciertos" males, defectos o como quiera llamárseles, de la sociedad objeto de la crítica cervantina. (180–81)

> Chanfalla and Chirinos are simply the "conscience" of the society that Cervantes is going to criticize. This conscience, or these characters, show evidence of the evils, or rather "certain" evils, defects or whatever you would like to call them, of the society that is the object of Cervantine criticism.

Although I do agree with Ramos de Castro's idea of the "conscience" of the play that serves to point out society's flaws and prejudices, I believe that no one character embodies the "conscience" of society, but rather, they all work together to relay Cervantes' message. Therefore, I believe that Ramos de Castro is confusing the issues of the characters' motives and Cervantes' goal in writing the *entremés.* Zimic also disagrees with Ramos de Castro:

> A Chanfalla y Chirinos no interesa en absoluto "poner en evidencia los males y defectos de la sociedad." Consiguen este efecto, es cierto, pero sólo con una intención fríamente portunista y explotadora. (167)

> Chanfalla and Chirinos are not at all interested in "highlighting the evils and defects of society." They achieve this effect, it is true, but only with a coldly opportunistic and exploitative intention.

The characters Chirinos and Chanfalla are motivated by financial gain from a group of gullible country folk. They do not seem to be condemning the villagers for being obsessed by lineage, but they do use this obsession to their advantage. The suggestion of impure lineage or Jewish heritage is the greatest weapon that Chirinos and Chanfalla have against the village. They use this weapon to blackmail the villagers and make money without having to do much work. The swindlers use ignorance and prejudice to their advantage, and they will continue to make money from their nonexistent puppet show as long as people are afraid of being discovered as *conversos.* Thus, the swindlers use the silly villagers' insecurity about their pure Christian heritage to transform them into marionettes controlled by these manipulative puppeteers.

THE PUPPETS

The marionettes, or the spectators of the *retablo*, are the victims of the elaborate prank, and they are excited to show off their ability to view the mystical spectacle and prove their *pureza de sangre*. The audience of the magic *retablo* includes the Mayor Benito Repollo, his daughter Teresa Repolla, and his cousin known as "Sobrino Repollo." The other members of the audience are the governor, the scribe Pedro Capacho, the alderman Juan Castrado, and his daughter Juana Castrada. Cervantes gives several characters the humorous last names "Capacho" and "Castrado," (castrated) which serve to emasculate them and make us wonder about the legitimacy of Juan's daughter Juana. Therefore, from the beginning of the *entremés*, we are made to doubt Juana's purported Old-Christian lineage. Also, the last name "Repollo" denotes the cabbage-like intelligence of these villagers whose pride and gullibility makes them an easy target for the swindlers.[10]

Benito is eager for the start of the show, and he declares, "Vamos, Autor, que me saltan los pies por ver esas maravillas" (Come on, Author, my feet jump to see those wonders) (225). With this quote, Cervantes subtly compares, with comic effects, the character Benito to a marionette. It is as if Benito's feet, which are jumping with anticipation, were attached to invisible strings controlled by the tugging of Chirinos and Chanfalla, the puppet masters. Teresa also cannot wait for the *retablo* to begin so that she can show herself to be as "honorable" as she thinks she is:

Ya sabes, Juana Castrada, que soy tu prima, y no digo más. ¡Tan cierto tuviera yo el cielo como tengo cierto ver todo aquello que el Retablo mostrare! ¡Por el siglo de mi madre, que me sacase los mismos ojos de mi cara si alguna desgracia me aconteciese! ¡Bonita soy yo para eso! (225)

You know, Juana Castrada, I am your cousin, and I say no more. If only I were as sure of heaven as I am that I will see everything in this show! Upon my mother's life, may my eyes be removed from my face if I am disgraced! I am perfect for this show!

First, in order to prove her honorable lineage, Teresa links herself to Juana Castrada, whose father's last name (Castrado) throws doubt upon Juana's legitimacy and therefore upon her *pureza de sangre*. If anything, Teresa's relation to Juana makes her less likely to meet the requirements needed for seeing the magical show. Teresa is so vehement about her pure heritage that she is willing to have her eyes plucked from her face if she is unable to see the *retablo*, thus blinding herself to the "reality" of her imagined disgrace. What she does not know is that she is already so blinded by her belief in her own purity that she will not recognize the nonexistent show as a hoax. Needless to say, although Teresa's eyes are not gouged out when she fails to see the play, she blindly follows the rest of the rustics in claiming to see the imaginary fantastic figures of the *retablo*. Teresa and the other townspeople believe so strongly in their ethnic purity that they vehemently boast of their lineage and confidently look forward to seeing the puppet show.

STEREOTYPES AND THE RUSTIC CHARACTERS

Jewish heritage is a key issue in *El retablo de las maravillas*; therefore, one must consider the idea of stereotypical characterizations of Jews and *conversos* during the time period that Cervantes wrote this interlude. Many stereotypes of Jews existed in the seventeenth century. Martínez López explains several and their importance in *El retablo de las maravillas*:

> Más importante uso tiene la caracterización del judío o confeso como listo, agudo, "leído y escribido" y, en algunos casos, "reprochador de voquibles", frente al cristiano viejo como ignorante y/o necio. . . . De acuerdo con estas premisas Cervantes divide a sus personajes en tontos y agudos. (80)

> The important use is the characterization of the Jew, or confessed, as intelligent, sharp, "well-read and able to write" and, in some cases, "disapproving of uttered stupidities," in front of the old Christian as ignorant and / or foolish. . . . According to these premises, Cervantes divides his characters into fools and those that are clever.

Martínez López uses these stereotypes to analyze all aspects of the *rústicos* in order to label them according to their perceived *pureza de sangre*. Thus, Martínez López divides the villagers into groups of "smart" *conversos* and "stupid" Old Christians. Although Martínez López thoroughly and skillfully discusses the idea of stereotypes, I disagree with the concept of labeling the townspeople because I believe that in doing so, one completely misses the message of Cervantes' play. Categorizing the rustic characters is inconsistent with the theme of the play since Cervantes is making fun of the idea of ridiculous labels. The point is that it does not matter what one's lineage is, and one should not obsess about it. Cervantes sees Spaniards' preoccupation with *pureza de sangre* as foolish and, thus, portrays the lineage-obsessed *rústicos* as silly people who will go to any lengths in order to prove that they are of noble, pure Christian decent.

Martínez López goes on to specify who he believes is of *converso* origin and who is a *cristiano viejo* based on his interpretation of the characters' actions, which he believes show intelligence or stupidity:

Hablando de tontos y listos conviene reconsiderar aquí la imagen corriente de los labradores del entremés como epítome de la credulidad cuando sólo al Gobernador, el único libre de mancha, corresponde esa estampa, que era la del estereotipo del castizo que él representa. No ocurre así con los demás. Todos-ya se verá- tienen alguna tacha que ocultar y, preocupados de no levantar sospechas, tienen necesariamente que entrar en el juego aunque lo hacen dando a entender que no son bobos y están en el ajo. (95–96)

Speaking of fools and clever people, one can reconsider the current image of the farmers of the theatrical work as the most gullible characters, when only the Governor, the only one free of stain, corresponds to that type, which was that of the stereotype of the pure Christian he represents. Not so with others. Everyone will see—they have some flaw to hide. Since they are worried about not raising suspicions, they must enter the game although they do it implying that they are not stupid and are in on the scam.

Martínez López bases his opinion that the governor is the only true Old Christian, and, therefore, the only *tonto*, upon his erroneous belief that the governor is "el único de los personajes que jamás dice si ve o no ve las figuras del retablo . . ." (the only one of the characters who never says whether he sees the figures in the puppet show) (91). In fact, the governor makes several comments admitting that he does not see the imaginary play. In an aside, the frustrated governor states:

Basta; que todos ven lo que yo no veo; pero al fin habré de decir que lo veo, por la negra honrilla. (229)

Enough; Everyone sees what I don't see; but in the end, I will have to say that I see it, for the sake of my damned honor.

The governor values his reputation as an honorable man, and, therefore, he can express his doubts only through comments directed at the audience.

I also do not agree with Martínez López's declaration that the other villagers are intelligent and know all about the hoax. Cervantes repeatedly shows the townspeople to be rather dimwitted as evidenced by their malapropisms and misunderstandings:

Chirinos: ante omnia nos han de pagar lo que fuere justo.
Benito: Señora Autora, aquí no os ha de pagar ninguna Antona ni ningún Antoño; el señor regidor Juan Castrado os pagará más que honradamente, y si no, el Concejo. ¡Bien conocéis el lugar, por cierto! Aquí, hermana, no aguardamos a que ninguna Antona pague por nosotros. (221)

Chirinos: ante omnia they must pay us whatever is fair.
Benito: Madam Author, here you don't have to pay any Antona or Antoño; the councilman Juan Castrado will pay you more than honestly, and if not, the Council. You know the place well, by the way! Here, sister, let's not wait for any Antona to pay for us.

Chirinos asks for their payment in advance by using the Latin *ante omnia*, and Benito clearly misunderstands this phrase. We see that these proud, yet dimwitted country folk are the perfect victims for Chirinos and Chanfalla. Although the rural characters are portrayed as ignorant people, Martínez López seems arbitrarily to label them as intelligent and, then, takes this supposed intelligence as a sign that they are of Jewish heritage.[11] Martínez López states that the townspeople are cornered into acting as if the play exists, and that they understand that Chirinos and Chanfalla have come to extort money from them. There is no evidence supporting the idea that the townspeople comprehend this, and, in fact, based on the information in the characters' comments, each one believes himself or herself to be the only one unable to view the marvelous show. The exasperated governor questions his inability to see and feel what Chanfalla describes as miraculous rain from the Jordan River:

[Aparte.] ¿Qué diablos puede ser esto, que aún no me ha tocado una gota donde todos se ahogan? ¿Mas si viniera yo a ser bastardo entre tantos legítimos? (230)

[Apart.] What the devil could this be, not a drop has touched me while everyone else is drowning? Could I be a bastard among so many legitimate people?

The governor, like all the others, feels alone in his failure to view the spectacular images that everyone else enthusiastically claims to see. I believe that Martínez López is giving the ridiculous *rústicos* too much credit for their understanding of the magical *retablo* since all are shown to be unintelligent because they believe Chanfalla and Chirinos' story completely. The gullible characters simply cannot fathom that they are the victims of a money-making scheme. The witless village people believe they must keep up the charade if they are to uphold their image as legitimate, pure Christians.

I do not believe that it was Cervantes' intent to divide villagers into groups of *listos* and *tontos* or *conversos* and *cristianos viejos,* but rather to show them all in the same light: as rather silly people who are so terrified to confront their imaginary "true" selves that they are willing to put on a show for others and themselves to maintain their so-called integrity.

Jews were also negatively stereotyped as being emasculated cowards, while Old Christians were brave men ready to fight for honor. According to Martínez López,

A los personajes del pueblo que Cervantes ha presentado como listos los volverá a caracterizar de confesos con otros tópicos también procedentes del discurso antisemita y que conviene señalar. Motivo central en él, y correlativo a la antinomia tonto/listo, es la contraposición hombre con bríos/cobarde para aludir a la del cristiano viejo, guerrero matamoros frente al confeso dedicado a menesteres pacíficos y descendiente de quienes, según el estereotipo irónicamente repetido por fray Antonio de Guevara, "son de su mismo natural, para las ciencias muy hábiles, y para las armas muy cobardes." (107–108)

The townspeople that Cervantes has presented as intelligent will again be labeled as converts, and it should be noted that other topics also stem from anti-Semitic discourse. The central motive in it and corresponding to the opposing characteristics of stupid / clever, is the comparison of the valiant man / coward to allude to that of the old Christian, a warrior braggart, as compared to the convert and his descendants who were dedicated to peaceful needs, according to the stereotype ironically repeated by Fray Antonio de Guevara, "they are of their own nature, very skilled in the sciences, and very cowardly with war and weaponry."

Although I agree with Martínez López on the existence of these stereotypes, contrary to what he proposes, I do not believe that Cervantes portrays his small-town characters as cowardly in order to brand them as *conversos*. In fact, Cervantes seems to give us mixed signals in assigning stereotypically Jewish and Old Christian characteristics to the country folk who are probably not of Jewish origin. The *rústicos* act frightened of the imaginary images conjured up by Chirinos and Chanfalla. The fearsome images strike terror into the hearts of these characters, thus, bringing out stereotypically "cowardly Jewish" behavior in people who are most likely Old Christians. The question is: can these country folks be described as timid and fearful just because they are reacting to the imaginary images in a predictable way? Why did they not act bravely when confronting the frightening images? Their biggest fear is not the imaginary tiger they pretend to see, but the fact that they could be *conversos* or bastards. Their lineage is brought to the forefront of their consciousness because of this play that supposedly tests their purity. Every day, these people are forced to act normally, or act as they feel Old Christians should act. In this case, they feel that normalcy dictates showing fear of the nonexistent characters in the play. Their fear of having an impure lineage is amplified and enhanced when confronted by this fantastical *retablo*.

These villagers are shown to be unintelligent and cowardly, two traits that are stereotypical characteristics of Old Christians and Jews, respectively. Therefore, since Cervantes applies different stereotypical qualities to these characters, he is showing that anyone can have these attributes, whether one is of *converso* origin or of *sangre pura*. It is interesting to note that these characters are trying to act like *cristianos viejos*, but by displaying terror over imaginary images, they are unwittingly playing into the stereotype of the cowardly Jew. Therefore, the stereotypes are not valid. This irony could cause the audience members to question their own heritage and also question stereotypes associated with certain groups of people.

EL FURRIER: THE SCAPEGOAT

The *Furrier,* or Quartermaster, exclaims he does not see the performance, and, therefore, he becomes the scapegoat who is accused of being a Jew. The imaginary performance is interrupted by the sound of a trumpet followed by the arrival of the *Furrier.* The *Furrier* is the military officer who has the responsibility of finding food and lodging for the other soldiers. When he announces that thirty soldiers will be arriving within the half-hour, expecting the villagers to accommodate them, Benito announces, "Yo apostaré que los envía el sabio Tontonelo" (I bet that the wise Tontonelo has sent them) (233). Benito continues to vehemently insist that the Quartermaster is part of the magical show since the appearance of this man is as frightening to Benito as the other "images" in the *retablo.* Ramos de Castro explains:

> No podemos olvidar la situación real de la época, en la que la penosa y constante obligación de dar alojamiento a las tropas en plena paz tenía que resultar harto enojosa y desagradable. La postura de las autoridades al advenimiento del furriel es doblemente evasiva, o mejor dicho, su negativa a aceptar esta otra realidad, responde a una doble motivación-aunque una de ellas sea inconsciente-: la inmersión en el *Retablo* y el deseo subconsciente de eludir la obligación del alojamiento. (185)

> We cannot forget the situation of the time, in which the difficult, constant obligation to give accommodation to the troops during times of peace had to be very irritating and unpleasant. The position of the authorities at the quartermaster's arrival is doubly evasive, or rather, Benito's refusal to accept this other reality, responds to a double motivation, even if one of them is unconscious: immersion in the puppet show and the subconscious desire to avoid the obligation of accommodation.

The arrival of soldiers would be a great burden for the villagers. Besides having to provide meals and a place to stay for the soldiers, the townspeople would also have to worry about these strangers taking advantage of their daughters and wives. Therefore, Benito and the others would rather believe that the *Furrier* is a character in the show. The gullible villagers are so immersed in the idea of the *retablo*, they cannot separate reality from fantasy. They slowly and grudgingly come to the realization that the Quartermaster is not part of the spectacle, and they try to bribe him to leave their town. Juan Castrado announces:

> Por vida del Autor, que haga salir otra vez a la doncella Herodías, porque vea este señor lo que nunca ha visto; quizá con esto le cohecharemos para que se vaya presto del lugar. (234)

> Upon the life of the Author, let the maiden Herodias appear again, so that this man can see what he has never seen; maybe with this we will bribe him to leave this place quickly.

It is humorous that the country folk believe in the reality of the hoax so completely that they are using the dancing girl, a nonexistent character, as a bribe in an attempt to get rid of the *Furrier*. Since they have all conjured up an image of Herodias in their mind's eye, they believe that the unbelievable beauty and grace of this swaying damsel will tempt the Quartermaster, and he will leave the town in exchange for a glimpse of the sensuous dance. Benito then cheers on his nephew, who he believes is engaged in a high-spirited dance with the imaginary girl. Of course, the *Furrier* is an outsider and therefore has no knowledge of the rules and regulations for viewing the *retablo*, so he has no reason to pretend to see anything:

> *Furrier:* ¿Está loca esta gente? ¿Qué diablos de doncella es ésta, y qué baile, y qué Tontonelo?
> *Capacho:* ¿Luego no vee la doncella herodiana el señor Furrier?
> *Furrier:* ¿Qué diablos de doncella tengo de ver? (235)

> *Furrier:* Are these people crazy? What the hell kind of maiden is there to see, and what dance, and what Tontonelo?
> *Capacho:* Then Mr. Furrier does not see the Herodian maiden?
> *Furrier:* What damn maiden? I don't see anything!

To the Quartermaster, it seems as if all of the villagers have gone completely mad. Thus, Chirinos and Chanfalla have perpetuated a type of insanity throughout the whole village, which is highly contagious. The symptoms of this psychological sickness include the delusional behavior of the villagers who see visions that do not really exist. Wardropper explains:

> But these peasants are not so stupid that, to protect their own interests, they are incapable of pretending to see what they do not see. This initial attempt to

deceive others quickly turns into self-deception, and eventually into hallucination. It is a hallucination created both by the statutes of *limpieza de sangre* and by the trickster Chanfalla. (31)

The fact that the villagers are "crazy" is highlighted when the *Furrier* comes to town. Since he is the only one unaware of the conditions for seeing the *retablo*, he is struck by the insanity of the townspeople. Cervantes demonstrates that the obsession with lineage is a psychological sickness by showing the insane behavior of the *rústicos*, which is accepted as normal by everyone in the town. The villagers are willing to act like lunatics in order to preserve their illusion of a pure lineage.

The frustrated *furrier* does not understand the situation, and the villagers take this as a confession of Jewish heritage:

Capacho: Basta: de *ex il[l]is es.*
Gobernador: De *ex il[l]is es,* de *ex il[l]is es.*
Juan: Dellos es, dellos el señor Furrier; dellos es. (235)

Capacho: Enough: from ex il [l] is es.
Governor: From ex il [l] is es, from ex il [l] is es.
Juan: You are one of them, Mr. Furrier; one of them.

When the *Furrier* declares he sees nothing, he is branded an outcast of society. The hostile villagers use him as a scapegoat, and he alone stands accused of being ". . . 'one of them,' a member of the despised and hated caste of New Christians" (Wardropper 31). These characters succeed in projecting their self-doubt and skepticism about their *pureza de sangre* onto the "unseeing" Furrier. They no longer must harbor suspicions about themselves and their neighbors as Old Christians; they have found someone who openly denies seeing the spectacle, and therefore they can point their fingers at the Quartermaster for being the "true Jew" among them. This actually goes against the stereotype of the Old-Christian soldier (Martínez López 108).

The use of the Latin phrase "de *ex il[l]is es*" to ridicule the *furrier* calls to mind the trials of Jesus Christ as written in the New Testament[12]:

> Now Peter sat without in the palace: and a damsel came unto him, saying, Thou also wast with Jesus of Galilee. But he denied before them all, saying, I know not what thou sayest. And when he was gone out into the porch, another maid saw him, and said unto them that were there, this fellow was also with Jesus of Nazareth. And again he denied with an oath, I do not know the man. And after a while came unto him they that stood by, and said to Peter, Surely thou also art one of them; for thy speech betrayeth thee. Then began he to

curse and to swear, saying, I know not the man. And immediately the cock crew. And Peter remembered the word of Jesus, which said unto him, Before the cock crow, thou shalt deny me thrice. And he went out, and wept bitterly. (Matt. 26.69–75)

Peter, a disciple of Jesus Christ, is labeled as being "one of them" or a follower of Christ. He strongly denies association with Jesus three times in an attempt to distance himself from the situation. Ironically, the phrase used to label Peter as one of the original *cristianos viejos* is the same used to imply that the Quartermaster is of Jewish lineage. In using these words, the townsfolk unwittingly compare the Quartermaster to a disciple of Christ; thus, their attempt to shame him by calling him a Jew backfires since they are really associating him with the first Christians who were, of course, all Jews. This biblical reference draws attention to the confusion of the rural characters in terms of their perceived identity.

The unintelligent villagers taunt the Quartermaster and incite him to violence:

> Benito: Nunca los confesos ni bastardos fueron valientes; y por eso no podemos dejar de decir: dellos es, dellos es. (235)

> Benito: Converts and bastards were never brave; and that is why we cannot stop saying: You are one of them, one of them.

Benito believes the stereotype that Jews and bastards are not brave and uses it to insult the *Furrier* by labeling him a cowardly *converso*. Of course, the livid Quartermaster strikes out against the townspeople, and a huge brawl ensues. Benito and the others have foolishly succeeded in causing a fight with a man of arms who is skilled in the art of combat. Although all decorum has been shattered, the villagers' belief in the magical spectacle does not waiver, and the hoax is a success. According to Reed:

> The fictional spectators in *El retablo de las maravillas* likewise remain deceived in the only Cervantine interlude which does not end with a song or dance. In this play, Cervantes makes no attempt to provide closure, not even ironically. (174)

Unlike in the folktale of *The Emperor's New Clothes* and enxemplo 32 in *El conde Lucanor* where the hoax is revealed and the swindlers are shown to be frauds, the illusion of the *retablo* remains intact. The triumphant tricksters are free to use their canard and "show" their theatrical work to the whole town now that it has been approved by the town's administrators. If one should side with the Quartermaster on the nonexistence of the *retablo*, one's *pureza de sangre* is lost. Although the *Furrier* is firmly rooted in reality and could have broken the enchantment of the spectacle, the *rústicos* are too trapped in the fragility of their personal identity to allow that to happen.

SELF-HATING "JEWS"

Since they cannot see the magical puppet show, each villager's mind is reeling with thoughts of self-doubt, denial and hatred of the new Jewish identity that has taken root in his or her psyche. In an aside, the governor exclaims:

> ¡Milagroso caso es éste! Así veo yo a Sansón ahora, como el Gran Turco. Pues en verdad que me tengo por legítimo y cristiano viejo. (228)

> Miraculous case is this! I see Samson now, like I see the Great Turk. The truth is, I consider myself a legitimate, pure Christian.

The governor is shocked and dismayed at his inability to see the *retablo*, but he must express this in an aside so that the other characters do not catch on to his "blindness." The *rústicos* cannot share their feelings of fear, doubt, and hopelessness stemming from the inability to see the *retablo;* therefore, they are all isolated from each other. Outwardly, they demonstrate confidence in seeing all the magical scenes, and they make a grand show of reacting to the nonexistent characters with theatrical flair. As a defense mechanism, the rustic folk create personal illusions to match the tricksters' descriptions of the spectacle. Teresa Repolla melodramatically shrieks about the supposed numerous mice running about:

> Yo sí soy la desdichada, porque se me entran sin reparo ninguno. Un ratón morenico me tiene asida de una rodilla. ¡Socorro venga del cielo, pues en la tierra me falta! (229)

> I am the unfortunate one, because they run around and on me with no qualms. A little dark mouse has grabbed ahold of my knee. Help must come from the heavens, for I lack it here on earth!

Teresa's cousin Juana Castrada frantically reacts to the mice before Teresa does, but Teresa Repolla will not be outdone. Teresa creatively adds details to the scene, hoping to prove to be a legitimate Old Christian by showing her interaction with the *retablo* mice. Teresa announces that one mouse has seized her knee, and then she dramatically begs for help from heaven. Chirinos describes a large group of multicolored mice, but he does not mention that one has run up Teresa's leg. These characters must fashion their own version of reality in order to hide from the terrifying question swimming in their minds: Could I be a Jew? Their attempts to dismiss this idea are futile; their self-perception is changed forever. Like the magical images dancing in their mind's eye, their new identities are also illusions created for them by Chirinos and Chanfalla. Realistically, the villagers are all probably Old Christians (Gerber 128), but what matters is that they now believe that they are of Jewish heritage and they hate themselves for it.

Sander Gilman describes the concept of Jewish self-hatred:

> Self-hatred results from outsiders' acceptance of the mirage of themselves generated by their reference group-that group in society which they see as defining them-as a reality. (2)

The rustic characters of Cervantes' interlude are part of the reference group that stereotypes Jews. They have already accepted these stereotypes as fact when they become outsiders themselves after failing to view a theatrical work that supposedly only reveals itself to pure-blood Christians. They apply the negative stereotypes to themselves and instantly loathe the newfound link with their supposed Jewishness, and, therefore, they resist their classification as Other. Gilman explains:

> The Other comprises precisely those who are not permitted to share power within the society. Thus outsiders hear an answer from their fantasy: Become like us-abandon your difference-and you may be one with us. (2)

If the townspeople were to acknowledge their inability to see the show, they would label themselves as Other, thus losing their power in the community. These characters avoid becoming outcasts of society and instead choose the Quartermaster to fill the role of Other. The villagers point to the confused *Furrier* who admits he sees nothing:

Benito: Basta: dellos es, pues no vee nada.
Furrier: ¡Canalla barrentina[13]!: si otra vez me dicen que soy dellos, no les dejaré hueso sano!
Benito: Nunca los confesos ni bastardos fueron valientes; y por eso no podemos dejar de decir: dellos es, dellos es. (235)

Benito: Enough: he is one of them, because he sees nothing.
Furrier: Rotten villagers! If they tell me again that I am one of them, I will not leave one unbroken bone!

Benito: The converts and bastards were never brave; and that is why we cannot stop saying: one of them, one of them.

By accusing the Quartermaster of being "one of them," the villagers shift the attention away from themselves and affirm their position in the dominant group accepted by society. They refuse to acknowledge and accept their perceived difference and continue to act as if they belong to the reference group. The *rusticos* do not admit their inability to see the show, but since the Quartermaster says he cannot see the *retablo*, the villagers label him as the impure *converso* and angrily insult him with anti-Semitic comments. These rustic characters would rather find a scapegoat than apply these derogatory remarks to themselves. Thus, the imagined Jewish identity sparks a deep self-hatred in the *rústicos*.

SYMBOLIC ELEMENTS OF THE MAGICAL "SHOW"

The symbolic images of the fantastical *retablo* are directly linked to the peasants' anxiety concerning lineage and *pureza de sangre*. The apprehensive audience of *rústicos* awaits as Chanfalla utters the incantation to start the mystical puppet show:

> ¡Atención, señores, que comienzo! -¡Oh tú, quien quiera que fuiste, que fabricaste este Retablo con tan maravilloso artificio, que alcanzó renombre *de las Maravillas:* por la virtud que en él se encierra, te conjuro, apremio y mando que luego incontinenti muestres a estos señores algunas de las tus maravillosas maravillas, para que se regocijen y tomen placer sin escándalo alguno! (227)

> Attention, gentlemen, what a beginning!—Oh you, whoever you were, who made this show with such marvelous artifice, that it achieved fame and is called *Marvelous*: by the virtue that is held in it, I conjure you, I urge and command that you show these gentlemen some of your marvelous wonders at once, so that they can rejoice and take pleasure without any scandal whatsoever!

The mysterious spell intrigues the gullible country folk, and, of course, Chanfalla reminds them all again about the scandal and misfortune that could befall them if they fail to see the theatrical work. Chirinos and Chanfalla narrate the scenes following the incantation. The scenes of the *retablo* seem to be an odd conglomeration of animal images and stories from the Bible, but they all serve to frighten or titillate the villagers. The scenes also become symbols of deceit, treachery, lineage, Judaism, sexuality, and legitimacy. Chirinos and Chanfalla describe six different scenes:

the biblical figure, Samson, preparing to tear down the Philistine temple (Judg. 16.3–31); a raging bull; scampering mice; a shower of water direct from the Jordan River; dozens of lions and bears; and the seductive dancing woman referred to as Herodias but believed to be Salome (Matt. 14.2–11).

In what follows, I give a brief overview of all the scenes included in the *retablo*. I explore the symbolic images of Herodias and the mice in more detail in the following sections because these two elements of the magic show require a more thorough analysis in terms of their connection with lineage and Jewish heritage.[14]

The first and last scenes are stories from the Old and New Testament, respectively. Moner notes the link between the biblical figures of these two stories:

> Lo que llama la atención, en el caso de Sansón y Salomé, es que ambos pertenecen, indudablemente, a la raza odiada de los Hebreos, cuando, precisamente, el retablo funciona en la obra como un instrumento de discriminación que pretende excluir a los judíos. (810)

> What stands out, in the case of Samson and Salome, is that both undoubtedly belong to the hated Hebrew race, when, precisely, in the theatrical work, the puppet show functions as an instrument of discrimination that seeks to exclude Jews.

At first, the villagers do not seem to notice that Samson is indeed Jewish since they are terrified that they will be crushed flat by the temple he is destroying. They do question the appearance of the Jewish dancing girl, which I analyze in the following section. As noted by Wardropper, "they are classical examples of treachery" (29) since Samson is betrayed by Delilah, the woman he loves, and the dancing girl Salome, as instructed by her conniving mother, brings about the death of John the Baptist. The tales of deceit and trickery should act as a warning to the credulous townspeople, but they have no clue that the theme of treachery mirrors their reality as they fall victims to a hoax.

The scene involving the rain of holy water from the Jordan River falls between the other biblical scenes, and Chanfalla explains that the shower will make the women's faces shine like polished silver and will gild the men's beards. The women hope to be touched by the water while the men try not to get wet. According to Spadaccini, the men avoid the sacred rain to keep their manliness intact since golden beards would feminize them (230). Wardropper subscribes to another explanation of why the men evade the magical water:

> Neither the text nor its editors explain why the men are so afraid of the prospect that their graying beards might turn golden. The answer surely is that, according

to legend, Judas Iscariot had a red beard, a facial feature that by extension was identified with all traitors. (29)

Although it fits in with the theme of treachery, this explanation sounds too far-fetched, and I believe that the male characters are concerned with their outward appearance in terms of their masculinity and would abhor being perceived as feminine. Molho's interpretation of Benito's interaction with the water supports the idea that the rain feminizes the men:

> El único en dejarse penetrar por la lluvia espermática, que por las espaldas le ha corrido lomos abajo hasta el orificio de la canal maestra, es—como era de prever—Benito Repollo, que su mismo nombre representativo de un vientre o sexo de mujer, predestinaba a recibir el buen licor de vida. (209)

> The only one to let himself be penetrated by the sperm-like rain, which has run down his back to the orifice of the master canal, is—as expected—Benito Repollo, that his same name, representative of a woman's womb or vagina, predestined to receive the good liquor of life.

Benito's exclamation that the rainwater has entered his "canal maestra," (230) or anus, is an allusion to sodomy which therefore suggests his threatened masculinity. The emphasis on the male characters' femininity also challenges their legitimacy as fathers, therefore, casting doubt upon the lineage of their offspring.

The scenes involving animals symbolize virility, lineage, and legitimacy. The charging bull frightens the rustic characters, and Juana Castrada exclaims to her father, "ya me vi en sus cuernos, que los tiene agudos como una lesna" (I already saw myself in his horns, which are as sharp as an awl) (228). The bull is a potent symbol of sexuality, and its sharp horns are phallic symbols ready to gore anyone who gets in their way. Molho asks the question, "¿Qué lezna será ésa, dura y aguda, con que el toro apunta a la muchacha inmovilizada entre sus cuernos?" (What awl could it be, hard and sharp, with which the bull points to the immobilized girl between his horns?) (207). The horns are also a symbol of the cuckold or *cornudo*, and since Juana sees herself on the bull's horns, one wonders if she is the legitimate child of Juan. The issue of Juana's legitimacy also calls into question her Old Christian heritage if she does not know who her biological father is. Lions and bears, in addition to being virile animals, are symbols of heraldry found on coats of arms. According to Moner:

> Efectivamente, los blasones nobiliarios no son, en definitiva, sino símbolos genealógicos que pretenden garantizar la limpieza de sangre y el abolengo de quienes los ostentan. (815)

Indeed, the noble coats of arms are ultimately genealogical symbols that seek to guarantee the cleanliness of blood and the ancestry of those who hold them.

These ferocious animals are coveted images on a coat of arms since they represent the *pureza de sangre* of honorable Old Christian families, but here they frighten the villagers, thus showing that the coat of arms is a frightening concept because of the power it lends to people who wield it.

The hordes of mice, while not frightening in the same sense as the bull, lions and bears, also terrify the villagers. They represent the absurdity of the peasants' obsession with lineage since Chirinos describes these mice as the direct descendants of the original pair of mice on Noah's ark. Of course, all mice are related to the first two mice, and all humans share a similar background as well, making the intangible idea of blood purity a ridiculous concept. The various scenes of the *retablo* may seem like a hodgepodge of miscellaneous images, but they are all connected by the central theme of genealogy and heritage.

"LA BELLACA JODÍA": SALOME/HERODIAS

The last image of the marvelous *retablo* is the dancing girl Herodias; the hypocritical rustic characters desire to dance with this Jewish biblical figure, even though they reject others whom they believe to be of impure Jewish lineage. Chirinos announces her:

> Esa doncella que agora se muestra tan galana y tan compuesta es la llamada Herodías, cuyo baile alcanzó en premio la cabeza del Precursor de la vida. Si hay quien la ayude a bailar, verán maravillas. (232)

> That maid who now appears so gallant and so composed is the so-called Herodias, whose dance awarded her the prize of the head of the Precursor of life. If there are those who help her dance, they will see wonders.

This image recalls the New Testament story of a scheming Jewish woman named Herodias who uses her daughter Salome to bring about the murder of John the Baptist.[15]

It is actually Salome, not Herodias, as Chirinos indicates, who dances for Herod Antipas, Herodias' husband and Salome's stepfather, in this New Testament story. Cory Reed explains:

> It is clear that this dancing girl—she is referred to several times as "la doncella" or "la doncella herodiana" (179–182)—is Salome, and not her mother Herodias. While scholars have attempted to explain this discrepancy, such explanations themselves have been largely inadequate. Robert Marrast considers the name

> substitution an intentional ploy used by Chanfalla and Chirinos to expose the ignorance of these Old Christians concerning their familiarity with religious scripture. Wardropper more sensibly suggests that the substitution is necessary since the theme of treachery requires the appearance of Herodias, the agent of the betrayal of John the Baptist. In fact, recent research on the Salome legend has shown that the synthesis of the mother and daughter into one representative figure was actually a common practice in medieval and Renaissance Europe, resulting from a point of view which considered Salome the mere instrument of Herodias' betrayal of John the Baptist. Salome was regarded as only a means to her mother's ends; she did not demand John's head on her own accord, but did so only at Herodias' request. Cervantes, therefore, gives his Salome figure the name of the actual betrayer, Herodias, as if she herself had danced for John the Baptist's head. (9)

I believe that Cervantes was familiar with the legend of Salome, and that he emphasized the sexual nature of the female character and also highlighted the aspects of trickery and deception in the story by fusing Salome and Herodias into one woman. Salome is coached by her mother Herodias into ordering the beheading of John the Baptist when offered a prize after dancing for Herod. The sin of murdering John the Baptist is, therefore, on Herodias' head, and she is seen as the treacherous woman who is able to manipulate all in order to accomplish her evil goal.

Chirinos refers to John the Baptist as "el Precursor de la vida" (the Precursor of life) which refers to the fact that John the Baptist was the harbinger of new life for people who converted to Christianity. John's action of anointing Jesus Christ with holy water in effect gave birth to Christianity. Thus, with the murder of John the Baptist, Herodias has killed a man who possessed the godly power to give life. Therefore, Chirinos calls attention to the fact that not only is Herodias a Jewish woman involved in the *retablo*, but that she is also the one responsible for the death of Jesus's baptizer. It is obvious that the villagers do not focus on this important aspect of the malevolent dancing woman; instead, they choose to concentrate on the promise of a spectacle that flaunts Herodias' overt sexuality. Chirinos declares, "Si hay quien la ayude a bailar, verán maravillas" (If there are those who help her dance, they will see wonders.) (232). This statement brings to mind a bawdy strip tease, and the male characters practically foam at the mouth for a chance to watch the seductive undulations of a Jewish dancing girl—albeit an evil, deceitful one who does not even exist.

Because she is Jewish, Herodias is another symbolic character in the imaginary play that evokes the theme of Judaism. Reed remarks on the portrayal of Jews in the legend of Salome and Herodias:

Indeed, the original Salome tale itself is often seen in terms of a Christian-Jewish opposition, although, perhaps, due more to medieval reinterpretation of the story than to the legend itself. The same Catholic tradition which blamed the Jews for the death of Christ seems to have vilified many of the other Jews represented in the New Testament, implicating them in treachery against Christianity. Among these treacherous Jews are, naturally, the Herods, who are guilty of murdering the very man who baptized Christ. (14)

The story can be simplified and put in terms of evil Jews vs. good Christians, but if we delve deeper into the underlying story of Salome, we see that it is not so simple. According to Reed:

As political representatives of Rome in Judea, Herod and his family are not strictly Jewish (as evidenced by his refusal to obey Jewish law) nor are they true Romans. Herod's distrust of the Jews is revealed by his fear of a Jewish uprising against his own authority supported by Rome, one of his reasons for imprisoning John. (15)

Therefore, one cannot say that Herod's family was truly Jewish because their actions did not follow Jewish law. I believe that Cervantes did not focus on the anti-Semitic sentiment of the tale of Salome or strive to interpret the political details in the story, but rather that he chose to reveal the hypocritical nature of his characters and the irony of their actions. These men willingly and enthusiastically cavort with an imaginary woman of Jewish descent who caused the death of the original Baptist; yet, they emphatically reject any connection to a Jewish heritage.

None of the characters object to the fact that a Jewish woman would be a participant in a theatrical work that ironically cannot be viewed by anyone with a Jewish family history. Therefore, I disagree with Reed's statement that "The villagers clearly dislike Salome primarily for being Jewish" (14). The peasants are definitively enthusiastic about the inclusion of a beautiful dancing woman in the *retablo*, and they like her, or more accurately, lust after her. Benito encourages his nephew to dance with Herodias who will perform the erotic *zarabanda* and *chacona* dances, "bailes populares considerados inmorales en la época" (popular dances considered immoral at the time) (Spadaccini, 232):

Benito: ¡Esta sí, cuerpo del mundo!, que es figura hermosa, apacible y reluciente. ¡Hideputa, y cómo que se vuelve la mochac[h]a!—Sobrino Repollo, tú que sabes de achaque de castañetas, ayúdala, y será la fiesta de cuatro capas.
Sobrino: Que me place, tío Benito Repollo. (232)

Benito: This girl, yes, her body is out of this world! what a beautiful, pleasing and shining figure. Sonofabitch, that girl can dance!—Nephew Repollo, you who know all about castanets, help her, and it will be the party of four capes.
Nephew: That pleases me, Uncle Benito Repollo.

One imagines that the villagers are ogling the nonexistent beauty who is supposedly dancing in a very seductive manner. It is interesting to note that, judging from their excited reactions to the woman, the men would have no problem with dirtying their "clean" lineage by engaging in sexual relations with the imaginary Jewess, thereby theoretically enabling her to procreate and foster an impure lineage.

The villagers do not "dislike" Herodias or object to her appearance, but rather they are a bit puzzled about how she could appear in the play even though she herself is Jewish and not supposed to have the ability to see the play. This confusion is evidenced by the fact that Benito exclaims, "Pero, si ésta es jodía, ¿Cómo vee estas maravillas?" (But, if she is a Jew, how does she see these wonders?) (232). Chanfalla replies, "Todas las reglas tienen excepción, señor Alcalde." (All rules have an exception, Mr. Mayor.) (233). We can imagine a wry mocking smile playing about the lips of Chanfalla as he essentially negates the whole purpose of the play. It is also interesting to note that Benito refers to Herodias as "jodía" which Cervantes might have included to draw attention to this rustic man's uneducated, and therefore humorous, way of speaking.[16] Also, it is similar to the word "jodida" (screwed) which could refer to the dancing woman's status as Jewish and, therefore, not acceptable in the eyes of Spanish society.[17] This woman cannot deny the fact that she is Jewish, and her heritage would hamper her if she existed in seventeenth-century Spanish society. Benito's term for her could also be a reference to the fact that Herodias committed adultery with her husband's brother (Spadaccini 232–33). Either way, the Jewish Herodias is doubly "jodida."

The villagers choose to ignore the negative aspects of the beautiful dancing girl conjured up by the tricksters. They instead focus on the fantasy of the girl's attractive appearance. Kirschner explains:

> Sin embargo, esta figura tan atrayente, placentera y excitante, que Chirinos, buena conocedora de su público, hace surgir desencadenando con ella la furia erótica (116) en el sobrino del alcalde, es la "figura" que debería causar más horror. Ella encarna todos los estigmas aludidos: la sexualidad abierta, el claro linaje judaico y el adulterio, ya que abandonó a su esposo para convivir con Herodes Antipas, Tetrarca de Galilea. (826)

> However, this figure so attractive, pleasant, and exciting, that Chirinos, a good connoisseur of his audience, unleashes the erotic force (116) on the mayor's

nephew, and is the "figure" that should cause much horror. She embodies all the aforementioned stigmas: open sexuality, the clear Jewish lineage and adultery, since she abandoned her husband to live with Herod Antipas, Tetrarch of Galilee.

The townspeople are terrified of most of the images included in the magical show, and although they do not fear Herodias, they should be more frightened by her than they are of the hordes of rats, fierce lions and rampaging bulls. The dancing girl's lovely facade hides the false soul of a traitor. Herodias embodies all the characteristics that the villagers fear most, but rather than be terrified and repulsed by the sexually charged Jewish adulteress, these silly people are attracted to her, thereby making all their reactions and pretenses seem all the more foolish.

Although Cervantes' character Salome dances the sexually suggestive *zarabanda*, according to Reed, the dance of the seven veils is commonly associated with the legend of Salome (16). Reed draws parallels between this dance and what he believes is the primary goal of the entremés:

> Just as Salome's dance of the seven veils is a dance of unmasking and revelation, the imaginary retablo unmasks the unsuspecting villagers in Cervantes' play, stripping them of their social identities in order to reveal the ugliness of their prejudice. (16)

Among the villagers, the dance of Cervantes' Salome helps to mask their imagined "impure" identities. The suggested image of a beautiful dancing woman is something that the townspeople are easily able to imagine and react to energetically; thus, they are able to hide the fact that they see nothing. Also, they can participate in the action of this magical dance, which makes the whole scene seem more real. They easily imagine Benito's nephew dancing with a young, beguiling woman. Although this dance serves to help hide the rustics' perceived identities from each other, in reality, it exposes and unmasks their hypocritical nature to the audience.

In this play, Cervantes reveals the ridiculous nature of the rustic characters who must don masks to cover their perceived "impure" identities after failing to view the fantastic *retablo*. Inside, these characters are filled with self-doubt about their real identities, but outside, they uphold a facade that displays their unblemished heritage, and, therefore, they react very dramatically to all the nonexistent characters. As self-doubt clouds their minds, they must accept the heavy burden of the mask that hides what they believe to be their true identities as *confesos* and bastards. However, as the *rústicos* try harder to conceal their imagined identities from the others, they are unveiled to the audience as intolerant, unintelligent people, obsessed with blood purity.

OF MICE AND MEN

One scene of the magical show involves the image of a swarm of multicolored mice, and this scene evokes the idea of lineage since these rodents seem very different, yet Chirinos exclaims that they are all relatives of the same pair of mice. The character Chirinos describes this image to the townspeople:

> Esa manada de ratones que allá va, deciende por línea recta de aquellos que se criaron en el arca de Noé; dellos son blancos, dellos albarazados, dellos jaspeados y dellos azules; y, finalmente, todo[s] son ratones. (229)

> That herd of mice that goes there, direct descendants from those who grew up in Noah's ark; they are white, they are of various, mixed colors, they are speckled, and they are blue; and finally, all are mice.

Chirinos depicts a group of scampering mice of every hue, all direct descendants of the mice on Noah's ark. It seems as if this would make these mice special or of a higher class than other mice, but, according to the Bible, all mice are descendants from the original two on the ark. This brings up the question of lineage, and we see that Cervantes is making the point that lineage is not an important issue since Chirinos states, "finalmente, todos son ratones" (finally, all are mice). Moner explains the significance of the symbolic mice:

> El significado de la alusión no puede ser más claro dentro de este contexto: estos roedores, en apariencia tan diferentes y en realidad tan parecidos, y que proceden todos de una misma pareja original, presentan demasiadas analogías con el género humano-tal como lo pinta la mitología bíblica-para que se nos escape la alusión. De hecho, no podemos dejar de pensar que Cervantes se complace aquí en subrayar que los judíos, así como los cristianos, descienden todos, al fin y al cabo, de Adán y Eva. ¿Cómo imaginar entonces que una sangre diferente pueda correr en sus venas? (812)

> The meaning of the allusion cannot be clearer in this context: these rodents, in appearance so different and in reality, so similar, and that all come from the same original couple, show so many analogies with the human race—as the Biblical mythology portrays it—that the allusion cannot escape us. In fact, we cannot stop thinking that Cervantes is pleased here to underline that the Jews, as well as the Christians, all descend, after all, from Adam and Eve. Therefore, how could one imagine that a different blood could run in their veins?

We see the parallel between the many colored mice and people of distinct backgrounds. The fact is that we are all human beings, despite the existence of different ethnicities in the world. Therefore, the obsession with lineage is absolutely absurd. The symbol of the mouse is also interesting in that Cervantes is communicating the message that people are self-important beings who focus on their own silly little worlds, when, in reality, we are more like mice than we want to believe. The arrogant characters presume that they are an incredibly significant Old Christian part of society when they are actually unimportant, foolish villagers.

CERVANTES VERSUS "EL MONSTRUO DE NATURALEZA"

El retablo de las maravillas can be read as a parody of Lope de Vega's popular seventeenth-century *comedias* about courageous, honorable, hardworking Old Christian peasants who were of pure lineage. Lope feeds the common man's ego by upholding the idea of the valiant Old Christian. He reinforces the belief that it is good to be of pure blood by showing examples of brave and virtuous Old Christians in his theatrical works. According to Forastieri-Braschi:

> Justamente, contra quien la emprende burlona y deconstructivamente Cervantes en *El Retablo de las maravillas* es contra el mito lopesco del villano cristiano viejo de limpia sangre que Lope popularizó en las primeras dos décadas del siglo XVII. De trasfondo a una crisis económica y agrícola, la imagen del campesino geórgico y rico figuraba en paradigmas castizos como Peribáñez, Juan Labrador y Tello de Meneses quienes medraron a una hidalguía estamental hasta la hipérbole embustera de que el nieto de Tello de Meneses llegó a ser rey de España, como antes lo había sido el labrador Bamba. (349)

> Precisely, In El Retablo de las Maravillas, Cervantes mocks and deconstructs the Lope-esque myth of the old, pure-blood Christian peasant that Lope popularized in the first two decades of the seventeenth century. Against the background of an economic and agricultural crisis, the image of the rich, farming peasant appeared in traditional paradigms such as Peribáñez, Juan Labrador and Tello de Meneses who all achieved nobility, and even the untruthful tall tale that the grandson of Tello de Meneses became King of Spain, as the laborer Bamba had been before.

The public could relate to these theatrical works that portrayed the common man as someone who could one day rise to be king.

Lope also seems to believe that *pureza de sangre* is an important element in an individual's worth since his peasant characters are of Old Christian stock and uphold the image of the courageous countryman of pure lineage. Lope plays to the tastes of the uneducated masses, and Cervantes greatly resents the enormous popularity of Lope's works, which to him seem like random collections of scenes with no unity. Cervantes imitates this type of play in *El retablo de las maravillas*, and we see the disjointed quality of the images of the magic *retablo* that seem to have no common thread.

Unlike what Lope does with his theatrical works, Cervantes uses *El retablo de las maravillas* as a vehicle to express his thoughts on society's prejudices. Unfortunately for this playwright, Spanish society was not ready to see a play that included social commentary about their obsession with blood purity and, therefore, would cause them to question their own identity. They would rather watch a play that would entertain them and inflate their sense of self-worth. Thus, the theatrical companies rejected Cervantes' interludes and longer plays because they understood that this playwright's works would not draw a crowd.

Cervantes deems Lope de Vega a monster because of Lope's prolific writings and his ability to churn out amazing quantities of theatrical works in little time. We also know that Cervantes did not hold the works of Lope de Vega in the highest regard. Cervantes calls Lope "el monstruo de naturaleza" (the monster of nature) in the prologue to his *Ocho comedias y ocho entremeses nunca representados*:

> Tuve otras cosas en que ocuparme; dejé la pluma y las comedias, y entró el monstruo de naturaleza, el gran Lope de Vega, y alzóse con la monarquía cómica. (93)

> I had other things to occupy me; I left the pen and the comedies, the monster of nature arrived, the great Lope de Vega, and he ascended in the comic monarchy.

Cervantes disapproves of Lope de Vega's apparent disregard for the classical precepts of theater, as seen in Lope's *Arte nuevo de hacer comedias (The New Art of Writing Plays)*, and he openly criticizes the style of the Spanish *comedia* in general.[18] In *Don Quijote*, Cervantes uses the canon's speech to voice his own opinions on the sad state of theater during this time:

> Si estas [comedias] que ahora se usan, así las imaginadas como las de historia, todas o las más son conocidos disparates y cosas que no llevan pies ni cabeza, y, con todo eso, el vulgo las oye con gusto, y las tiene y las aprueba por buenas, estando tan lejos de serlo, y los autores que las componen y los actores que las representan dicen que así han de ser, porque así las quiere el vulgo, y no de otra manera, y que las que llevan traza y siguen la fábula como el arte pide, no sirven para cuatro discretos que las entienden . . . (484–85)

> If these [comedies] that are now seen, as well as those imagined as those of history, all or more are known nonsense and things that do not have feet or head,

and, with all that, the uneducated masses hear them with pleasure, and attend them and approve of them as good, although they are not so, and the authors that compose them and the actors that play roles in them say that they must be, because that is how the common man wants them, and not otherwise, and that those that have a clue and they follow the fable as the art says it should be, it's not worth their effort for the meager group of four people who understand them.

Here, Cervantes attacks many of the statements in the *Arte nuevo*. According to Cervantes, ignorant fools, who are also obsessed with blood purity, are dictating the current theatrical form, and the playwrights are committing a grave error in letting the foolish lead them astray from the classical art of drama. The artists have "sold out" in order to please the ludicrous desires of the *vulgo*, who is too stupid to appreciate classical theater. They would rather watch a play that caters to their ideas about lineage and society, and therefore, exults the *vulgo* as an example of a virtuous pure Christian. Also, the *comedia nueva* is ridiculous in Cervantes' view since it ignores the Aristotelian unities, and, thus, he considers it to be irrational, disjointed rubbish. The masses liked the *comedia nueva* because it was entertaining and portrayed the common man in a favorable light.

In *El retablo de las maravillas*, Cervantes is making fun of both Lope's style and the people who were fans of Lope's theatrical works. These were simple folks who had vulgar, unsophisticated tastes in entertainment and were constantly preoccupied with *pureza de sangre*. The reaction of Juana Castrada to the non sequitur actions of the marvelous puppet show in Cervantes' interlude mirrors the reactions of the general public to a play by Lope de Vega:

Castrada: Señor Benito Repollo, deje salir ese oso y leones, siquiera por nosotras, y recebiremos mucho contento.
Juan: Pues, hija, ¿de antes te espantabas de los ratones, y agora pides osos y leones?
Castrada: Todo lo nuevo aplace, señor padre. (231)

Castrada: Mr. Benito Repollo, release the bear and lions for us at least, and we will enjoy it.
Juan: Well, daughter, didn't you get scared of the mice before, and now you ask for bears and lions?
Castrada: All that is new is pleasurable, Mr. Father.

Although the suggested image of the nonexistent scampering rats terrifies Juana Castrada, she gleefully cries out for more frightening scenes simply for the cheap thrill of being frightened by more intimidating creatures. The enthusiastic reactions of the villagers in the play reflect the Spanish public's appreciation for what Cervantes deems *comedias* of little worth. The character Juana Castrada represents the views of the easily amused *vulgo* when she exclaims, "Todo lo nuevo aplace" (All that is new is pleasurable). Gerli notes:

> The skewed logic and factual errors of the show represents a travesty of the Lopean precept of variety. Yet the performance is wildly applauded by Chanfalla's boorish audience. (489)

For Cervantes, plays created according to Lope's formula were inferior and illogical works written for the ignorant masses, and the *retablo* exhibits the ludicrous nature of such plays.

Juana's silly response indicates that the public does not judge a theatrical work on its merit as an artistic piece, but rather is delighted by anything new that grabs their attention. One can compare Juana Castrada and her kind to babies who rely on their base senses to direct them to grasp at any shiny bauble that catches their fancy. This bauble could be a piece of plastic of little value; yet, they still hold it in high esteem simply because it is new, and it pleases them for no particular reason other than its sparkle. For Cervantes, Lope's plays are like the cheap pieces of plastic that pacify babies who do not know the value of the diamonds that are Cervantes' theatrical works. In *El retablo de las maravillas*, Cervantes criticizes the majority of Spaniards by portraying them as unintelligent oafs who are obsessed with *pureza de sangre* and who applaud a nonexistent play that would be terrible if it did exist.

METATHEATER IN *RETABLO*

The tricksters Chanfalla and Chirinos are completely cognizant that their theatrical performance, which includes their presentation of the nonexistent puppet show, manipulates the gullible villagers' sense of identity and causes them to doubt their blood purity. In Lionel Abel's theory of metatheater, the theatricality of life is reflected in dramatic works where reality and fantasy are intertwined and are unable to be distinguished (64). In *El retablo de las maravillas*, Chirinos and Chanfalla bend the rules of reality to create a fantastical play that cannot be seen by those of impure lineage. The foolish townspeople are so obsessed with *pureza de sangre* that they believe in a created reality where puppet shows will not reveal themselves to unworthy spectators. Thus, the rustic characters become actors who must prove to themselves and to others that they have the ability to see the *retablo*. These characters react to the nonexistent spectacle, and in playing the actors' roles, they don masks to hide their imagined Jewish identity.

El retablo de las maravillas is a metatheatrical work on many levels. Within the play itself is the marvelous *retablo* supposedly created by Chirinos and Chanfalla. Two swindlers narrate the action of this nonexistent play thereby creating a sort of ghost play that elicits the reactions of the characters who act as the audience. Arboleda discusses the idea of metatheater in Cervantes' interlude:

> La primera palabra, la interjección "¡Atención!", es tal vez la mejor que haya podido escoger Chanfalla para iniciar su representación que, digamos de paso, es improvisada. Esta palabra divide exactamente el texto en las dos secciones que hemos venido mencionando. Lo que sigue a esta palabra es precisamente lo metateatral, el teatro dentro del teatro. Dicha palabra, dicho grito, no sólo cumple con su función de marcar la frontera entre los dos textos; al llegar a la mente de los espectadores inmediatamente los está invitando a concentrar su atención en lo que la compañía va a representar a través de la palabra, su instrumento teatral por excelencia. Con la magia y el poder que sólo el actor metateatral sabe dar a la palabra, se desarrollan las seis escenas de la obra interna. (44)

> The first word, the interjection "Attention!", is perhaps the best that Chanfalla has been able to choose to start his representation which, let's say, is improvised. This word divides the text exactly into the two sections that we have been mentioning. What follows this word is precisely the meta-theater, the theater within the theater. This word, this shout, does more than fulfill its function of marking the border between the two texts. Upon reaching the minds of the spectators, he is immediately inviting them to concentrate their attention on what the company will perform through their voice, their theatrical instrument par excellence. With the magic and the power that only the metatheatrical actor knows how to give to words, the six scenes of the internal theatrical work are developed.

Chirinos and Chanfalla use the villagers' fear of an impure identity to create the illusion of a magical play since the townspeople must act as if they see the spectacle in order to protect their identities as Old Christians. The impostors aim to deceive the townspeople, and, therefore, act as though they truly believe in the power of the discriminatory puppet show they have created. Even though the puppet show is not real, it is real enough to transform the *entremés* into a metatheatrical work.

The peasants are compelled to react to the imaginary characters in the *retablo* to prove that their lineage is untainted by Jewish blood; thus, the country dwellers' actions become another theatrical work inside the bigger frame of the play as a whole. According to Forastieri-Braschi:

> Los villanos espectadores del retablo son ellos mismos el retablo verdadero, el verdadero espectáculo. (351)

> The villager spectators of the puppet show are themselves the true show, the true spectacle.

In responding to the false images of the *retablo*, the characters become the unwitting actors in a theatrical work of their own creation, thereby becoming the spectacle. Thus, Cervantes' work recalls Abel's definition of metatheater which includes the idea that "the world is a stage" (105) and the characters "are aware of their own theatricality" (60).

The villagers become actors who pretend that they are watching a fantastically vivid and amazing display. Pedro Capacho enthusiastically describes the mystical rain from the Jordan River:

> ¡Fresca es el agua del santo río Jordán! Y aunque me cubrí lo que pude, todavía me alcanzó un poco en los bigotes, y apostaré que los tengo rubios como un oro. (230)

> Fresh is the water of the holy Jordan River! And although I covered myself as well as I could, my mustache got a bit wet, and I will bet that it is now golden.

Pedro takes his acting cue from Chanfalla who tells of the gilding power of the magical waters, but Pedro embellishes Chanfalla's depiction of the rain by announcing that the water falls fresh and cool upon his face. Therefore, Pedro's acting abilities help him prove that he is able to see as well as feel the cascade of rain. These characters deceive their neighbors and create a drama in order to avoid being labeled a Jew. The intensity of their performances escalates as they intend to prove their pure backgrounds. Reality and fantasy blend as the townspeople trick even themselves into believing that they see the marvelous images. Psychologically, they must assure themselves that they are *cristianos viejos* and push away the doubt that clouds their minds. They are actors who are compelled to continue the charade to prove a supposedly superior identity, and they can never drop the mask that hides their identity, or they risk revealing a terrifying truth of origin to themselves and their neighbors. This scenario mirrors the reality of Spaniards in the seventeenth century who feel obligated to become actors to uphold their status as Old Christians.

Abel also states:

Metatheatre glorifies the unwillingness of the imagination to regard any image of the world as ultimate. (113)

The rustic characters demonstrate this characteristic of metatheater by refusing to accept reality. Although they do not see the fabulous figures spectacularly described by the tricksters, they create their own reality, which includes the existence of the magical *retablo*. The creative motivation that drives these unwitting actors is the fear of being Jewish or of otherwise impure lineage.

There are two types of audiences that see the performances. Kirschner describes these audiences in terms of the real and fictional public:

> Por de pronto, el teatro en el teatro crea automáticamente dos públicos: El público del escenario, formado por una sola clase, la de los campesinos ricos, que van a reaccionar como grupo homogéneo al espectáculo, y el público de la época cervantina al que se dirige el entremés (sea éste el auditorio ciudadano del corral en el que se mezclaba la aristocracia, la burguesía y el pueblo; sea el no menos amplio mundo de lectores). (823)

> Suddenly, the theater within the theater automatically creates two audiences: The stage audience, formed by a single class, that of the rich peasants, who will react to the show as a homogeneous group, and the audience of the Cervantine era to which the interlude is directed (be it the public courtyard auditorium in which the aristocracy, the bourgeoisie and the villagers were mixed; or the ample world of readers).

Therefore, Cervantes directs his message, which condemns the obsession about *pureza de sangre*, to all who represent Spanish society of the seventeenth century. Cervantes creates a metatheatrical work by including rustic characters who form an internal, or fictional, audience to a nonexistent play created by other characters in the playwright's interlude. The townspeople become actors who theatricalize their lives. The ridiculous, exaggerated actions of the country folk reflect the lives of the external audience or the Spaniards who feel they must be actors every day in order to uphold their status as Old Christians. Therefore, Cervantes' interlude allows us to peer into the mind of a typical Spaniard of the seventeenth century and see his greatest fear. This *entremés* acts as a mirror showing the metatheatricality of Spanish life.

The idea of the imaginary puppet show in the interlude *El retablo de las maravillas* can be compared to the idea of lineage. There was no way to see one's own lineage since it is not a tangible object, and the question of blood purity could never be answered because there was simply no complete way of knowing one's exact heritage. At that time, people did not have the option of DNA testing to discover their hidden roots. Therefore, one's lineage was as intangible as the imaginary *retablo*. Cervantes' frustration with Spanish society's obsession with *pureza de sangre* is reflected in his writing, and the rustic characters are portrayed as ridiculous, self-important buffoons who will go to any lengths to protect their supposed reputations as honorable Old Christians. The tricksters, Chirinos and Chanfalla, act as the puppet masters who, instead of controlling figurines, pull the strings of the puppet-like townspeople and create a spectacle. As described by these masters of deception, the nonexistent, metatheatrical *retablo* parodies the illogical theatrical works that were popular at the time and serves both to mock and frighten the absurd characters who are fixated on blood purity.

The fantastic *retablo* acts as the poisoned dart that is shot deep into the heart of the rural characters' self-identity and, therefore, cracks and poisons the vulnerable core of the self. The result is self-doubt, resistance to the possibility of impure lineage, and insecurity about identity, all caused by the obsession with *pureza de sangre*. The villagers' imagined "Jewish identity" is the catalyst that stirs up paranoia and suspicion. This dart changes their views of themselves and of others, and the life-altering theatrical production colors their whole world by suggesting their tarnished heritage. *El retablo de las maravillas* serves not only as a parody of Lope de Vega's popular *comedias* about Old Christian peasant heroes, but also as a scathing social commentary meant to highlight and criticize the injustice of ethnic prejudices in seventeenth-century Spanish society.

NOTES

1. For more information on the Inquisition and Spanish society, see Kamen. See Gutwirth for an analysis of *converso* humor in Spain.

2. See Byron, Canavaggio, and MacEoin for more general information about the life of Cervantes.

3. Artigas studies the issue of the *converso* in *El licenciado vidriera (The Lawyer of Glass)*, another work by Cervantes. Cervantes is familiar with the details of student life in Salamanca, as evidenced by his descriptions in *El licenciado vidriera*. Cervantes most likely studied at the University of Salamanca (MacEoin 7).

4. (Molho 47–71). It is interesting to note that Anderson's fable did not come from oral tradition, but rather from a German translation of *enxemplo* 32 of *El Conde Lucanor* (Molho 47).

5. See Terracini for a detailed comparison of the deception tales by Don Juan Manuel, Cervantes and Anderson.

6. For more in-depth information about the other trickster tales, see Molho.

7. Larson analyzes *El retablo de las maravillas* by exploring the speech-act theory and discussing the use of language in the play. Smith uses reception theory to analyze the reactions of both the internal, or fictional audience comprised of the simple townsfolk characters, and the external, or real audience of this Cervantine interlude. Bravo and Zahareas both examine society with relation to the theatrical works of Cervantes. Brown compares Cervantes' plot elements in *El retablo de las maravillas* to old testament allegories and explores the recurring theme of phallocentrism in the play. Patterson writes about how the issue of blood purity is approached in modern performances of this theatrical work.

8. See Egginton for an examination of the character Chanfalla's role in the theatrical work. For an analysis of the character Chirino, see Gracia Guillén. Llosa Sanz discusses the importance of the character Benito Repollo in this *entremés*. Cartagena-Calderón explores the issue of masculinity in *El retablo de las maravillas* and Spanish society of that time. See Mujica for an in-depth discussion of skepticism in this theatrical work. Chevalier studies the folktale *El embuste del llovista (The Rainmaker's Hoax)* and its relation to this *entremés* since it is mentioned by the character Chanfalla at the beginning of the play.

9. For a general overview of many of the elements in *El retablo de las maravillas*, see Volpe. Casalduero and Zimic give brief descriptions and analyses of many of Cervantes' theatrical works, including *El retablo de las maravillas*. Azcue Castillón compares this interlude with a scene in *Don Quijote* about the helmet of Mambrino. González studies the link between *Retablo* and *El arpa y la sombra* by Alejo Carpentier. See Oliva for a comparison between *Retablo* and a similar theatrical work entitled *Nuevo retablo de las maravillas y olé* by Lauro Olmo.

10. For a more detailed analysis of the character names in *El retablo de las maravillas*, see Molho.

11. Martínez López believes that in comparing the characters' village to Algarrobillas, Chanfalla is labeling all the townspeople as *confesos*. He mistakenly thinks of Algarrobillas as a town thought to be populated by people of Jewish heritage. According to Spadaccini, "Las Algarrobillas era un lugar en la actual provincia de Cáceres, famoso en la época por sus jamones, carne prohibida a los judíos" (Las Algarrobillas was a place in the current province of Cáceres, famous at the time for its ham, prohibited meat for Jews) (218). Therefore, in mentioning Algarrobillas, a town of Old Christians, Chanfalla makes an allusion to the *pureza de sangre* of the characters. The governor and other town leaders take this comment as a complement, not an insult.

12. Wardropper, Spadaccini and Molho also recognize the Latin phrase as one from the Bible, and they all offer interpretations of this reference.

13. The "barrentina" is a traditional, sack-like hat worn by rural Christian communities in Spain in Catalonia and Valencia. I translated this to "rotten villagers" since the Quartermaster is referring to the rustic characters by associating them with their typical clothing. Interestingly, around 1,400, this type of hat was once associated with Jews who had to wear one to distinguish them from Christians. With this symbolic reference, the cap further acts to label the villagers as "the other".

14. For a more detailed discussion of the other elements in the *retablo*, see Kirschner, Molho, Moner, and Wardropper. For a broader discussion of how reality,

appearance, and baroque thought and philosophy relate to *retablo* and George W. Bush's theatrical politics, see "The Baroque as a Problem of Thought" by Egginton.

15. And said unto his servants, This is John the Baptist; he is risen from the dead; and therefore mighty works do shew forth themselves in him. For Herod had laid hold on John, and bound him, and put him in prison for Herodias' sake, his brother Philip's wife. For John said unto him, It is not lawful for thee to have her. And when he would have put him to death, he feared the multitude, because they counted him as a prophet. But when Herod's birthday was kept, the daughter of Herodias danced before them, and pleased Herod. Whereupon he promised with an oath to give her whatsoever she would ask. And she, being before instructed of her mother, said, Give me here John Baptist's head in a charger. And the king was sorry: nevertheless for the oath's sake, and them which sat with him at meat, he commanded it to be given her. And he sent, and beheaded John in the prison. And his head was brought in a charger, and given to the damsel: and she brought it to her mother (Matt. 14.2–11).

16. In seventeenth-century Spain, it was common for the "o" to replace the "u" in popular speech, and therefore "judía" becomes "jodía" (Spadaccini 232).

17. The word "jodida" is an adjective derived from the verb "joder." According to the Collins Spanish dictionary, "joder" means "to fuck" in Spanish. Therefore, the adjective "jodida" has a sexual connotation since it literally means "fucked". One can interpret this word to also mean "screwed" which means, "to be caught in a difficult situation that one cannot escape."

18. After having written 483 plays, Lope de Vega wrote *El arte nuevo de hacer comedias en este tiempo* which describes his guidelines for the creation of a new kind of theater. This treatise serves as an explanation and a defense of Lope's ideas. In the *Arte nuevo*, Lope de Vega shows that he is not ignorant of classical theory and explains that he writes for the demands of the seventeenth-century Spanish public. Lope does not adhere to most of the Aristotelian rules of drama. According to Aristotle, there should be one coherent action or theme within a play, and this action should ideally occur in the span of one day. Also, Aristotle declares that tragedy and comedy are to be two completely separate theatrical concepts. Lope de Vega begins his list of rules by attacking one of the most important Aristotelian concepts of drama: he proposes the idea of mixing tragic and comic elements. For more regarding Aristotelian rules, see Aristotle's *Poetics*. See Lope's *El arte nuevo de hacer comedias* for more details on this playwright's theory of seventeenth-century theater. Brioso Santos discusses how Cervantes expresses his opinion about Lope de Vega using his play El *retablo de las maravillas* as a satirical representation of the new theater.

Chapter 2

A "Monstrous" Problem

Examining Issues of Race in Virtudes vencen señales

Luis Vélez de Guevara (1579–1644) always aspired to belong to a higher class than the one into which he was born. The son of middle-class parents in Écija, Spain, Vélez was by no means considered to be of royal lineage. Although he never became a rich nobleman, Vélez held positions in several houses of nobility throughout his life, and he even worked in the palace as the doorkeeper of the royal chamber (Spencer xv–xvii). Vélez de Guevara was a very popular playwright, poet, and novelist of seventeenth-century Spain, and it is said that this prolific writer penned more than 400 plays throughout his career, but only about 80 of these theatrical works have been found (Cotarelo 621–22).[1] Vélez was greatly influenced by the writing style of Lope de Vega, and Wilson describes him as "One of Lope's most successful contemporaries, and one of the closest to him in poetic and dramatic spirit" (79). Vélez was praised by other playwrights of his time, and unlike Cervantes, he embraced Lope's popular techniques instead of disdainfully rejecting them. Paulson remarks on Vélez's style of writing:

> Whether we consider the lesser-known playwright a slavish imitator of Lope or a creative adapter of *lopista* techniques, the fact remains that he is an excellent representative of the Lope school of drama. (47)

In fact, Vélez de Guevara adheres so firmly to Lope's rules of drama that there is some confusion as to whether to attribute certain plays to Vélez de Guevara or to Lope de Vega (Paulson 46). Like the great playwright Lope, Vélez focuses more on the themes and action in his plays rather than character development. According to Spencer:

Vélez' interests lay in development of the action rather than in well-rounded portrayal of character. He was either incapable of or indifferent to detailed psychological analysis. This explains the fact that the personages whom he can most successfully present are the heroic on a supernormal scale, and the comic in an unusual number of humorous types. (xxiii)

Vélez uses quickly moving plotlines and exciting and intriguing themes to grab the audience's attention, and his characters tend to be flat, one-dimensional caricatures. Many of his characters are honorable, brave, virtuous superheroes; witty, yet cowardly clowns; or cruel and heartless villains.[2]

VÉLEZ DE GUEVARA'S IDENTITY CRISIS

It is no secret that the playwright Luis Vélez de Guevara was of *converso* origin.[3] Vélez did not deny his Jewish lineage, and even tried to use it to his advantage at times. Vélez served the Count-Duke of Olivares, a man who was sympathetic to *conversos* and who openly spoke out against anti-Semitism (Fra-Molinero 344). Davies comments on the playwright's status as a *converso*:

> What is interesting, and perhaps surprising, in Luis Vélez's case is the openness with which the *cristiano nuevo* connection is admitted and exploited, in the little we know of his private dealings as well as on the stage. (25)

Although Vélez might have used his *converso* origin to secure a position with the Count-Duke of Olivares, the playwright bitterly resented the fact that his lineage hampered him in terms of his employment and attainment of personal goals. Hauer explains:

> A personal wish of Luis Vélez was to become a member of one of the military orders—a prerequisite for entrance was "sangre limpia." Vélez never succeeded in attaining the prized honor. (16)

Vélez, like many Spaniards in the seventeenth century, found it very difficult to be of *converso* heritage, and, therefore, he masked rather than embraced his Jewish origin. Luis Vélez de Guevara's real name was actually "Luis Vélez de Santander." Cotarelo comments on the writer's name change:

> Sabemos ya que los verdaderos apellidos del poeta eran Vélez (dejando fuera el patronímico de Rodríguez) *de Santander,* que usó en sus primeros escritos. Pero ahora toma el de *Guevara,* que no le correspondía, pero que era famoso

en nuestra nobleza, habiéndole usado desde el siglo XIV una ilustre familia: los señores de la casa de Guevara, del valle de Leniz y de Salinillas . . . (637)

We already know that the real last names of the poet were Vélez (leaving out the paternal last name Rodriguez) *of Santander*, which he used for his first works. But now he takes that of Guevara, which did not belong to him, but which was famous in our nobility, pertaining to an illustrious family since the fourteenth century: the lords of the house of Guevara, the Leniz valley and Salinillas . . .

Vélez picked a name that would mask his real lineage and reflect an imagined noble heritage. He traded his *converso* last name in order to "upgrade" to one that could elevate him to a higher status. A man by the name of Luis de Santander from Écija was burned at the stake by the Inquisition, and Vélez did not want his name to attach him to the stigma of unclean blood. As Cotarelo points out:

Apellidarse Santander y ser de Écija, no era, pues, gran recomendación para obtener un hábito de Orden caballeresca. (638–39)

Having the last name Santander and being from Écija were definitely not recommended if you wanted to obtain a badge from a noble order.

Thus, by altering his name, Vélez attempts not only to erase the stain of *converso* blood but also to gain a historically noble lineage.

By many accounts, Vélez was a vain man who freely spent his meager earnings on clothes befitting a rich nobleman (Hauer 16–17).[4] According to Hauer:

Vélez apparently longed to be something that he was not, thus he created a world suitable to his desire but he was never able to have sufficient funds to manage to live as he would have liked and constantly wrote *Memoriales* begging for money. (17)

The popular playwright was always poor, but by donning fancy apparel and changing his name, he appropriated the identity of a wealthy *cristiano viejo* of noble descent. Vélez's insecurity about his Jewish origin is reflected in his writing, as will be seen in the following discussion.

CRITICAL APPROACHES TO *VIRTUDES VENCEN SEÑALES*

Luis Vélez de Guevara probably wrote *Virtudes vencen señales* between 1618 and 1622.[5] In this play, we see abhorrent racist ideas espoused and upheld as accepted among Spanish society of the time. This racism is apparent in the portrayal of the main character of this play, Filipo. Filipo is a Black man born to white parents who are the king and queen of Albania. He is heir to the throne, but his color is taken as a bad omen by the king, and, therefore, he is locked away in a tower.[6] Filipo escapes his prison tower and is thrust into a world where all who see him instantly and unjustly reject him because of his different appearance. At first, this Black man is isolated because of his racial difference, but he uses his innate "virtuous nature" in order to overcome his "monstrous" appearance. I will use a linear approach to analyze *Virtudes vencen señales* in order to show Filipo's transformational journey that begins with his escape from his prison tower and ends with his coronation as the king of Albania. He embarks on a voyage of discovery of both the outside world and himself. After his escape, he first sees his dark countenance reflected in a pool of water and immediately rejects his Black identity and expresses horror and dismay at his appearance. Throughout the play, Filipo is unchanged in certain aspects of his character: He remains a pillar of nobility and morality and shows himself to be a forgiving man. He also consistently rejects his dark appearance while emphasizing his noble, white soul. Yet, he also demonstrates important changes, which I will show by analyzing his development from an unsure, wandering fugitive who is ignorant of his noble lineage to an overconfident superhero who becomes king of Albania. Throughout the play, Filipo's attitude changes, and he becomes increasingly more confident to the point of being annoyingly overly confident. At the end of the play, Filipo is self-righteous and boastful as he declares, again and again, that he is the one and only rightful king of Albania. In each scene, Vélez shows Filipo's nobility and virtue through brave deeds and reactions to the various problems that become more difficult as the play progresses.

The bigoted characters who interact with Filipo change as well, all following a predictable path of development. At first, they fear and despise Filipo because of his Black skin. Then, they fall under the spell of his highly virtuous nature. All people, including Filipo's enemies, follow his command after he proves himself to be virtuous, despite his appearance. After a show of his bravery, his enemies literally lie whimpering at his feet.

This racist theatrical work cannot be interpreted as a story of the acceptance of a different racial identity or the proof of equality of those who are of African descent. Conversely, we see the rejection of an identity that does not mesh with the dominant reference group. The same message is repeated numerous times: inside Filipo's "monstrous" black body exists a virtuous, pure white soul. If Filipo could, he would shed and abandon his Black skin in exchange for a white one, which he believes would reflect his true inner self. The playwright intends to erase Filipo's Black identity, but never actually succeeds in doing so since his black skin is continuously mentioned.

Cervantes wrote *El retablo de las maravillas* in order to criticize Spanish society's obsession with *pureza de sangre*. He disapproved of discrimination against the New Christians, and in his play, he parodies the ridiculous fixation on lineage prevalent in seventeenth-century Spanish society. Like Vélez, Cervantes himself is thought to be of *converso* origin, although this Jewish lineage is more certain with Vélez. Therefore, Cervantes resented being labeled and marginalized in society. Cervantes' play is quite subversive since he openly ridicules society's ideas about blood purity. On the other hand, Vélez is not at all subversive in his treatment of issues of identity in *Virtudes vencen señales*. He does not object to society's terrible assessment of Black people and to their marginalization. It does not seem that Vélez would have had much contact with Black people, as it is generally known that Blacks in seventeenth-century Spain were primarily slaves from Africa. Fra-Molinero discusses this subject with respect to the portrayal of those of African heritage in sixteenth and seventeenth-century Spanish literature:

> In all cases africanity—being of African descent—and slavery are represented as synonymous. Furthermore—and here lies the change from the Middle Ages to the early modern times—slavery is not an accident of fortune . . . but a natural condition for Blacks on Spanish soil . . . . (337)

Vélez does not contest the repulsive idea that Black people were thought of as savage, violent, and monstrous. These imagined qualities are mentioned every time Filipo's appearance is described. Vélez points out Filipo as an exception to the perceived rule that Black lineage denotes an ignoble and wild nature. He does not set out to prove the unfair, hateful nature of racial stereotyping. In fact, he reinforces it by having his character renounce and reject his "monstrous" Black identity and identify with the noble whites of mainstream society. In his introduction to the critical edition of *Virtudes vencen señales* by Manson and Peale, the Golden Age scholar Ruano de la Haza discusses racism in the play and counts nineteen uses of the word "monstruo" or "monstro" to describe Filipo directly. He states that one could argue that the characters in this play call Filipo a monster not because he is Black, but because he was born Black to white parents, and this is against the natural order. Ruano de la Haza explains that this reasoning could apply to Filipo's father, the king, but this does not explain the reaction of the other characters in this theatrical work who call Filipo a monster before they discover the extraordinary circumstances of his birth, and, therefore, it is the color of the prince's skin that makes him "monstrous" (21–22). Filipo is an exception to the abhorrent concept, prevalent in Spanish society at the time, that Black skin is the mark of an uncivilized, evil, monstrous man.

Besides thoroughly analyzing the character Filipo in terms of his racial identity, I draw a connection between Vélez's *converso* identity and his character's issues with race. I also discuss issues of gender because Leda, Filipo's sister, is a *mujer varonil (manly woman)* who believes herself to be heir to the throne of Albania. At first, Leda rejects Filipo as king and rebels, but the feisty female is put in her "rightful" place since a woman has no business obtaining a position of power in seventeenth-century Spain. My main focus, however, is the protagonist Filipo who rejects and denies his Black identity and embraces his perceived white, noble soul as he shows himself to be the perfect king of Albania.

Although Vélez de Guevara was a very well-known writer in the seventeenth century, interest in his works has waned over the years, and many of his theatrical works have not been thoroughly studied and analyzed.[7] *Virtudes vencen señales* has received little attention; hence, there are few critical studies that analyze it. Some critics compare it to *La vida es sueño* by Calderón, while others focus on the differences between the two manuscripts of *Virtudes vencen señales*.[8] I value the critical analyses of Michael Kidd and Baltasar Fra-Molinero since they both skillfully delve into the subject of racial and gender identity with regard to the characters of this theatrical work. These literary critics aid me in developing my own ideas and conclusions as I thoroughly analyze the race and gender issues present in the play.

To analyze the main character's problems of racial identity, I use the theory of Sander Gilman, as he describes it in *Difference and Pathology: Stereotypes of Sexuality, Race, and Madness*, to better understand the psychology of the marginalized Other and the reference group's reactions to this unique person. People fear the Other, or the member of a minority group, because of this person's difference. When members of the dominant group lack understanding of the difference, their fear of this difference motivates them to label and stereotype the Other in order to regain control of their world (Gilman 17–30). In Vélez's play, King Lisandro immediately stereotypes his son Filipo and sees his color as an ominous sign, therefore, labeling his Black son an evil villain even before he could talk. Filipo's Blackness is a mystery to Lisandro, and the king knows that he will not be able to control people's reactions to his son. Lisandro's fear stems from his loss of control, and therefore he struggles to regain control of the situation by hiding his son's difference and isolating Filipo from white society. Lisandro's temporary solution is to ignore the Other as if he didn't exist.

I also employ Gilman's theory of Jewish self-hatred to analyze Filipo's reaction to his difference and his rejection of Black identity. Even though Filipo is Black and not Jewish, the theory is applicable since it serves to study the actions of all marginalized minorities who wish to be part of the reference group. Filipo is immediately overcome with self-loathing when he realizes his racial difference. He longs to discard his black skin to be accepted in society. Filipo's status as an outsider motivates him to reject his identity and attempt to become like those in the dominant group. Although Filipo longs to be accepted in this group, he can never fully abandon his difference. Thus, the theories of Gilman help me to better understand the character's motivation with regard to identity.

XENOPHOBIA AND "GIRL POWER"

From the beginning of *Virtudes vencen señales*, foreigners, or those who are outside of the dominant group, are labeled as dangerous because of their perceived difference. The play takes place in Albania, which is a symbolic setting since *el alba (the dawn)* denotes shining radiance and whiteness, and the residents of this foreign land are white (Kidd 120). Fra-Molinero explains:

> To be Albanian, like being a Christian in 17th-century Spain, one had to be white, and of certifiable ancestry. Skin color was the sign of difference . . . Albania is a metaphor for Spain. It is one of those mythic kingdoms so typical of European Renaissance theater, like Poland, Denmark, or Muscovy. They belonged inside the pale of Christendom. (339)

In the first scene, the character Leda is introduced, and we immediately see that she is an independent, strong woman. Her name symbolically links her to the figure of Leda from Greek mythology.[9] Bell discusses this important mythological figure:

> The beautiful Leda drew the attention of Zeus, who was expert at circumventing the interference of husbands. One night he assumed the appearance of a swan and ravished Leda as she walked in the palace garden. (276)

Thus, like her mythological counterpart, Leda evokes thoughts of a pale beauty. Kidd explains:

> The princess's name is metonymically linked to the figure of the swan traditionally associated with beauty and grace (as well as with whiteness). (120)

Leda is the daughter of the king of Albania, and she believes herself to be heir to the throne. Her masculine demeanor and affinity for hunting show that she has assumed a male role. She is an opinionated *mujer varonil* with her own agenda, and her father Lisandro shows confidence in her virtue and ability to eventually govern the Albanian people as queen. Lisandro defends

Leda as the successor to the Albanian throne, and no foreign suitor will take this power away from his daughter, even if Enrico, the king of Sicily desires to marry her. We can interpret Leda's masculine nature as a manifestation of her father's desire for a male heir. After negatively responding to her suitor, Leda exclaims:

y es la respuesta que os doy,
y quedaos, porque me voy
a matar un javalí. (74–76)

and it is the answer I give you,
stay here because I am leaving
To kill a wild boar.

She flaunts her male attributes by briskly taking leave of her company and declaring that she would rather be off hunting wild boar. Since there is no male heir, Leda must play the part of the king's son and, therefore, she displays masculine characteristics to prove she is worthy of the throne. Lisandro's desire affects reality and changes his daughter's identity.

Leda refuses to marry anyone from another country. Thus, from the beginning of the play, xenophobic tendencies are revealed, and there is a fear of the foreigner, or the Other, in Albania. In response to the marriage proposal from Enrico, Leda declares that although she is a woman, she represents the male heir of Albania, and she does not intend to marry a foreigner.

Leda does not want royal power to fall into the hands of a foreigner who is seen as a threat to Albanian society. Kidd discusses the xenophobic tendencies of the Albanian royal family:

> Perhaps a metaphor for Spain's increasing isolation and withdrawal from European culture in the seventeenth century, Albania's xenophobia makes Leda's marriage to a foreigner out of the question and opens up a power vacuum that can only be filled by turning the princess into a prince. (123)

For lack of a brother, Leda must fill the position as male heir to the crown, and she sees it as her duty to marry an Albanian and, therefore, maintain the purity of the Albanian royal family and society in general. Thus, social norms are off-kilter here, and the stage is set for something to balance this feminine defiance of a male-dominated society. A male heir to the throne must be found, and the audience is ready to accept one with a flaw, as long as he is male. Neither a queen nor a foreign king will be acceptable in the eyes of seventeenth-century Spanish society since adherence to social rules does not allow power to be handed to the Other.[10]

THE PRODIGIOUS PRINCE

There is a remedy to the king's problem, but social order is left askew since a male heir exists, but his appearance is deemed frightening and symbolizes the threat of the outsider. After other characters show concern over the lack of a male heir, the king finally admits that he has a son, but that he was born Black. Upon his birth, the king takes his son's skin color as an ominous sign and, therefore, locks him away in a tower for twenty years. The king is fearful of his unusual son who is labeled as Other in an all-white Albanian society. In *Difference and Pathology*, Sander Gilman analyzes people's fear of the Other:

> Difference is that which threatens order and control; it is the polar opposite to our group. This mental representation of difference is but the projection of the tension between control and its loss present within each individual in every group. That tension produces an anxiety that is given shape as the Other. (21)

Lisandro could not predict that his son Filipo would be born Black; therefore, he finds himself in a situation that he cannot control. His son's undeniable difference represents Lisandro's loss of control. Filipo is automatically labeled as Other and therefore is a foreigner in his own land. Albanian society is threatened by the existence of this dark-skinned prince. The king's fear of his son's racial difference motivates him to act in a cowardly manner in order to escape the stigma of having a Black son. Lisandro falsely announces Filipo's death and imprisons the Black prince in a tower to permanently separate him from "normal" white Albanian society. In this way, Lisandro "kills" his son, thereby destroying the Other, at least in the eyes of the public. The king regains control by isolating Filipo and restricting all aspects of the young prince's life to the confines of a tower.

The king launches into a description of the magical and mysterious circumstances of the birth of his Black son:

Solicitava el desseo
engendrar su semejante,
natural inclinación
de todos los animales,
una noche que tenía
puesta en los ojos, delante,
en un tapiz de oro y seda,
una figura admirable
de la Reyna de Etiopia
Sabaa, donde al acabache

negro dio espíritu brioso . . .
tan atento, que pudieron
las especies visuales
dar a la imaginativa
fuerca para que engendrase
lo mismo que estavan viendo
los ojos; que en estos trances
es universal doctrina
de todos los naturales
que lo que se vee se engendra, (285–309)

I had the desire
that your fellow man has as well,
the natural inclination
of all animals,
one night I had
placed in front of my eyes,
a tapestry of gold and silk,
of an admirable figure
the Queen of Ethiopia
Sabaa, where the shining jet
black gave a spirited energy . . .
so strong, that the visual image
could give the imagination
the force to engender
the same thing that the eyes were viewing
that in these trances
it is universal doctrine
of all in nature
that what one sees, one begets,

Lisandro explains that he contemplated a beautiful silk and gold portrait of the queen of Ethiopia hung above his royal bed during the conception of his son. The Black queen's image causes his son's dark skin. Kidd explains the theory behind this odd tale:

> The pseudoscientific basis for this bizarre story, rooted in the natural philosophy of antiquity, reappears in the neoplatonic belief that images could enter through the eyes and physically damage the soul, a notion that persisted in both the popular and literary imagination of the Renaissance. (125)

Vélez must have been inspired by similar stories of strange births caused by the vision of an exotic image.[11] *Virtudes vencen señales* is a rewriting of

Heliodorus's Ethiopian story (Kidd 125). The story is the same, but the colors are reversed, and the white baby is regarded as different.[12] *El collar de la paloma*, by Ibn Hazm de Córdoba, includes a story with very similar elements (Fra-Molinero, 351). In this tale from eleventh-century Spain, a Black baby is also born to white parents, but here the mother of this baby is the one who is guilty of gazing upon the portrait of a Black man.[13]

In *Virtudes vencen señales*, the character Lisandro never admits to actively staring at the portrait and reacts as if the portrait just happens to be there when his son is conceived. The king beholds the tapestry that is hanging above his bed (una noche que tenía/*puesta en los ojos, delante,*/en un tapiz de oro y seda,/ una figura admirable) (289–293) (one night I had/placed in front of my eyes/a tapestry of gold and silk,/of an admirable figure) and he portrays himself as a passive victim who cannot avoid looking upon the beautiful portrait. The male gaze is thus inverted and subverted by this description, and it is Sabaa's portrait that gazes down at the king. Kidd comments on this inversion of power:

> While the king seeks actively to conquer and contain the image of the negress, the linguistic ambiguity of the passage leaves open the possibility of a reversal of the process, in which the reader or onlooker would instead become bewitched by the object of his attention. (126)

By describing his encounter with the enchanting Black queen's portrait in this way, Lisandro tries to avoid the guilt of actively lusting after a Black woman, which is taboo in his society. Therefore, he removes himself from active involvement with the Ethiopian queen's portrait and, instead, portrays himself as a passive victim of her power. The figure of Sabaa dominates and controls the king's gaze.

The minority race becomes dominant here as Sabaa usurps the power of the king to impregnate the Albanian queen. We could interpret this scenario another way as well since Lisandro directs his gaze at the attractive Ethiopian queen's portrait in order to become sexually aroused, therefore committing adultery with her image. As Sabaa drives the king's lustful thoughts, she replaces the Albanian queen as the object of desire, thus usurping the power of the white queen. In this interpretation, the Albanian queen becomes a mere vessel for the child of King Lisandro and Queen Sabaa. Lisandro's desire for the Black queen shapes reality when a Black boy is born as a result of the supernatural encounter. In either interpretation, the Black queen remains the dominant figure in the scene. I agree with Kidd's progressive reading of this scenario:

> In the eroticized landscape of the royal bedroom, the gaze of the colonizer is subverted or, more literally, inverted by the gaze of the colonized subject, as the

image of the black queen penetrates and dominates the eyes, soul, and future offspring of the white king. (128)

A love triangle exists between Lisandro, Sabaa, and the queen of Albania, and the king's power is undermined since the Black queen uses him to engender an offspring. It is the image of Sabaa that succeeds in impregnating the queen, and, therefore, Lisandro is the vehicle through which the seed of Sabaa travels.

The portrait of the Black queen is literally above the Albanian royal couple, which puts her in a position of power over them. Kidd interprets the placement of the tapestry:

> The portrait of Sabaa hangs above the bed of the king and queen, so that the king must cast his glance upward in order to view it from a reclining position. The image of Sabaa, by contrast, rests at a vantage point that would most likely allow the trajectory of her gaze to sweep the entire room. In Foucauldian terms (Foucault 146–148), this vantage point places her in a position of power derived from the epistemological superiority of the panopticon, once again inverting the perceived relationship between colonizer and colonized. (127)

One could interpret this part of the play as Vélez's way of fictitiously giving power to the marginalized *converso* population of Spain by allowing the image of a Black female figure, a symbol of the *converso* or Other, to control a white couple of the highest nobility.

The progressive interpretation may be applied to the tale of the conception of Filipo, but on the whole, we cannot ignore the negative connotations of Black identity in Vélez's play. We are not allowed to forget the perceived monstrosity created by the dominance of the Black image. The image of the queen usurps the power of the white king, but we are reminded that his sexual contemplation of her image is very wrong, and the king feels he is punished when his son is born Black. Every character remarks on Filipo's appearance and deems him hideous. Their reactions imply that Filipo is a monstrous, deformed freak of nature, not just a man with Black skin. For the bigoted characters who exist in the world of this theatrical work, Filipo's appearance marks him as the unfortunate offspring of an evil union that produces what they see as a terrible, savage-looking creature. Therefore, we can analyze the curious circumstances of Filipo's conception progressively, but the harsh reactions to the Black prince's appearance overshadow and negate the progressive interpretation of Filipo's conception. The story shows the racist idea that the intermingling of the Black and white races produces unfortunate outcomes. We see that the result of the Ethiopian queen's virtual interaction with the king motivates him to hide his son, the only male heir to the throne, and lock him up in a prison like a criminal. Filipo's only crime is being Black in a prejudiced, xenophobic society, the consequence of the "unholy" union of his white father and a Black female figure depicted on a tapestry. In fact, Filipo's own father calls him a "prodigioso ultraje" (enormous insult) (338), and the king condemns his son's appearance as hideous and monstrous:

> que quando [en] Filipo estrañe
> el color, lo monstruoso,
> lo no visto, lo espantable,
> lo diferente, lo fiero,
> lo prodigioso, lo errante,
> lo feo, lo peregrino,
> virtudes vencen señales. (452–58)

> that when with Filipo, one was shocked
> the color, the monstrous,
> the unseen, the frightening,
> The different, the fierce
> the prodigious, the wanderer,
> the ugly, the pilgrim,
> virtues overcome signs.

In the eyes of the other characters, the prince is redeemed by his virtuous nature, but it is made clear that this is inherited from his royal, white Albanian parents since his Black color is not considered to be connected to his noble lineage.

FILIPO'S DICHOTOMY: BLACK BODY, WHITE SOUL

From the moment Filipo views himself, he is filled with self-hatred and vehemently rejects his perceived "horrifying" appearance and declares that his superior, virtuous soul is trapped in an ignominious, Black body. In his first appearance, the stage directions state that the actor who played Filipo would be a white man who painted his face black. Kidd provides an interesting analysis of Filipo's description:

> In order to maximize the dramatic effectiveness brought about by Filipo's bewilderment at his own appearance, Vélez may have wished him actually to appear with a white body and a black face, the only part of his body he would never have seen during his life in captivity. Since the face is so central to self-identification, once Filipo saw his countenance in the pond he would be instantly transformed into a black man in his mind's eye. Whatever the case,

the protagonist's physical appearance implies a technical flaw that is ultimately unsolvable. On the one hand, if Filipo in reality has a black face and white body, it hardly seems possible that the other characters would fail to comment, as they do, on this striking contrast. On the other hand, if the absence of a black body is a simple stage convention and Filipo is understood to be completely black, then he would surely have recognized his blackness long before contemplating his image in the fountain. (121n)

One thing is for sure: we know that the actor who plays Filipo uses makeup to blacken his face, which symbolically transforms the actor into a Black man. Vélez never expects a real Black man to play the part of the prince. For the seventeenth-century Spanish audience, the white actor's portrayal of the prince further serves to fictionalize people of African heritage since the actor must paint his face to represent the Other. The white imposter chosen to portray Filipo is not even disguised to look like a true Black man since only his face is darkened.

From the moment that the Black prince appears on stage, it is impressed upon the audience that Filipo's poetic and refined language is incongruous with his seemingly "monstrous" appearance, and immediately, one is struck by the eloquence of this character's speech (571–80). Filipo's lofty commentary on his new state of freedom causes him to philosophize about God's power, and his thoughtful intelligence is revealed in his first words. According to John Lipski, most of the Black people living in seventeenth-century Spain did not speak Spanish differently than the white Spaniards, but the seventeenth-century Spanish audience expected Black characters to show their difference in their speech, as well as their appearance. Lipski explains:

> Given the formulaic nature of the black character roles (e.g., reference to African place names, frequent singing and dancing and lamenting the fate of the slave while adopting seductive poses) and the frequent repetition of stereotyped phrases such as *aunque neglo gente somo,(although we are black people)* it is clear that the theater-going public of 16th and 17th century Spain had well-developed expectations as to the overall behavior patterns of Africans. (10)

The character Filipo obviously does not resemble other stereotyped Black characters in seventeenth-century Spanish theater, and, therefore, his speech defies his Blackness.[14] He does not speak a broken, accented Spanish or refer to Africa as the audience anticipates. Filipo's skill with language shows that he is a native speaker, not a foreigner, even though his appearance indicates otherwise. In fact, he speaks more eloquently than the other characters in order to compensate for his Blackness. Hence, Filipo uses his poetic discourse to show the xenophobic public that his white soul shines through his Black exterior, and, therefore, he attempts to erase his difference.

There is a connection between the Antilles Black man as described by Franz Fanon and the Black character in this play:

> The Negro of the Antilles will be proportionately whiter—that is, he will come closer to being a real human being-in direct ratio to his mastery of the French language . . . . A man who has a language consequently possesses the world expressed and implied by that language. What we are getting at becomes plain: Mastery of language affords remarkable power. (18)

Filipo's mastery of Spanish gives him the power to communicate his whiteness to the other characters. Kidd explains that "Filipo's polished Spanish clearly becomes one of the signs of his "white" interior" (119). Through his language, Filipo transforms himself from a monstrous creature into a human being in the eyes of the characters and the audience.

Filipo's happiness over his newfound freedom suddenly turns to sadness and confusion when he wishes to quench his thirst and sees himself reflected in a pool of water. Water has the power to sustain life, but here water ends Filipo's life as he knows it. The water changes this character's self-perception forever by ending his ignorance and reflecting his true appearance. Filipo is shocked by his black skin:

Mas, ¡cielos!
¿Soy yo este feo
monstro que dentro el cristal
a la noche miro igual?
¡Yo soy el mismo que veo!
Aun mirándome no creo
que soy yo, que tan altiva
alma ¡o plata fugitiva!
parece, aunque me copiaste,
que en tan baxo y torpe engaste
es impossible que viva. (611–20)

But, heavens!
Am I this ugly one?
monster in the crystal mirror
Am I the same shade as night?
I am as I see myself!
Still looking at myself, I do not believe
what I am, such a lofty

soul. O errant mirror!
it seems, although you show me as I am,
in such a dull and crude jewelry setting
I find it impossible to exist.

Upon beholding himself in the fountain pond, he is frightened at his appearance and does not believe that the Black image he sees is his own because it does not match the way he sees himself in his mind's eye. He immediately rejects his Black identity, which he connects with difference, ugliness, and immorality. Fra-Molinero comments on Filipo's reaction to his self-discovery:

> He is both aware of racial differences and at the same time ignorant of his own body. Through some kind of natural instinct, he seems to know that he should abhor a black body, yet he is unaware of being Black himself. (341)

The prejudiced idea that black skin denotes evil tendencies is ingrained in Filipo, and he cannot bear to see himself reflected like this. Fanon explains the negative associations with black skin:

> In Europe, the black man is the symbol of Evil. . . . The torturer is the black man, Satan is black, one talks of shadows, when one is dirty one is black—whether one is thinking of physical dirtiness or of moral dirtiness. It would be astonishing, if the trouble were taken to bring them all together, to see the vast number of expressions that make the black man the equivalent of sin...and, on the other side, the bright look of innocence, the white dove of peace, magical, heavenly light. A magnificent blond child—how much peace there is in that phrase, how much joy, and above all how much hope! (189)

Filipo accepts the concept that his Blackness is monstrous, and he longs to be white. As he gazes at himself in the water, he exclaims that his lofty soul could never live in such a "baxo y torpe engaste" (such a dull and crude jewelry setting) (619). Filipo believes that his beautiful, pure soul is like a shining jewel, and it deserves better than his Black body, which is compared to a debased metal mounting. This scene can be compared to the story of Narcissus from classical mythology:

He was pursued by many lovers, male, and female, but he rejected them all. One of the lovers killed himself and called upon the gods to avenge him. Narcissus fell in love with the beautiful youth he saw looking up at him from the depths of a pool. The fact that he pined away because this lover was unattainable suggests he had less than a strong grasp on reality. He was changed into the flower known as the narcissus. (Bell 277)

The difference between these two stories is that when Filipo sees himself reflected in the pond, he is repulsed rather than attracted to what he sees. Kidd compares the classical myth to the Spanish play:

> In the scene in question, Vélez clearly inverts the Narcissus myth insofar as Filipo's self-discovery is brought about negatively or, in Freudian terms antinarcissistically, that is, through an identification not with but rather against the ego. (121)

We see the character Filipo as the polar opposite of Narcissus. He perceives himself to be repulsive and hideous whereas Narcissus perceives himself to be desirable and beautiful. Narcissus cannot uproot himself from the side of the pond where he sees his unattainable lover. Narcissus loves himself so much that he ends up destroying himself because his mind is held prisoner by his own beauty. The moment he sees himself, Filipo is conversely held prisoner by his ugliness. He can never escape from his Black body, and, therefore, he hates, rather than loves himself. Thus, self-love and self-hatred can both have destructive powers, and Filipo's reason for self-hatred is his Black identity.

Unbeknownst to Filipo, his sister Leda is behind him on the mountainside, and Filipo sees Leda's image reflected in the fountain waters as well. He instantly compares her white, godlike appearance to his own undesirable reflection:

O el alma se engaña o ve
aquí dentro otro traslado.
¿Qué deidad nueva confía
deste cristal su arrebol?
Junto a mi sombra está el sol,
junto a mi noche está el día:
¿si es el alma propria mía
que me ha querido enseñar
su essencia inmortal? (629–37)

Is my soul deceived, or has
another copy materialized.
What new deity appears
and glows within this crystal?
next to my shadow is the sun,
next to my night is the day:
Does my own soul
want its immortal essence
to be revealed to me?

When Leda appears, Filipo believes that she is the bright, shimmering jewel that is the image of his true essence. To Filipo, Leda's reflection represents what he should look like, and he immediately falls in love with this image. Therefore, Filipo is narcissistic in a sense, since he believes that Leda's beautiful, white body is a true representation of his soul. In this way, he falls in love with himself. Although I agree with Kidd's commentary on the Black prince's antinarcissistic sentiment, I believe that there is a very narcissistic element to the character of Filipo, and, as I show later in this chapter, his narcissism grows throughout the play. This is not narcissism in a traditional sense of loving one's outward appearance, but rather it is narcissism on a different level. Filipo places an extremely high value on his self-worth, and he praises his lofty, virtuous soul more often as the play progresses and even compares himself to God. He hates his body but loves his soul, and he wishes he could separate the two. He connects Leda's beauty to the beauty of his own soul. Thus, begins the appearance of Filipo's narcissistic tendencies, although he is a self-hating Black man who despises his body and wishes he could dispose of it in favor of a white one that he deems more suitable.

Filipo's interaction with Leda is his first contact with a human other than his teacher and companion, Tebandro. Leda is frightened upon first seeing Filipo:

¿Quién eres, di,
monstro portentoso y fiero? (665–66)

Who are you? Speak,
astonishing and fierce monster?

This meeting serves only to confirm Filipo's fears concerning his perceived monstrous appearance and reinforces his self-hatred. Leda's fear dissipates, however, when Filipo eloquently speaks of her in glowing terms. Leda believes that anyone who could flatter her so poetically must have a virtuous soul, and his complements make him more acceptable and less monstrous in her eyes. Therefore, his praise of a member of the dominant white group allows him to become more accepted despite his difference. Leda remarks:

¡Qué alma tan hermosa encierra
cuerpo tan feo! No sé
después que hablar le escuché
que jamás el alma yerra,
qué inclinación le he cobrado
en la fiereza que ofrece.
¡Nuevo misterio parece

averme a un monstro inclinado!
No sé la sangre que tiene,
que su persona me agrada. (719–28)

What a beautiful soul is contained in
such an ugly body! I do not know
After he spoke, I heard him
that the soul never errs,
Although he seems fierce,
I am becoming fond of him.
A new mystery it seems
I am inclined to like this monster!
I do not know of his bloodline,
But he is pleasing to me.

Leda's praise is a double-edged sword in that she is surprised that such beautiful words could come from someone who she regards as ugly. She therefore reinforces the repugnant idea that being Black is equal to being savage and evil, and Filipo is an anomaly because he is both Black and has a good heart. Leda also wonders if Filipo's Black body might be incongruous with his heritage since she makes a reference to his bloodline. She reiterates Filipo's thoughts that his pure white soul is trapped in what she considers an ignoble, Black body. Thus, the Black prince's racial difference is magnified because of his "white," noble way of speaking.

Leda's exaggerated, dreadful reaction to Filipo, as well as other characters' responses, would cause one to think that Filipo is not only Black but also a hideous, terrifying, deformed creature unworthy of being called a human being. Fra-Molinero explains the lamentable discriminatory view of Black people in Renaissance society:

> Blacks were a special case in the order of nature. In the Renaissance version of the Great Chain of Being, or natural scale of Creation, Blacks were placed just above apes, Black slaves coming to represent in art the fallen condition of man. . . . Blacks were considered not only intellectually inferior to whites, but more important, Blacks were *morally* inferior, their black skin being the outer sign of sin and lack of virtue. To be Black in Spain in the Renaissance was a social curse. (343)

Therefore, the seventeenth-century Spanish audience accepted racist ideas and would not question the characters' exaggerated reactions to Filipo's appearance and their incredulous remarks upon hearing his eloquent diction and observing his virtuous deeds. As far as we know, Filipo's only difference is his Black skin. Therefore, in the bigoted eyes of seventeenth-century Spanish society, discrimination is completely acceptable and being Black is synonymous with being subhuman.

Filipo's reaction to his reflection sparks a feeling of self-loathing that he can never completely squelch. When he sees Leda, he instantly wants to *be* her. Gilman explains:

> Thus, outsiders hear an answer from their fantasy:
> Become like us—abandon your difference—and you may be one with us....
> The first sign—be like us, and you will become one of us—implies accepting one's own difference. But the more one attempts to identify with those who have labeled one as different, the more one accepts the values, social structures, and attitudes of this determining group, the farther away from true acceptability one seems to be. For as one approaches the norms set by the reference group, the approbation of the group recedes. In one's own eyes, one becomes identical with the definition of acceptability and yet one is still not accepted. For the ideal state is never to have been the Other, a state that cannot be achieved. (2–3)

Filipo aspires to be a part of the reference group; therefore, he must show that his soul is whiter and more virtuous than everyone else. His lofty language also reflects his desire to be accepted as a white man. He despises his Black identity and rejects it to show others that he is really a white man encased in a Black body. He truly believes himself to be white, but his appearance prohibits others to accept him, and his difference marks him as an outsider throughout the play. Filipo can be a self-hating Black man and boast of his honorable soul continuously, but this can never erase his Blackness. He can never abandon his difference. Filipo will inherit the throne, but his "monstrous" appearance is an enormous obstacle in this society that causes others to rebel against him.

FILIPO'S NOBLE ACTIONS OVERSHADOW HIS APPEARANCE

Vélez intends to prove, not only through articulate speech, but through courageous deeds as well, that Filipo's ominous Blackness does not define him as a person. In the second act of *Virtudes vencen señales*, Filipo shows himself to be a golden-tongued poet and a brave and heroic man. The Black prince encounters Tirrena, a singing peasant girl who predictably cries out in terror after he approaches her (974–976). Tirrena is frightened and repulsed by Filipo's appearance, but upon hearing his noble speech, she becomes less afraid of him. Since Filipo has not eaten since he escaped from the tower, he is famished and asks Tirrena for food. She offers him onions and bread, and he takes the bread but refuses the onions, which Tirrena interprets as a sign of noble blood:

Quien con hambre haze desprecio
De las cebollas no tiene
Mala sangre. (1044–1046)

One who is hungry and scorns
Onions must not be of
Bad blood

In this play, the onion represents the lowborn peasant because this vegetable is an inexpensive, foul-smelling bulb that is plentiful and easily attainable. Also, it grows in the ground, symbolizing the common man who works with the earth and is not of noble lineage. Historically, onions are regarded as a lower-class food:

> From ancient history up to the 19th century, onions were relegated as the food for the poor. The Code of Hammurabi, known as the ancient law of Mesopotamia, shows great concern for the needy by providing them a monthly ration of bread and onions, a ration that comprised the mainstay of the peasant diet. As disagreeable as the onion was to the aristocrats, the peasants devoured them completely raw. Apparently, onions took on dual status in the attitudes in the ancient world. In Egypt they were highly revered by the poor and eaten extensively along with bread and beer. (Allen)

For Vélez, Filipo's refusal to eat the onions is yet another way to prove this Black man's noble and virtuous nature.

Filipo then comes across Clarín, the humorous servant character of the play whom Filipo has met before. Clarín tumbles down a mountainside in a sack, a victim of a group of malicious bandits. He lands at the feet of Filipo who demonstrates his forgiving nature by pardoning Clarín for his earlier rude behavior and unkind words. The grateful servant and Filipo engage in a discussion of money, and since Filipo has never seen or used currency, Clarín explains its great worth in society. Once again, Filipo shows his amazing virtuous nature by rejecting the concept of money because he sees it as idolatrous (1298–1310). People covet and worship money, and Filipo sees this as blasphemous and, therefore, throws the coin to the ground. In this scene, the prince shows his highly spiritual nature and his indifference toward material goods. This is yet another example to prove that Filipo's pure, noble soul overcomes the bad omen that is his Black appearance.

Filipo shows his incredible bravery when he hears Tirrena's screams for help, and he hastily runs to rescue her from a band of evil thieves. The captain of the band, Sergesto, was about to rape her and strip the poor woman of her honor when Filipo and Clarín arrive, ready to fight the vile men. After a short battle, the robbers surrender and pledge allegiance to Filipo. They then declare Filipo captain of the thieves. It is amazing how quickly these men change from terrible pillagers to loyal subjects who are willing to change their evil ways and follow their new leader. The bandits' rapid transformation is attributed to the persuasive powers of Filipo's honorable and courageous character.

In this scene, Filipo begins to boast more about his virtuousness and innate kingly nature. Filipo declines the title of captain and demands to be called king of the countryside thus showing that leadership is his calling:

no quiero que me llaméis
capitán: por Rey juradme
destos campos y llamadme
Rey, que en mi valor veréis
que este título merezco,
y que assienta en mi valor
el de Rey mucho mejor
que otro alguno; aunque parezco,
por las muestras naturales
del negro color del rostro,
fiero y prodigioso monstro,
virtudes vencen señales. (1445–456)

I do not want you to call me
Captain: pledge allegiance to me as King
of these fields and call me
King, that in my courage you will see
I deserve this title,
and that is consistent with my value
the title of king is much better
than any other, although it seems
that the black color of my face
is naturally proof that I am
a fierce and prodigious monster,
virtues overcome signs.

Filipo is confident that he deserves the title of king, but he must reject his "repugnant" appearance to gain acceptance. He tells the others to ignore his black skin, but in doing so, he calls attention to his difference. Filipo becomes increasingly narcissistic in the sense that he believes in the complete superiority of his noble soul as he announces his position as king of the countryside, even though he is not aware of his true lineage yet. As this foreign-looking prince continues to show his valor with increasingly impressive deeds and lofty thoughts, it becomes clear that Vélez is determined to demonstrate that *virtudes vencen señales*. Filipo must overcompensate for his perceived "monstrous" color if he is to gain the respect of a xenophobic, racist seventeenth-century Spanish audience that believes Black people are animalistic and innately less intelligent and moral than whites. The fact that Filipo rescues Tirrena and defeats the thieves elevates his status into that of a brave hero. For the audience to accept Filipo as king of white Albania, he must erase his difference by becoming a superhero whose virtue far surpasses the virtue of all other Albanians.

FILIPO BECOMES KING

Filipo proves, without a doubt, that his prodigious color does not affect his noble "white" soul. Filipo is aware of his virtuous nature before he meets his father, and his deeds and words show that he is ready to assume the responsibilities as king of Albania. Filipo finally meets his real father, King Lisandro, and the truth of his royal origin is revealed. Upon seeing his son, the king remarks on the difference of Filipo's unsettling appearance, but he senses the blood that runs through their veins is the same:

Ricardo, dexa
que llegue hablarle, que, puesto
que la espantosa presencia
puede admirarme, la sangre
que en él con tanta excelencia
está diziendo que es mía
con la que tengo en las venas
parece que se procura
juntar. (1657–64)

Ricardo, let him
arrive so that I can speak to him,
in his frightening presence
he can come admire me, the excellence
of the blood within him
is saying it is mine
with what I have in my veins
it seems to yearn to
join with mine.

Of course, Filipo's frightening appearance is mentioned here, but Vélez intends to show that the prince's virtuous blood is the same as his white father's blood. Thus, the difference of Filipo's Black race is obscured by his noble bloodline.

Filipo has already been named king of the countryside, but now he discovers that he is heir to the throne of Albania. Unfortunately for Filipo, he also discovers that the beautiful woman with whom he has fallen in love is his sister (1894–1912). Filipo mourns the fact that Leda is his sister, but his amazing, honorable nature and self-restraint allow him to forget his love for this woman and avoid a taboo relationship. Fra-Molinero explains:

> Sexual union with a Black man belongs in the realm of the forbidden, and to signify the interdiction Vélez de Guevara chose the image of the incest taboo. (346)

Filipo's restraint is further proof that he does not give into the animalistic, savage, and immoral tendencies that a biased seventeenth-century Spanish society wrongfully ascribed to the Black man.

In the third act, Lisandro has died and Filipo is king. He shows himself to be haughty and narcissistic in this part of the play since he continuously boasts of his own virtuous soul and kingly essence. He must be overconfident and announce that his soul is royal and virtuous to prove to the Albanians that his monstrous appearance does not denote an unfit and savage king. The Black king addresses his Albanian subjects in a speech that shows he has democratic tendencies since he eloquently announces his plan to share his power with his subjects (2015–2032). Besides touting himself as a god on earth, he offers all Albanians a chance to participate in the governing of their country. Filipo speaks to his subjects in a familiar, friendly way, hoping to endear himself to them. Hence, a Black king becomes more palatable to the white public because he declares that all will share in his power. Filipo makes this speech in hopes of winning over the Albanians and making them forget his odd appearance. The Black king also wants the support of his subjects because he knows that other countries will fear and resist him, and they will attempt to reject his authority. Filipo needs the loyalty of the Albanians if he is to stay in power as king.

Filipo tries to come across as humble in his first speech as king, although his humility is lost when he speaks of his divine nature. His humble attitude gives way to one of stubborn determination as he demonstrates his superiority. Filipo contradicts himself in the way he treats Clarín, his trusty servant. When the thieves name Filipo king of the countryside, he assures the clownish servant, "Clarín, no os echo en olvido" (Clarín, I will not forget you.)

(1495) and tells Clarín that he will serve by Filipo's side as his confidant and adviser (1499–502). It is clear that Clarín does not aspire to be more than Filipo's servant, but the prince names him as his adviser. Later, when Filipo is king of Albania, he gives the admiral of Albania, a man secretly plotting to kill Filipo, the title of royal chamberlain. After the new king gives out several more titles, Clarín complains bitterly (2098–2104). Clarín has served Filipo faithfully, and he feels that his friend has forgotten him as soon as he assumed power as king of Albania. Although Clarín never asked for a position of power, Filipo gave him one, and when the king conveniently forgets to give Clarín a title, the servant feels slighted and underappreciated. After Clarín has voiced his opinion, the king has some rather harsh words for the servant:

Nunguno, por accidente
de gusto ni de passión,
ha de subir escalón
de merced indignamente, . . .
Clarín, humilde has nacido:
conténtate con tener
de vestir y de comer
cerca de un Rey. (2133–36, 2141–44)

None, by accident
of desire or passion,
can ascend the stairs
of honor if unworthy, . . .
Clarín, humble, you were born:
be content to have
clothing and eat
near a king.

Filipo has a condescending attitude, and unfairly chastises Clarín for wanting the recognition that was promised to him earlier. The king also points out Clarín's low-class status, thus highlighting his own noble blood. He squelches Clarín's hope by exclaiming that one of such common lineage should never hope to fill positions meant for nobility. Therefore, Clarín can never escape the social class into which he is born. In insulting Clarín and pushing him down, so to speak, Filipo desires to lift himself up as an example of someone whose noble blood entitles him to kingly power. By belittling someone of ordinary lineage and emphasizing his royal bloodline, Filipo hopes to make the Albanian public look beyond his difference and focus on his royal roots.

REBELION AGAINST THE BLACK KING

Filipo's difference is not ignored, but rather it is used as an excuse to denounce him as king since he represents the outsider. Several characters feel that they deserve the crown, and they cannot accept that a Black man is the king of Albania; thus, rebellion ensues. One by one, Filipo puts the power-hungry characters in their place. The seed of rebellion is planted in Leda who furiously voices the unfairness of the situation. Her long rant makes it seem as if she is throwing a tantrum like a child whose toy has just been taken away. Vélez uses Leda's angry reaction to prove that "hysterical" women are not suited for the throne:

a la memoria sagrada
de mi padre, de quien sé
que soy viva semejanca,
sin que el color contradiga
a la verdad de la estampa.
Sólo en mí mi padre es Rey,
después del cielo éste manda,
como mi Rey y mi padre,
en mi vida y en mi alma. (2224–2232)

to the sacred memory
of my father, who I know
I am made in his likeness
without color contradicting
the truth of our similarity.
Only in me my father is King,
after heaven, he commands,
like my King and my father,
In my life and in my soul.

Leda would have been queen of Albania, but a Black man has taken the power away from this white woman. The princess bitterly complains because her status has fallen, and her long-lost brother, whom she sees as an unworthy, frightening creature, has usurped her position. Leda attacks Filipo's weak spot by calling attention to his dissimilarity. She exclaims that she will not obey this strange person who looks nothing like her father. In pointing out his difference, Leda hopes to introduce doubt about Filipo's legitimacy and, thus, question his right to the Albanian throne.

In his long-winded rebuttal, King Filipo reprimands Leda and proclaims that he will be respected as the one and only king. Filipo reiterates the fact that he is the true king of Albania several times and scolds Leda for her rebellious words as if she were a small child (2319–2335). In this speech, Filipo announces that Leda does not have the right to the throne since she is a woman and, therefore, inferior to a male heir. He states that his color does not affect his superiority as a man. Filipo contradicts himself since earlier he tells his Albanian subjects that they are all kings and have the right to help make decisions in their country. Filipo fiercely defends his duty to be the sovereign king of Albania. The Black king even raises himself up to the level of a godlike being (2334–2349). Filipo supports his right to wield power by comparing himself to God and exclaiming that he was divinely chosen to lead the Albanian people as their king. Filipo is completely confident in his ability to be the perfect king, and his haughty attitude of supremacy is evident.

After Filipo proclaims his superiority, Leda repents immediately. She is humbled and submissive and bows before her brother and begs his forgiveness. She blames her rebellion on the fact that she is a weak woman who cannot resist the manipulation of the sinister admiral who is planning to murder the king (2354–2362). Leda's reaction here is a far cry from the strong, independent, *mujer varonil* she once was. Kidd comments on Leda's change:

> Yet, when Filipo appears on the scene and proves himself a capable ruler, Leda's "maleness" and, along with it, her right to male privilege, is immediately subverted. (123)

Leda attributes her rebellious actions to the fact that she is a woman. She generalizes that women are susceptible to deception because they believe everything that they hear:

Corrida estoy de aver sido
tan fácil que [a] las palabras
de un hombre tan mal seguro
diesse crédito, que es falta
general en las mugeres
no recatarse de nada
y creello todo. (2401–2407)

I run ashamed from the fact that I was
so easily lead by the words
of a man so evil, I was sure to
have faith in him, which is a common fault
in women
who cannot rescue themselves from anything
and will believe everything.

In this way, Vélez reiterates the message that women are too emotional and gullible to be trusted with power, and Filipo is far better suited to be king, even if his strange color differentiates him from others.[15] Amazed, Leda instantly bows down to Filipo, and she even reiterates Filipo's words and comments on his mysterious, divine nature (2398–2400). Like all other characters, Leda changes quickly as a reaction to the awe-inspiring power of her brother, the king.

Filipo's inflated sense of self is evident in this final scene, and he feels he must continuously praise his virtuous, godlike soul in order to inspire others to do so as well. Therefore, he rejects and erases his Black body and embraces his virtuous soul and noble white Albanian lineage.

Vélez wraps up the play rather hastily by exposing the plots to murder the king. Filipo's Black physiognomy makes him a target for those who wish to take away his royal power. These characters use Filipo's difference as an excuse to rebel against him. Filipo is Black, and therefore, according to white European society, unfit for the throne. The admiral believes he is a much better choice for king, but his treason is revealed when Filipo finds an incriminating letter. Filipo confronts the admiral, and when he is challenged, the traitorous character does not unsheathe his sword, but rather collapses into a shaking pile of jelly at the feet of Filipo. The admiral confesses and is reduced to a whimpering, submissive, repentant man in awe of the king's noble character. As in earlier scenes, Filipo shows clemency to a mortal enemy, and he pardons the traitor and allows him to live. Once again, the king's virtuous soul shines bright, and he has the ability to transform enemies into loyal subjects.

Not only is the admiral plotting to kill the king, but also outsiders are in cahoots with this traitor, thus emphasizing the idea of the dangerous foreigner who gains power and dilutes the purity of Albanian society. The king of Sicily, Enrico, and his sister Alfreda are the treacherous foreign characters. Although foreign in appearance, Filipo is not included in this group of outsiders since he is a native Albanian with a royal, white heritage. His Black appearance is an accident, and noble, Albanian blood runs through his veins.

Enrico and Alfreda are en route to Albania for both of their weddings. In theory, Enrico will marry Leda, and Alfreda will marry Filipo. Alfreda acts as if she were going to her own funeral rather than her wedding because she dreads marrying Filipo, and she is repulsed by what she regards as a monstrous and savage appearance:

Desdichada fue mi estrella,
pues me obliga a que me case
con un humano portento,

un Etíope, un salvaje; . . .
Yo moriré, si pudiere, (2743–746, 2763)

Unlucky was my star,
it forces me to marry
a shocking human,
an Ethiopian, a savage; . . .
I would die, if I could,

Alfreda declares that she would rather die than marry someone she considers a foreign barbarian, therefore, emphasizing abhorrent, racist, xenophobic beliefs common in seventeenth-century Spanish society.

Enrico reassures his sister Alfreda, and he divulges the plan to kill Filipo by recruiting her to poison the Albanian king on their wedding night. The treacherous foreigner has something else up his sleeve since he also plans to kill the admiral, thereby, securing the crown for himself. The foreigners are the real enemies, and, in contrast, although Filipo may look completely different from his fellow countrymen, he is a true Albanian who will protect his society from threats by foreign powers (2909–2911). Filipo is extremely confident in his ability to govern the nation, and his inflated sense of self-worth serves to compensate for his difference. As with all other characters who at first oppose Filipo, Alfreda is struck by the Albanian king's virtuous nature:

A que le amen
obliga; perdone Enrico,
que solo no he de matalle,
pero le he de defender,
porque el alma, hermosa imagen
de Dios, tanto le parece
que el cuerpo hermoso le haze. (2887–892)

He obliges others
to love him, forgive me, Enrico,
I will not kill him, on the contrary,
I must defend him,
because his soul, his beautiful image
is so like that of God, that it appears
his body is made beautiful.

Alfreda is in awe of the king, and his beautiful soul erases his ominous Black color in her eyes, which are opened to Filipo's godliness. She vows that she will not carry out the murderous plan, and, in fact, she pledges to protect him. Filipo confronts the Sicilian king, and Enrico immediately confesses and surrenders himself to the Black king. Filipo again shows his generous and forgiving nature by pardoning all these deceitful foreigners, thereby proving once again that he is the epitome of a great hero even though he must constantly negate his Black identity.

It is not realistic that the characters would change their negative opinions so quickly, but Vélez would like the audience to believe that Filipo is a superhuman capable of miracles. The characters rapidly fall under the spell of Filipo's magnetic personality as he poetically boasts of his virtuous soul and compares himself to God. He seems to have the characteristics of a cult leader who uses intense charisma to mesmerize and entrance others to get them to follow him. The Black king uses his ability to convince others of his noble blood and virtuous nature to overcome what others view as his portentous appearance.

VÉLEZ'S CONNECTION WITH HIS CHARACTER FILIPO

We can connect this playwright's own rejection of his Jewish lineage with the identity-obsessed main character he creates in his theatrical work. Michael Kidd comments on the use of Vélez's play as a vehicle to broach the topic of *pureza de sangre:*

> Moreover, if questions of race and gender—of otherness, that is—act as a type of screen under which issues of ethnicity and religion are delicately broached ... then the play offers what I believe to be a significant commentary on Vélez's *converso* status. (117)

Vélez projects his feelings onto the character Filipo. Just as Filipo tries to disassociate himself from his Black identity and attempts to claim a white one, the writer divorces himself from his *converso* roots by changing his last name. The switch to "Guevara" is an attempt to hide his real lineage and obtain an Old Christian identity that he feels is more suitable for his "noble" soul. Vélez lived as if he were a rich noble of pure blood, but his expensive clothes and new name could never erase the fact he was of *converso* origin.

People of Jewish lineage could try to blend into Spanish society since their appearances did not signify their difference. Fra-Molinero explains:

> In order to belong to the national community, one has to look the part, that is, one has to be undifferentiated from the rest of society. *Converso* descendants *looked* like the rest, and were excluded from honors and government appointments. (344)

Although the *cristianos nuevos* looked like other Spaniards, they could never really blend in because it was usually known which families were of Jewish origin. Therefore, there was no escaping ethnic difference. It was the *converso*'s last name, family history, occupation, and activities that alerted others to their connection to Jewish ancestry. Castro comments on this issue:

> Para agravar la situación y hacerla aún más confusa, los españoles de ascendencia hebrea se movían en una esfera de intereses distinta de la usual entre cristianos viejos; no siendo el mismo su estilo de vida, no era difícil barruntar quiénes eran cristianos nuevos, a veces sin necesidad de demostraciones documentales. (98)

> To make the situation worse and even more confusing, Spaniards of Jewish descent moved in a sphere of interests that were different from the usual among old Christians; since the lifestyle was not the same, it was not difficult to determine who were new Christians, sometimes without the need of any documents.

One's ethnic heritage could not directly be discerned just by appearance alone, but people could easily guess who was of *converso* origin. One could attempt to deny a Jewish heritage by changing a name. In comparison, racial difference cannot be denied because one's appearance immediately calls attention to a unique lineage. Filipo can never deny that he has black skin, but he constantly voices his disgust at his appearance and attempts to compensate for it by declaring that his soul is white and virtuous. Vélez uses his character Filipo to show that although someone may be of a different race or ethnicity, this person can be virtuous and honorable, *despite* his or her difference. Therefore, we can connect Filipo's situation to the predicament of a *converso* writer struggling to prove his self-worth to a society that puts a high value on *pureza de sangre*.

Thus, Vélez deals with his own issues of identity by using his character Filipo as an example to show that although born of a different race, one can be virtuous and noble because of innate characteristics. In this case, a Black man is heir to the throne of Albania, a country inhabited by white people. It is interesting to note that if Vélez is trying to prove that people of Jewish lineage can be just as virtuous and noble as *cristianos viejos*, then he is, in a sense, shooting himself in the foot. His implicit comparison of the exemplary Black prince and the *conversos* of Spain backfires by emphasizing the fact that Filipo's noble lineage is untouched by his Black appearance. His skin color is supernatural since his parents are not Black. Therefore, in the eyes of the Albanians, he is a white man who mysteriously happens to have black skin. Filipo is a pure-blooded noble white man even if his appearance is peculiar. One can assume that if Filipo was actually an African of Black ancestry, he would never have been portrayed as the virtuous heir to the Albanian throne, but, rather, he would have been depicted as a wild, savage man as suggested by the descriptions of the other characters who are surprised by Filipo's monstrous form. In this case, the Albanians would have never accepted the Black prince. Only Filipo's appearance is affected by an impurity, and his royal, Albanian blood is pure and untainted. His difference is skin deep, but the *converso*'s difference is more profound because it runs through his veins and influences the very core of his being. Thus, the *converso* will always be connected to his Jewish roots even if the religion is long forgotten. One cannot escape the fact that according to seventeenth-century Spanish society, the blood is contaminated forever by Jewish ancestry.[16] Using this logic, we can assume that if someone is of Jewish lineage, this lineage runs through the blood, therefore, marking this person and his or her descendants as impure in terms of ethnic heritage.

Through *Virtudes vencen señales*, Vélez would like to convey the message that the *conversos'* difference is not important, and they should be considered as equals to the *cristianos viejos*. The playwright's approach to this issue does not necessarily support what he desires to prove. The nature of Filipo's difference is indeed a superficial one since his white lineage is unchanged by his Black appearance. However, the *conversos'* heritage is unchanged, according to Spanish society, generation after generation. No matter how often they change their names and attempt to pass as a *cristiano viejo*, the *conversos* cannot avoid having "Jewish blood."

Instead of seeing this play as an argument for the *conversos*, as Vélez would want, Spaniards of the seventeenth century could interpret it in a different way. They would understand that Filipo deserves to be a king because he has white, noble blood, and his difference is truly superficial. His blood is untainted. According to common belief, the *conversos* have the opposite problem since they look like other Spaniards. Their difference is not superficial, but rather, much more profound since they cannot extract the impurity from their blood. Vélez constantly repeats that Filipo has white, royal blood, and it seems rather ironic that the playwright would pay so much attention to the "blood purity" of this character when that is precisely what is called into question in terms of the *converso*. Therefore, what Vélez wants to prove, and what Spaniards of the seventeenth century could interpret from the play, are two different ideas. In vying for equality in Spanish society for those of *converso* origin, Vélez inadvertently argues against those who have blood tainted by Jewish heritage. Thus, Jewish heritage runs deep in the veins of the *conversos*. However, Filipo's Black color is superficial since internally he is as pure, white, and noble as his Albanian father.

The characters of Vélez's play have their own interests in mind, and they seem to be a group of self-centered, narcissistic, cowardly characters who are motivated by power. Filipo's dark skin, which is interpreted as an ominous sign, frightens his father Lisandro. Filipo's skin color signifies evil to the king of white Albania, and, therefore, the king fears that his son might threaten his power. Lisandro's anxiety motivates him to imprison his son in a cowardly attempt to avoid problems stemming from his son's skin color. Lisandro's self-centered personality is the cause of Filipo's many years of unjust imprisonment.

Leda, Filipo's sister, is portrayed as an egotistical woman who possesses manly attributes. She expects to inherit the crown and throws a childlike tantrum when Filipo becomes king. She uses her brother's Blackness as an excuse to denounce his right to wear the crown. It is clear that Leda's "womanly condition" leaves her vulnerable, and she is convinced to rebel against the king. Although Leda is white, she is also a woman, and her feminine quality renders her weak and unfit to rule a nation. Therefore, we see that the playwright is definitely not an advocate for the equality of women.

The admiral and Enrico are power-hungry, self-centered characters who plot to kill Filipo. Both regard Filipo as a monster, and each character believes himself to be better suited to the Albanian throne. Enrico is doubly deceitful, and he plans to kill the admiral after Filipo is murdered. The foreigner Enrico is treacherous, and he turns out to be a big threat to the Albanian nation. From the beginning of the play, we see the xenophobic tendencies of the Albanian royalty, and Enrico's evilness reinforces the idea that foreigners are not to be trusted.

The main character Filipo is characterized as a superhero. As the story progresses, he becomes increasingly self-aggrandizing, and he constantly boasts of his valor and godliness. At first Filipo does not aspire to be king, but once he has assumed the power, he constantly repeats that he is the one and only king.

Throughout the play *Virtudes vencen señales*, we see the development of the character Filipo who is transformed into the self-confident king of Albania. Vélez might have created Filipo as a reaction to issues with his own *converso* identity. Filipo begins his journey outside of his prison tower as a virtuous and poetic man who is frightened of his own Black appearance and unsure of his origin. It becomes clear to Filipo that royal, white blood runs through his veins, and he continuously rejects and denies his Black identity. As Filipo performs increasingly heroic deeds and demonstrates his noble and forgiving nature, his sense of self-worth grows greater. When he becomes king, he continuously compares himself to God, proclaims his ability to govern, and dismisses his unique appearance as an accident of nature. For the play's characters and the seventeenth-century Spanish audience to accept this Black man as the rightful king of a white Christian nation, Filipo must deny his Blackness and become "whiter" than everyone else. The Black king's secret for obtaining power lies in the ability to abandon his marginal status and imitate the dominant culture. Filipo must show superiority to the members of the reference group to become king. Unfortunately for Filipo, his Black color is never forgotten, and consequently can never be completely erased. Filipo has an inflated sense of self-worth to compensate for his difference, and, therefore, he disengages himself from his black skin.

The racist idea that Filipo has an ugly, monstrous appearance, but has the most wonderful, honorable, courageous, merciful, noble, pure white soul is repeated ad nauseam. Filipo becomes more narcissistic as he shows his true valor and overcompensates for what others see as his "monstrous" appearance. He must be superhuman for his personality to eclipse the color of his skin. Although Vélez aims to create a valiant superhero by emphasizing this unusual character's numerous eloquent speeches and brave deeds, Filipo is really a pompous, haughty man whose deep-rooted self-hatred prompts him to vehemently reject and deny his Black identity and vociferously boast of his noble white lineage.

NOTES

1. See Profeti for a description of criticism of Vélez's works, including commentary from Vélez's contemporaries. Profeti mostly cites those who praise the writer's ability to create literary works.

2. For more on Vélez's biographical information and descriptions of his literary works, see Davies, Hauer and Spencer.

3. In *Los españoles: cómo llegaron a serlo (The Spaniards: How They Came to Be)*, Castro comments on Vélez de Guevara's Jewish heritage (33–34n). Besides discussing Vélez's *cristiano nuevo* identity, Davies also comments on the playwright's portrayal of *converso* characters in several of his theatrical works (21–26). Cotarelo and Hauer also examine Vélez's history with respect to his *converso* origin.

4. In her book, Hauer includes an itemized list of Vélez de Guevara's wardrobe. The playwright has a number of costly, elegant items in his collection such as black silk stockings, leather jackets, taffeta garments, and a green velvet traveling bag (16–17).

5. For an explanation of why Vélez is thought to have written *Virtudes vencen señales* during this time period, see Kirk and Schevill. Schevill states, "Judging from the language and style, it belongs to Vélez's middle period before he succumbed to an excessive use of *culto*. Of this there is relatively little in the play. His natural descriptions have an unusual simplicity and directness. I venture to suggest that the date of composition may be placed between the fall of the Duke of Lerma (1618) and the coming into power of the Conde Duque de Olivares under Philip IV (1622)" (190).

6. Parker explores the theatrical idea of unjust imprisonment in a tower and analyzes several of Calderón's plays with respect to this mythical element.

7. Hauer discusses Vélez's popularity throughout the centuries. She notes that there are not very many extensive studies of his works, and therefore this lack of attention relegates Vélez to the realm of a rather obscure dramatist, although now there seems to be some renewed interest in his work (11–33). He is best known for his novel *El diablo cojuelo (The Limping Devil)* (Wilson 79).

8. See Schevill for an in-depth comparison between *Virtudes vencen señales* and *La vida es sueño (Life is a Dream)*. Schevill believes that Vélez's play influenced Calderón as he wrote *La vida es sueño*, which was perhaps written after *Virtudes vencen señales* (191). Kirk also compares the plays by Vélez and Calderón and describes the two different texts of *Virtudes vencen señales*. Zugasti describes the characteristics of the palace play genre and compares *Virtudes vencen señales* to seven other theatrical works that focus on issues of royalty and fit the description of this genre. Profeti gives a detailed analysis of the differences between the two *Virtudes* manuscripts. In the introductory essay of Manson and Peale's edition of *Virtudes vencen señales*, Ruano de la Haza includes an analysis of its structure and versification, compares the works by Vélez and Calderón, and discusses racism as a theme in *Virtudes vencen señales*.

9. For further studies on mythology as portrayed in Spanish theater, see Kidd, *Stages of Desire*.

10. For more detail on the social conditions of Spain in this period, see *Spain 1469–1714: A Society of Conflict* by Kamen (196–257).

11. Huet discusses this idea and explores the issue of monstrous and supernatural births as portrayed in literature.

12. Your father then had intercourse with me, as he had been bidden to do, he solemnly averred, in a dream; and immediately I was aware that I was pregnant by his engendering. But when I brought you forth white, gleaming with a light complexion alien to the Ethiopian race, I understood the cause. During the intercourse with my husband the picture of Andromeda presented her image to my eyes, showing her entirely nude, just as Perseus was taking her down from the rock, and it had thus by ill fortune given to the seed a form similar in appearance to that of the heroine. I therefore decided to save myself from a shameful death, being convinced that your colour would subject me to a charge of adultery—for nobody would believe my account of that miraculous change. I pretended to my husband that you had died at the moment of birth, and I exposed you in complete and utter secrecy, placing with you as large a store of riches as I could, to be a reward for whoever should preserve your life. But, my sweet daughter of only an hour, if you should survive, be mindful of your noble descent (Heliodorus 95).

13. Se cuenta asimismo de un fisiognomista experto que le trajeron un niño negro nacido de dos padres blancos. Después de haber examinado todos sus rasgos, comprobó que era de ambos, sin duda alguna, y entonces pidió que le llevaran al sitio en que habían cohabitado los padres. Al entrar en la habitación en que estaba el lecho, vio la imagen de un negro en la parte del muro donde recaía la mirada de la mujer. "Por culpa de esta imagen—dijo al padre—has tenido este hijo" (Ibn Hazm de Córdoba 106).

There is the tale of an expert physiognomist who was asked to see a Black child born of two white parents. After examining all his features, the physiognomist found that the child was both white and Black, without a doubt, and then asked to be taken to the place where the parents had cohabited. Upon entering the room where the bed was, he saw the image of a Black man in the part of the wall where the woman's gaze fell. "This image is to blame—he said to the father—for the birth of this son."

14. For an in-depth description and analysis of Black characters in Spanish theater, see Fra-Molinero, McGaha, and Weber de Kurlat. McGaha compares the Black characters from *Othelo* and *Las misas de San Vicente Ferrer (The Masses of St. Vincent Ferrer)*. Weber de Kurlat focuses on Black characters in Lope de Vega's theatrical works and also studies the Black comical characters in Spanish theater.

15. According to fifteenth-century ecclesiastical ideology, women were seen as "intemperadas," "extremosas," "parleras y porfiosas," "móviles e inconstantes" ("Intemperate," "extreme," "talkative and stubborn," "constantly moving and fickle") (Vigil 13–14). According to Vigil, "Esta era, en líneas generales, la vision que desde la ideología eclesiástica del siglo XV existía sobre la condición femenina y sobre el papel que las mujeres debían desempeñar en la sociedad" (This was, in general, the vision that has existed since the ecclesiastical ideology of the fifteenth century on the feminine condition and on the role that women should play in society) (14). Attitudes about women had not changed much since the fifteenth century; therefore, these ideas can also be applied to seventeenth-century concepts about women.

16. For more information on the *conversos* of Spain and the idea of *pureza de sangre,* see *Inquisition and Society in Spain in the Sixteenth and Seventeenth Centuries* by Kamen.

Chapter 3

Struggling with the Mask of Conformity

Desire and Sexual Identity in El público

Wherever Federico García Lorca traveled, he delighted, amazed, and amused many with his wonderful talents. In addition to being a stupendous playwright and poet, he also could play the piano beautifully and sing folk songs. He could transcend any language barrier, and always found a way to communicate using music, poetry, and his sense of humor. No matter what country he was in, people were magnetically drawn to his glowing, outgoing personality. Unbeknownst to some, Lorca also had a melancholy, dark side that his friends and family occasionally glimpsed. It is as if Lorca were torn between showing himself to the world as an exuberant man who laughed loudly and loved life and revealing himself as a poet with a tortured soul. Often, his gleeful mask would fall way, and those who knew him best would see a man whose core ached with confusion, pain, and sadness. In *Federico García Lorca: A Life*, Ian Gibson writes about several of Lorca's companions who knew of Lorca's anguish.[1] One French writer even knew where the roots of Lorca's sadness lay:

> The French writer Marcelle Auclair did know her man, and, in her book *Enfances et mort de García Lorca*, published in 1968, analysed the homosexual aspect of the poet with sensitivity, reaching the conclusion that Federico's "greatest fear was, undoubtedly, that his parents would discover that he was an 'invert.'" The writer does not tell us if Lorca himself confided this fear to her, but at any rate we may be fairly sure that the necessity of having to lead a double life in a society where homosexuality was considered abhorrent played a large part in the poet's underlying sadness and, at times, despair. (xxi)

The enormous secret of Lorca's sexuality weighed heavily on him, and he could not bear to think that his parents might find out about what society would deem an "abnormal" sexual orientation. Therefore, he had to bear the heavyweight of the mask and cover up his true desires in order to be acceptable in Spanish society. This disguise suffocated him emotionally by denying him the right to reveal his genuine nature to the world.

The Spain of Federico García Lorca's lifetime was a turbulent, changing nation. In 1923, Primo de Rivera took over the leadership of Spain at a time of great unrest and violence between workers and employers. Supported by conservatives who wanted the power of a military authority, Primo de Rivera ruled as dictator until 1930 (Kamen 148). During this time, Lorca felt emotionally and artistically suffocated in this highly intolerant environment. According to Gibson, in 1925, Lorca's main goal was "to get out of Primo de Rivera's Spain, with its stifling sexual morality, its censorship, and its taboos, its constant harassment of non-conformers and intellectuals and its pettiness" (152). During this time, Lorca was extremely depressed, and he confided in his friend Benjamín Palencia who was also gay. From Lorca's letters to this painter, one can deduce that Lorca's melancholy stemmed from his deep feelings for Salvador Dalí, and, in later years, feelings for other men, which would be condemned by most people in the conservative Spanish society.[2]

THE MAIN DILEMMA IN *EL PÚBLICO*

The twentieth-century Spanish plays, *La llamada de Lauren* by Paloma Pedrero and *El público* by Federico García Lorca, both address the theme of sexual identity and the struggle with conformity within a rigid society. In *El público*, Lorca portrays several characters who are struggling to form an identity. They are in a constant battle to define their identity to others and to themselves. The characters are caught between showing their true inner selves and donning the mask of social conformity. The conflict in this play is that some of the characters are gay men who try to hide their sexual identity behind a heterosexual persona in order to be accepted by society. Although strong feelings pull the men toward same-sex relationships, fear of societal retaliation repels them from proclaiming their true sexual identities. The main question of Lorca's play is this: should the main character, the director, show his queerness and be condemned by an intolerant society, or should he disguise his real identity and be consumed by the desires of a forbidden love never realized? This dilemma mirrors Lorca's own problems, stemming from being a gay man living in the conservative, Spanish Catholic society of the 1930s. Martínez Nadal describes the principal messages of the play:

(1) Love is a phenomenon motivated by factors alien to the will of man.
(2) Thus love can manifest itself on all levels and with equal intensity or drama. Nor is the participation of two sexes, even of two human beings, poetically speaking, essential. (30)

The attraction of one being to another is an uncontrollable power that at times goes against societal rules which declare that real love exists only between a man and a woman.

Because of the disjointed and surrealistic nature of *El público*, I will not analyze it linearly. Instead, I will break down the play and examine the strange, ever-changing characters, magical beasts, and symbolic objects of the play. I will analyze the motivations of the characters who vacillate between revealing their queer nature and cloaking their true identities to survive in a vicious, judgmental world. Thus, the characters must make the difficult choice between dangerous liberty and the safety of emotional prison.

CRITICAL APPROACHES TO *EL PÚBLICO*

Lorca's play *El público* has been analyzed in a multitude of ways by different critics. Many critics tend to tackle one aspect of the play, such as the symbolic role of masks in the play.[3] In articles with a related theme, critics study the idea of cross-dressing and its effect on sexuality, showing that the characters' many costumes serve as a mask to disguise or reveal their changing sexual identities.[4] Others choose to focus on the few female characters in the theatrical work.[5] Some critics concentrate on the violent and sadomasochistic nature of some of the characters in the play.[6] The comparison of *El público* to other works by Lorca and, also, to literature by other writers is a popular theme in many critical essays.[7] Writers also study and analyze the audiences' reactions to presentations of this highly unusual theatrical work.[8] While some critics offer a general overview of the play, others prefer to narrow the focus and analyze it with regards to a certain theorist's ideas or focus on one symbolic element.[9] The varied and eclectic approaches to the analysis of *El público* have helped me to better understand this bizarre and fascinating play.

The critics aid me not only in comprehending this theatrical work, but also in forging my own ideas about it. Rather than look at a single symbolic element in the play or apply only one theorist's ideas to my work, my approach to examining *El público* is to create an in-depth, thorough psychological analysis of the characters, using several theories and critical articles to support my examination of the play. It is important to understand the characters' motivations for concealing or revealing their sexual identities.

Throughout my study of this theatrical work, I always keep the dramatist's situation in mind. Therefore, I analyze the characters in *El público* in the context of Lorca's battle with his own alternative sexual identity. Rafael Martínez Nadal provides invaluable insight into the psyche of Lorca since he was a close friend of the artist. Martínez Nadal's writings provide a window into Lorca's thoughts and feelings about *El público*. Therefore, I hold Martínez Nadal's writings about this play in high esteem, and I quote him frequently. Although Martínez Nadal explores many elements in *El público*, his work covers a broad range of themes and symbols from other writings by Lorca. I use Martínez Nadal's ideas to help me in my analysis, but I also develop my own opinions and interpretations to analyze and synthesize the plethora of elements in *El público* in terms of the theme of sexual identity.

The work of Sigmund Freud has also helped me significantly in the psychological analysis of the characters of *El público*. Freud's theories assist me in dissecting the actions and interpreting the motivations of sexually confused characters who are struggling with the fear of being rejected by society. I see that some characters constantly fight private desires in order to attempt to gain public acceptance. Another theorist, Bertolt Brecht, aids me in understanding the reasons behind Lorca's unusual style of writing in *El público*. Brecht describes using unconventional, experimental theatrical techniques to create an unreal, disjointed, disturbing theatrical work that does not mirror reality. He explains that this type of theater serves to shock and unsettle audience members. Although this reaction sounds negative, it actually shakes the audience from its complacent stupor and stimulates it to think critically about society. I apply Brecht's ideas concerning the experimental theater to Lorca's play because I believe that Lorca's goal was to spur the audience to ponder issues of identity by using a unique, surrealistic style, similar to the one described by Brecht. Thus, by applying different types of theory to my study of *El público*, and by delving into the psychological states of the characters, I create a distinct approach to the analysis of *El público*.

BACKGROUND ON *EL PÚBLICO*

Lorca's innermost feelings and thoughts on same-sex love inspired him to write his dramatic work *El público*. The playwright found a way to express his conflicted emotions and mental turmoil by allowing his ideas to flow onto paper. Gibson comments:

> It is difficult not to sense in *The Public*, as in several of the New York poems, a reflection of the anguish that took hold of the poet when his relationships with

Dalí and Aladrén foundered; and, in general, not to find in the play an attempt to come to terms with his homosexuality and the problem of having to live in large part a double life.[10] (296)

Lorca wrote most of *El público* during 1930 in Cuba, where perhaps the writer felt that he could give voice to his feelings since he was not engulfed in the restrictive atmosphere of Spain. It is obvious that Lorca agonized over every detail of the play since the original manuscript is rife with crossed-out words and scribbled corrections. Lorca's scrawled handwriting conveys a sense of urgency, and one senses that this story must be told. The manuscript was written on a hodgepodge of papers of different shapes and sizes, but much of it was written on stationary from the Hotel La Unión in Havana.[11] In late 1930 or early 1931, Lorca read the manuscript to several friends. He was extremely excited about his work, which was very different from his other plays, and he was eager to show others his new technique. After reading this unusual play, Lorca was met not with enthusiastic applause and acknowledgement of his talent, but with complete silence. His audience was bewildered and surprised by the theatrical work and could not grasp the meaning of this disjointed, illogical play, filled with fantastical creatures and odd transforming characters (Martínez Nadal 19).

Lorca revised *El público* over the years, and in July of 1936, he gave another reading of the revamped play. On July 16, 1936, two days before the start of the Spanish Civil War, Lorca's close friend, Rafael Martínez Nadal, helped Lorca prepare for his trip to Granada. After Lorca's bags were packed, he gave Martínez Nadal a package. Martínez Nadal describes Lorca's actions:

> We were on our way out when he went back to his room, opened the drawer of his desk and took out a package: "Take this and keep it for me. If anything happens to me, destroy it all. If not, you can return it to me when we next meet." (16)

When Martínez Nadal opened the package, he found the first draft of *El público*. On August 18th or 19th of 1936, Lorca met his untimely demise, assassinated by Franco's Nationalists.[12] Martínez Nadal did not destroy the manuscript and tried to get permission from Lorca's family to publish the play. His family did not want this unfinished version to be published, preferring to wait until they found a complete manuscript, which they never did. One could guess that they protested the publishing of this play because it dealt with the subject of sexuality and could be linked to Lorca's own sexual orientation, thereby, revealing the truth to those who refused to see beyond the mask. Although a completed version of the play was never found, Martínez Nadal was finally given permission in 1976 to publish an edition of *El público,* although apparently Act 4 was missing.

LORCA'S INNOVATIVE TECHNIQUES

Lorca worked on several plays that were very different from his more realistic theatrical works. Carlos Bauer describes this series of plays which includes *El público*:

> (Lorca) himself referred to these as his "impossible theater." With staging so complicated as to make them almost unperformable, and themes which audiences of the 1930s would certainly find appalling, the dramas seemed, at the time, impossible to produce. (xi)

In *El público*, the reader enters a world of surreal visions where the rules of reality do not apply, and one could imagine that this play would be almost impossible to take to the stage. In this irrational dream-like play, white horses blow golden trumpets and dance to the rhythm of their song. The play also has a nightmarish quality because of the many strange and grotesque images that abound in every sentence. Rafael Martínez Nadal comments on Lorca's technique in *El público*:

> The five *cuadros* at our disposal (about two acts and a half) suffice to prove that in 1930 Lorca, in his efforts to bring the most intimate problems on to the stage, was experimenting in techniques and ways of expression similar to those which twenty or thirty-five years later were to characterize the *avant-garde* drama of Europe and America. (27)

Lorca experiments with the use of shocking and disturbing images in his play in order to convey a message about sexual identity, and it is clear that this playwright does not abide by the Aristotelian rules of tragedy.[13] In fact, Lorca's play fits better into Brecht's idea of a new type of theater. María Ascensión Sáenz comments on Lorca's knowledge of theory:

> También Lorca, como conocedor de las últimas teorías teatrales, probablemente estaba de acuerdo con Brecht y la idea de su teatro épico de cambiar los modos convencionales de producción y recepción de la obra teatral. (683)

> Also, Lorca, who was very knowledgeable about the latest theatrical theories, probably agreed with Brecht and the idea of his epic theater that changes the conventional modes of production and reception of the play.

It seems that Lorca was aware of the innovative theatrical techniques that Brecht practiced, and the Spanish playwright wished to create an unconventional play that would make the audience think.

Brecht's experimental theater works completely against complacency and mimesis, and instead of having the actors mimic reality, it works to alienate the audience members and take them out of their comfort zone to call their attention to the action in the play:

> The artist's object is to appear strange and even surprising to the audience. He achieves this by looking strangely at himself and his work. As a result everything put forward by him has a touch of the amazing. Everyday things are thereby raised above the level of the obvious and automatic. (Brecht 92)

It is clear that *El público* is composed of anything but ordinary reality, and it definitely breaks away from the typical format of a play. This new theater of the twentieth century shocks the public and awakens it from its sleepy complacency in order to make it aware of social issues. The public then reacts, and thus learns from the actions in the theater. Because of the theatrical presentation, the audience develops a consciousness (if it is willing to do so), which in turn produces a change in society.

Felicia Hardison Londré explains the concept of the theater as a vehicle for social change:

> Lorca orients his examination of the nature of theatre in *El público* toward the individual, forcing the spectator to see himself in a new light and to become aware of the arbitrariness of certain ways of defining personal identity. (104)

Lorca knew that his play was unnerving, and that the members of the audience sometimes reject his ideas as too foreign. They refuse to view themselves in a different way because the prospect of changing their self-image and their concepts of acceptable identities is too frightening. This reaction occurred after Lorca read *El público* to a small group of friends. The writer Rafael Martínez Nadal, who was present at the time, comments:

> The gathering ended and we left the house together. Lorca spoke, not with resentment, but with confidence: "Either they've taken in nothing or they were afraid, and I sympathize with them. The play is most difficult and for the time being impossible to put on. But in ten or twenty years it will be a great success. You'll see." (19)

The odd juxtaposition of objects and characters serves to alienate the audience, and this did happen with Lorca's group of friends. Here, Lorca recognizes that the alienation effect (or as Brecht terms it, *verfremdungseffekte*) is so great that the audience is too frightened to ponder the meaning behind the play's many symbols; thus, they put up a wall to keep themselves from understanding the revolutionary ideas on love and identity. Lorca uses *El público* to hold a mirror up to the people in the audience, but they do not recognize themselves, and they shield themselves from their disturbing reflections. The playwright sees that it will take time for people to comprehend his message and begin to question society's strict rules pertaining to sexual identity. We do not know for sure if Lorca was conscious of his use of Brechtian concepts, but we can apply these ideas to this play because of his use of illogical images and unreal situations which serve to disturb the audience and make it ponder accepted social roles and identities. By using Brecht's ideas to analyze Lorca's play, we see that Lorca, like Brecht, desires to use an unconventional technique to better communicate his message. Also, in applying Brecht's theories to Lorca's work, we strive to understand Lorca's motivation behind his eccentric writing style in *El público*. Lorca might have employed this technique because it would be more effective in making the audience members pay attention and react to his work, although they would be uncomfortable seeing the bizarre images in the play. Lorca's highly symbolic theatrical work acts to stimulate the audience so that they ponder questions of sexuality.

LORCA AND SURREALISM

Lorca's use of odd, irrational characters, unreal creatures, and illogical, dream-like sequences may prompt people to classify *El público* as a surrealist play. Lorca does use some elements associated with surrealism; however, one cannot strictly categorize it as such. The playwright expresses himself with surreal symbols. Robert Goff explains: "These symbols represent a dimension that transcends the 'real' world and enters a realm that is more-than-real, or Surreal" (30). Lorca does indeed supersede reality and transport his audience into his personal world of complex, multi-faceted symbols, but he refuses to follow the mandates of André Breton, the poet and theorist who outlines the characteristics of true surrealism.

Breton gives his official definition of surrealism in both *The Manifesto of Surrealism* (1924), and again in *What Is Surrealism?* (1936) from which I have taken this particular definition:

> SURREALISM, n. Pure psychic automatism, by which it is intended to express, verbally, in writing, or by other means, the real process of thought. Thought's dictation, in the absence of all control exercised by the reason and outside all aesthetic or moral preoccupations.
>
> ENCYCL. *Philos.* Surrealism rests in the belief in the superior reality of certain forms of association neglected heretofore; in the omnipotence of the dream and in the disinterested play of thought. It tends definitely to do away with all

other psychic mechanisms and to substitute itself for them in the solution of the principal problems of life. (59–60)

Therefore, in true surrealist writing, the instincts are unleashed and the unconscious mind, or what Freud calls the id, controls the body. The surrealists attempted to tap into their primal selves by letting go of reality and their conscious states. Their unconscious impulses would then guide them in their writing which would be free from moral and logical constraints. By using automatic writing, or writing without conscious thought, the artists could represent their true inner beings. Martínez Nadal describes why Lorca does not subscribe to Breton's surrealist movement:

> Yet if by surrealism we understand what André Breton, Aragon and other theoreticians of the movement understood, *The Public* has nothing to do with that literary movement, and Lorca, one of the poets who has most brilliantly made use of surrealist techniques in many of his poems, will remain not only outside the movement but in open opposition to it. (71)

Lorca's manuscript version of *El público* clearly does not reveal an artist who uses free association and automatic writing. The multiple chaotic corrections in the manuscript show a writer who is fully conscious of his actions. Lorca honed his writing and carefully chose every word in the play. He was aware that his writing was surrealistic in nature, but he was quick to disassociate himself from the movement:

> In 1928, in the hey-day of *avant-garde* movements, Lorca wrote to his friend Sebastián Gash, at that time a young critic and *avant-garde* writer of Catalonia: "They-the poems that accompanied the letter-respond to my new 'spiritualist' vein, emotion bared and pure, totally free from all logical control. But beware! Beware! With tremendous poetic logic. It is not surrealism. Beware! The brightest of all forms of conscience illuminates them." (Martínez Nadal 71–72)

Lorca enjoyed utilizing irrational, surreal images with which he could better express his emotions in his theatrical and poetic works, but he was fiercely independent, and would not follow all of Breton's rules. Lorca would not sacrifice his artistic freedom for the sake of belonging to the surrealist movement.[14]

THE UNBRIDLED PASSION OF LORCA'S HORSES

In the beginning of Lorca's play, four white horses traipse through the scene, but these horses are unlike any existing horses. These surrealistic, symbolic horses play golden trumpets upon entering, and they speak to the main character, the director. As in other plays by Lorca, these horses represent passion, sexuality, virility, and primal instincts, but in El público, the horses take on a deeper dimension.[15]

The moment the white horses present themselves, the director feels he must take action to defend his mask of morality from these instinctual characters. The director immediately cries, "¡Mi teatro será siempre al aire libre!" (My theater will always be in the open air) (119) which implies that his theater will always be socially acceptable to the public, thus insulating him from any criticism. Although the mention of an open-air theater might suggest a liberating type of theater where all involved are free to express themselves, it is actually just the opposite. The open-air theater caters to mainstream society and only exposes what it wants this society to see. This theater is allowed to exist in the open. It pushes all that is unacceptable out of sight and underground and reflects only traditional viewpoints. The open-air theater conforms to the social constructs of a conservative society. It masks anything that is not "normal" for the public. The director then banishes the horses from his presence in an effort to protect his open-air theater from these animals. He desires to see the survival of his theater so that he can profit from his work and be accepted by his community. José Rubia Barcia interprets the appearance of the four horses as a bad omen for the director:

> The most famous horsemen in a group of four are those of the Apocalypse, harbingers of the destruction of the ancient world and the dawning of a new age. The trumpets sounded by the CUATRO CABALLOS of *El público* may well be associated with those of Jericho, reinforcing the idea of the fall or destruction. (255)

The director tries to prevent the destruction of his carefully planned theatrical creation, and he sees the horses as a threat to his efforts to maintain a socially acceptable façade. He screams:

> ¡Fuera de aquí! ¡Fuera de mi casa, caballos! Ya se ha inventado la cama para dormir con los caballos. (Llorando.) Caballitos míos. (120)

> Out of here! Get out of my house, horses! The bed for sleeping with horses has already been invented. (Crying.) Little horses of mine.

Martínez Nadal explains the director's contradictory words and actions:

> The Director not only accepts as normal the appearance of the four animals, but we know that he loves them with a secret impassioned love. On the one

hand he expels them, on the other he whispers in an aside: My little horses, and, in one of those revealing deletions from the text, Little horse of my heart. (211)

The director cries as he forces himself to expel the horses that he once loved, and we see that he is extremely emotionally confused. Here Lorca suggests that love need not exist only between a man and a woman. Love can transcend the boundaries of what society deems acceptable, and we do not have the power to control it. Therefore, love can blossom between two men. Lorca uses metaphor to extend this even further, and in his literary world, even a man and an animal can be drawn together by the inexplicable force of love.

The director feels he must uphold the open-air theater and that the audience of this theater would not condone his love for the horses. The director refers to the invention of a bed for sleeping with horses, and his knowledge of this invention suggests a prior sexual relationship with these animals. The horses cry and beseech the director to let them stay, but he forces them to leave and even threatens them with violence when he demands a whip. The director must abandon the horses, which represent his true inner desires, if he is to gain acceptance with his open-air theater.

From the beginning of the play, the horses are proponents of the new, unconventional theater, or el teatro bajo la arena. This theater beneath the sand is the true theater, which reveals the innermost thoughts and feelings of the characters without hiding their sexual identities. One would think that the metaphor of an underground theater would suggest limits and oppression, but in actuality, Lorca uses it to suggest release from the shackles of social precepts. Since it exists beneath the sand, this theater avoids the prying eyes of those who judge others based on their alternative identities. Eventually, several characters convince the director to create the theater beneath the sand, and by associating himself with this type of theater, the director uncovers a secret side of himself that society does not condone. He produces a new version of the play Romeo and Juliet which shows that genuine love can exist between two people of the same sex. The roles of Romeo and Juliet are both played by men. María Ascensión Sáenz discusses the horses' attitude toward the theater beneath the sand:

> En un principio parece que son estos caballos los defensores del teatro de vanguardia, resultando al final ser los delatores del nuevo teatro instaurado por el Director, el teatro bajo la arena, representante del nuevo teatro . . . (684)

At first it seems that these horses are the defenders of the avant-garde theater, but in the end, they are the traitors of the new theater established by the Director, the theater under the sand, representative of the new theater . . .

Sáenz concludes that the horses finally betray the new theater because of comments made by the characters, Student 4 and Student 2. The students explain that the director tries to hide the fact that his play really followed the principles of the theater beneath the sand by trying to conceal that Romeo and Juliet were actually played by a thirty-year-old man and a fifteen-year-old boy, but the horses destroy his plans to keep this secret (173). Student 4 describes why there is such uproar after the theatrical performance:

> El tumulto comenzó cuando vieron que Romeo y Julieta se amaban de verdad. (168)

> The uproar began when they saw that Romeo and Juliet truly loved each other.

Theater becomes reality when the two people who act as if they are in love on stage truly fall in love. No one is able to conceal the real love between the men who played the roles of Romeo and Juliet. Although this gay love is taboo, the men cannot deny their attraction. The director tries to pass this "abnormal" playoff as conventional. The horses reveal the truth about the actors, and the spectators cannot understand this and rebel. Therefore, I disagree with Sáenz's assumption that the horses turn against the new theater. They are loyal to the theater beneath the sand, and they reveal that the director is the traitor who tried to conceal the truth about the play.

THE FREUDIAN ASPECT OF THE HORSES

After the horses leave during the first scene, the servant announces the arrival of the audience, which consists of three men who are dressed identically. This announcement is almost exactly the same as the previous one for the arrival of the horses which were also described as the audience. One can see a parallel between the four white horses and the four men in the scene, one of which is the director. The horses represent the primitive, instinctual side of the characters, and, therefore, they can be analyzed in terms of Freudian psychology. According to Freud, the human mind is divided into three parts: the ego and the superego constitute the conscious parts of the mind, and the id is the unconscious part of the psyche. The famous psychoanalyst defines the id:

> It contains everything that is inherited, that is present at birth, that is laid down in the constitution-above all, therefore, the instincts which originate from the somatic organization and which find a first psychical expression here in forms unknown to us. (145)

These horses embody pure, uninhibited sexual drive as does the id which is the source of libido. The director then tries to repress his id or his unacceptable alternative sexuality when he forces the horses to leave his house. According to Goff:

> Since it is unnatural for instincts to be silenced, they forever seek to push their way into consciousness, regardless of social pressure from the ego to keep them repressed. (29)

The white horses refuse to be subdued and appear throughout the theatrical work showing their power and acting on their instinctual sexual impulses.

Julio Huelamo Kosma discusses the symbolism of the horse in *El público*:

> . . . los caballos buscan persuadir al Director empleando expresiones ligadas exclusivamente a realidades orgánicas y funcionales primarias: apelan a la saliva del Director, a su sudor, a sus uñas y hablan de la cama o del retrete. Atenidos a lo cual, es posible afirmar que esos Caballos constituyen la base amorfa, radicalmente animal, y, por tanto difícilmente racionalizable, del fondo inconsciente. (67)

> . . . the horses seek to persuade the Director using expressions linked exclusively to organic realities and primary functions: they appeal to the Director's saliva, to his sweat, to his nails and talk about the bed or the toilet. Because of these elements, one can affirm that these Horses constitute the amorphous base, the radically animal, and, therefore hardly logical idea, of the unconscious background.

The horses represent the deepest, darkest urges of the men. When the horses are pleading with the director to let them stay, they wish at least to maintain some kind of physical bond with the director, and they beg for organic material such as the director's saliva and fingernails. The use of these bodily substances connects the horses with the most instinctual needs of the flesh. Thus, the horses symbolize the unconscious element that drives the director to follow his libidinal impulses even if these instinctual behaviors are abhorred by society.

The white horses, representations of the id, struggle for survival and dominance throughout *El público*. Later, the character Juliet arises from her tomb and is sexually harassed by the four white horses:

> Los Tres Caballos Blancos: (Furiosos) ¡Queremos acostarnos!
>   Caballo Blanco I: Porque somos caballos verdaderos, caballos de coche que hemos roto con las vergas la madera de los pesebres y las ventanas del establo.

>   Los Tres Caballos Blancos: Desnúdate, Julieta, y deja al aire tu grupa para el azote de nuestras colas. ¡Queremos resucitar! (153–154)
>   The Three White Horses: (Furious) We want to go to bed!
>
>   White Horse I: Because we are real horses, carriage horses, and our canes have broken the wood of the troughs and the windows of the stable.
>   The Three White Horses: Undress, Juliet, and let your bare rump be whipped by our tails. We want to resurrect!

The horses' lust has reached a fevered pitch, and they become more and more frenzied because of their sexual frustration. The horses again embody the id as they are libidinous, primitive creatures who are slaves to their impulses. They vigorously shake their long, black lacquer canes, unquestionable symbols of the excited phallus. The first white horse repeats the phrase "Ya se ha inventado la cama para dormir con los caballos," (153) (The bed to sleep with the horses has already been invented,) which the director had cried out to the horses in the beginning of the play, and this repetition reminds us of the past sexual link with the director. The love between the horses and the director is a love that suggests gay love in the sense that it is not viewed as normal by society in the theatrical work.

Rebuffed by the director in the first scene, the horses must find an outlet for their pent-up sexual energy that has turned to aggression. Their tears have turned to anger. Pleading with the director did not have the desired effect, so they violently force themselves sexually on their victim, Juliet. The first white horse announces his animalistic masculinity by saying that his "cane" or penis is an unstoppable force that has destroyed his stable. This symbol of sexuality refuses to be caged, showing the horse's irrepressible nature. The rejection by the director does, in effect, keep the horses from acting on their instincts, and they must seek another route to relieve their frustrations. The horses shout, "¡Queremos resucitar!" (We want to resurrect!) which means that they want to be resurrected from their stifled state and express their sexuality. With the horses' resurrection, the id is then allowed to dominate. Juliet is not their first choice as a sexual partner, but she will have to do. Man 1 talks about the horses and reveals that even they have concealed desires:

Hombre 1: Deben desaparecer inmediatamente de este sitio. Ellos tienen miedo del público. Yo sé la verdad, yo sé que no buscan a Julieta y ocultan un deseo que me hiere y que leo en sus ojos.
Caballo Negro: No un deseo, todos los deseos. Como tú.
Hombre 1: Yo no tengo más que un deseo.
Caballo Blanco 1: Como los caballos, nadie olvida su máscara. (155–156)

Man 1: They must disappear immediately from this site. They are afraid of the public. I know the truth; I know that they do not look for Juliet and they hide a desire that hurts me and that I can read in their eyes.
Black Horse: Not a desire, all the desires. Like you.
Man 1: I have only one desire.
White Horse 1: Like the horses, nobody forgets their mask.

Man 1 knows the truth behind the horses' pursuit of the director, and Juliet is merely a substitute for their true desire. The black and white horses announce that even Man 1 has many hidden desires, and, therefore, what one believes to be a true need might really be a mask for deeper hunger. Martínez Nadal comments on this interesting passage:

> If the horses represent, in part at least, hidden instincts or desires, most psychoanalysts would accept the Lorquian idea that the instincts can also wear a mask. (213)

Thus, Lorca shows that it is not an easy task to interpret true desires and that the id is a complex, multi-faceted part of the human psyche.

THE BLACK HORSE: THE EMBODIMENT OF DEATH

The white horses have a polar adversary: the black horse. The mysterious black horse acts as the guardian of the deceased woman, Juliet, who desires to remain in her tomb and be left in peace. He is a symbol of darkness and death who protects her from the advances of the white horses, as Rubia Barcia explains:

> Interrupting the dialogue, the CABALLO NEGRO appears for the first time, with "un penacho de pluma del mismo color y una rueda en la mano"—the panache of black feathers, suggesting that he draws a hearse as a harbinger of death, and the wheel signifying the inevitable circle of time which leads there. (248)

This animal serves as a reminder that life is ephemeral, and although he could be interpreted as a negative symbol because of the traditional associations with the color black, he is a proponent of peace and tranquility. He wishes to see Juliet sleep eternally and avoid others who want to disturb her. Death is the ultimate escape for those who wish to permanently elude the inner voice that pushes them to fulfill their innate sexual desires and thus betray society.

In *El público*, the colors black and white do not hold the typical symbolic associations. Black does not automatically represent evil, nor is white always associated with good. The white horses are not innately good characters; rather, they represent the raw force of uncensored life. They are the beings who give themselves unabashedly to their carnal desires. On the other hand, the black horse does not represent evil. He is seen as the "good" horse since he acts as Juliet's protector against the white horses. The black horse is a symbol of death, but here death is not seen as wrong or evil; it is a state of eternal peace. In this play, white represents the vivid light of life while black is connected with death and the shadow of darkness which serves as a perpetual sanctuary.

The black horse, the first white horse, and Juliet discuss apples made of ashes, another symbol of death:

Caballo Blanco 1: A las orillas del Mar Muerto nacen unas bellas manzanas de ceniza, pero la ceniza es buena.
Caballo Negro: ¡Oh frescura! ¡Oh pulpa! ¡Oh rocío! Yo como ceniza.
Julieta: No. No es buena la ceniza. ¿Quién habla de ceniza?
Caballo Blanco 1: No hablo de ceniza. Hablo de la ceniza que tiene forma de manzana. (151)

White Horse 1: On the shores of the Dead Sea, beautiful apples made of ash are born, but the ash is good.
Black Horse: Oh freshness! Oh pulp! Oh dew! I eat ash.
Juliet: No. Ash is not good. Who talks about ash?
White Horse 1: I do not speak of ash. I speak of the ash that is in the form of an apple.

This dialogue highlights a juxtaposition of images concerning life and death. The apple is the ripe fruit of life, associated with nourishment, procreation, and vitality. However, the image of the apple in this play cannot be interpreted only as a symbol of life because the fruit is made up of a material associated with death. Although the symbol evokes life, this is a mere façade. Paul Julian Smith comments on the significance of the apples that grow on the shores of the Dead Sea:

> The motif has a long history: in the Renaissance Dead Sea apples served as emblems of the bitter truth of human mortality hidden beneath the seductive forms of sensual pleasure. In El público, on the other hand, the comforting opposition of inside and outside (form and content) is dissolved. No "allegorical" reading is possible; the apples betray their substance on their surface. Death is not a hidden secret, but open knowledge: as the Black Horse says, the dead keep speaking and the living use the lancet. (128–129)

The form of the apple does not hide the fact that it is made of ash, something that does not nourish. Ash is the result of destruction and death. All living beings die and return to the earth as dust or ash, and in this scene, Lorca reminds us of our mortality.

The idea of the Dead Sea is oxymoronic because the sea's water is the source of life, but in this play, the sea does not sustain life; it only supports the apple of death. It is fitting that the black horse, a symbol of demise, would like to feed off the fruit of decay. Martínez Nadal explains the significance of the Dead Sea with relation to the apples made of ash.

> Double meaning: shores of a sea near to one of the places where the Garden of Eden is supposed to have existed and shores of the sea of death. In both cases there are apples that by giving life become food for Death. Ash is good for the Black Horse. (216)

Martínez Nadal makes a reference to the Garden of Eden, and one can draw a parallel between the forbidden fruit of the garden and the apple created by Lorca. In the book of Genesis, God prohibits Adam and Eve from eating from the tree of the knowledge of good and evil.[16] Traditionally, the fruit of this tree is believed to be an apple; therefore, the apple made of ash could be interpreted as the fruit of temptation and sin that led to the expulsion from the heavenly garden. Whomever this apple tempts is thrown from the realm of the living. The ashen apple also represents the sin of sensuality and pleasures of the flesh and can be translated as the condemnation of alternative sexuality by a homophobic society who judges it as a deviant, sinful and empty behavior. The apple can represent carnal union and procreation, but the apple made of death's material shows that same-sex contact is fruitless, and the reason for it is pure sexual gratification, not the propagation of the human race. Hence, the apple that tempts the black horse can be analyzed as a symbol of temptation, sin in the eyes of society, and death.

THE GREAT MASK OF DECEPTION: "EL TEATRO BAJO LA ARENA" VERSUS "EL TEATRO AL AIRE LIBRE" (THE THEATER BENEATH THE SAND VERSUS THE OPEN-AIR THEATER)

Like the ash that is disguised as an apple, many elements in *El público* take on different forms or masks to hide their true nature. In fact, theater as a whole must be cloaked to fit in with society's expectations. In her introduction to the play, María Celementa Millán describes "la máscara teatral" as:

> un símbolo para Lorca en este drama de la falsedad del teatro al aire libre . . . la máscara simboliza en este sentido los convencionalismos sociales ante los que a veces hay que rendirse . . . (50–51)
>
> a symbol for Lorca in this drama of the falseness of the open-air theater . . . the mask symbolizes in this sense the social conventions to which one must surrender at times . . .

The open-air theater is a censored, sugar-coated version of reality, and it does nothing to test the rigid boundaries created by society.

We see the director's struggle with sexual identity through the use of the opposing images of the theater beneath the sand and the open-air theater. This character denies his feelings and is afraid to confront the truth of his queerness. Instead, he chooses to repress his true self and hide behind the mask of social conformity. The play *Romeo and Juliet* is a traditional play meant for "teatro al aire libre" (open-air theater) because it is a story of heterosexual love, which is the only acceptable love, according to the traditional public. By declaring that his theater will always be in the open air, the director denies his desires and, therefore, chooses to follow society's moral rules. In *Drama, Metadrama, and Perception*, Hornby states:

> For the individual, theatre is a kind of identity laboratory, in which social roles can be examined vicariously. In a safe environment, detached from everyday reality, the audience member can forget his own identity for a while, and identify with the characters he sees. (71)

I agree that the stage is an experimental setting where different types of identities are acted out, and the members of the audience are made to ponder identities that are dissimilar to their own. In fact, Hornby's assessment of the theater can be tied to Brecht's ideas because both writers believe that the theater should sever itself from reality in order to create an alternative space for the exploration of social roles. The audience learns about other identities which promotes awareness, understanding, and eventually acceptance. On the other hand, I disagree with some of Hornby's beliefs because we see that the theater is not truly a safe environment. The audience members will often only identify with the characters whose identities reflect their own. Therefore, a gay character is too foreign for a conservative audience accustomed to seeing the open-air type of theatrical work. The director knows that the audience is apt to rebel if the play does not portray characters with traditional identities and social values, so he feels restricted to producing a play that does not reflect his individuality.

The characters, Man 1 and Man 2, challenge the idea of the open-air theater. Man 2 asks about how Romeo goes to the bathroom and states that it would be lovely to see Romeo urinate (123), and, therefore, Man 2 questions the authenticity of the open-air theater and draws attention to the fact that this socially acceptable theater shows only one side of reality. "Repulsive" actions are hidden from the view of the public, as is the fact that the director is frustrated sexually. The director expresses a desire to protect the audience from such actions while Man 1 emphasizes the importance of the truth:

Director: ¿Y la moral? ¿Y el estómago de los espectadores?
Hombre 1: Hay personas que vomitan cuando se vuelve un pulpo del revés y otras que se ponen pálidas si oyen pronunciar con la debida intención la palabra cáncer; . . . Pero usted lo que quiere es engañarnos. Engañarnos para que todo siga igual . . . (124–25)

Director: And the morality? And the stomach of the spectators?
Man 1: There are people who vomit when the innards of the octopus are removed and others who turn pale if they hear the word cancer said with the right intention; . . . But what you want is to deceive us. Deceive us so that everything stays the same . . .

Man 1 insists that however unpleasant, the audience needs to see the truth. People will try to shield their eyes from the ugly truth and would rather gaze upon a beautiful falsehood. Here, Lorca suggests the Brechtian concept of shocking the spectators, which sometimes makes them uneasy, in order to reveal the real nature of the world.

The director is worried about protecting and shielding the audience from anything that might be deemed frightening or incomprehensible. He also wants his work to appeal to everyone so that he can ensure his financial success. The director knows that if people are made to feel intensely uncomfortable due to the subject of his play, they will not pay to see it.[17] If he creates a conventional theatrical work, he guards himself against economic ruin, and he will not have to face a scared, angry mob that will destroy all that goes against the social norm. He asks, "¿Qué hago con el público si quito las barandas al puente?" (124) (What do I do with the public if I remove the railings from the bridge?) and therefore, questions lifting the great theatrical mask to show the true face of theater beneath the sand. To ensure an incoming monetary flow and the safety of the audience and the actors, the mask must remain in place. Carlos Feal comments:

La barrera o baranda que separaba los dos mundos-mundo del espectador y mundo de los actores-, al derribarse, cesa de protegerlos. La ruptura de la convención teatral refleja la ruptura de las convenciones sociales y da lugar a un formidable estallido. (45)

The barrier or rail that separated the two worlds-world of the spectator and world of the actors-, when it is demolished, ceases to protect them. The rupture of the theatrical convention reflects the rupture of social conventions and gives rise to a formidable shattering of the rules.

If the theatrical world were to take away the safety rails and show its genuine face, the existence of the traditional world of the spectator would be in jeopardy. The safety of all concerned is threatened, and the director's own financial survival is at stake once social conventions are broken. Once the handrails are removed, both astonished and confused spectators and actors alike might lose their foothold on the slippery bridge of reality.

Man 1 realizes the importance of the truth, and he resents the fact that the cowardice of others prevents the existence of pure, undisguised theater. He sadly exclaims:

Tendremos necesidad de enterrar el teatro por la cobardía de todos. Y tendré que darme un tiro . . .
   Tendré que darme un tiro para inaugurar el verdadero teatro, el teatro bajo la arena. (123)

We will need to bury the theater because of everyone's cowardice. And I will have to shoot myself . . .
   I will have to shoot myself to inaugurate the real theater, the theater under the sand.

The subversive theater beneath the sand would reveal the true sexual identity of the characters, and this frightens the director. This fear stems from anticipating the reaction of audience members who might destroy the theater that represents an unacceptable veracity. In fact, the audience does rebel and reacts violently against the theater beneath the sand when it is revealed that Juliet is actually a man, and Romeo and Juliet, who are two men, really love each other. The director's real identity lies in the unconventional theater beneath the sand, but the sand has a suffocating effect and, once underground, the theater will be cut off from society.

The director is at first unwilling to give up being accepted in society, and he expresses his fear about the subversive theatrical work, which would reveal his hidden identity:

Vendría la máscara a devorarme. Yo vi una vez a un hombre devorado por la máscara. Los jóvenes más fuertes de la ciudad, con picas ensangrentadas, le hundían por el trasero grandes bolas de periódicos abandonados, y en América hubo una vez un muchacho a quien la máscara ahorcó colgado de sus propios intestinos. (124)

The mask will come to devour me. I once saw a man devoured by the mask. The strongest young people in the city plunged large wads of abandoned newspapers into his rear end with bloody spears, and in America there was once a boy who was hanged by the mask with his own intestines.

This grotesque image reveals the terrible punishment dealt to those who have dared to show their true sexual identity. The mask takes revenge on anyone who dares to take it off and discard it. María Estela Harretche examines the phenomenon of the mask in *El público*:

Ya en el cuadro primero del drama cuando el Director y el Hombre 1 dialogan sobre qué teatro hacer, la máscara es aludida como un ente capaz de devorar y aniquilar, al que sería temerario pensar siquiera en sacar a escena. (1815)

Even in the first scene of the drama when the Director and Man 1 discuss what kind of theater to do, the mask is referred to as an entity capable of devouring and annihilating, and it would be reckless to even think of bringing it to the stage.

The mask is a symbol for the rules of the dominant heterosexual society. It is a menacing figure that will destroy those who divulge their secret gay desires. The mask does not tolerate a deviation from the norm; thus, the director is terrified to show his true self.

One can never hide from the mask, for it is everywhere. The director observes that the mask presses down upon us at all times:

En la alcoba, cuando nos metemos los dedos en las narices, o nos exploramos delicadamente el trasero, el yeso de la máscara oprime de tal forma nuestra carne que apenas si podemos tendernos en el lecho. (156)

In the bedroom, when we put our fingers up our nostrils, or we delicately explore our butt, the plaster of the mask oppresses our flesh in such a way that we can barely lay on the bed.

The mask makes its presence known when we behave in a socially unacceptable manner or explore our sexuality, and again we see the clash of the id and the ego. The id tempts us to express our inner libidinous desires while the ego acts as the mask that prohibits us from expressing our instinctual behaviors. Here, we see that people cannot be true even to themselves, and the mask burdens them when they are alone. "Indecent" sexual acts, such as exploring one's own body, are deemed inappropriate by the mask, which will punish and oppress all who attempt to defy social precepts. Even sexual thoughts are censored by a mask that fastens buttons to cover up an indiscreet blush, the tell-tale sign of an "impure" contemplation. Therefore, the mask is often an internal construction that prevents one from ever revealing the total truth.

THE FEMININE MASK

Even a character can be used as a mask that obscures sexual identity. Elena is such a character, and she is constantly pursued by the masculine characters who believe that she could lend credibility to their feigned heterosexuality. Both her name and her appearance link her to the mythological Helen of Troy. Helen of Troy had many suitors who were probably more interested in her as a status symbol with many assets than an individual with a personality. She was used as a pawn of the gods and of mortals, and she had little say in her fate. Unfortunately, it was her face that spawned a deadly ten-year war.[18] Elena's appearance in the play reminds the audience of Helen of Troy (128). This character is dressed in the Greek style, and her revealing dress emphasizes her femininity. Her feet are encased in plaster, which symbolizes her immobility and helplessness. According to Hardison Londré, "she is the muse who inspires the Director's work within safe, traditional artistic forms" (108). Elena is like a statue and is meant to be objectified although she resists.

Like Helen of Troy, Elena is trapped in futile relationships with men who plan to use her to gain acceptance in society. Also, Elena's presence stirs up controversy and incites violence between Man 3 and the director and even between Man 3 and herself. Thus, she becomes at once the object of desire who is fought over, and the victim whose own adorer controls her by violent means. When the director first calls upon Elena, she is immediately characterized as a "mala mujer" (a bad woman) (127) although she has done nothing to warrant that title. Man 1, who "is the only one who hides neither his true personality nor his most intimate desires," (Martínez Nadal 59) expresses his dismay when the director calls for Elena. He does not wish to mask his sexual orientation by pretending to be interested in a woman, and he fears that this woman's presence will dash his hopes to reveal the truth. María Estela Harretche describes Elena's function:

> Elena es el personaje-máscara que, con mayor claridad y consistencia, funciona a lo largo de la obra escondiendo o ayudando a esconder algo. Elena es el refugio adonde acude el Director, desesperado por la gravedad del conflicto, como a un refugio que esconde y disimula y ayuda a mentir; Elena es la mujer que ayuda a los hombres en crisis por su homosexualidad, ocultando el problema con su presencia.... (1820)

> Elena is the character-mask that, with great clarity and consistency, functions throughout the work by hiding or helping to hide something. Elena is the refuge used by the Director, desperate because of the seriousness of the conflict, like a shelter that hides and conceals and helps to lie; Elena is the woman who helps men in crisis because of their homosexuality, concealing the problem with her presence.

I agree that Elena acts as a mask and has the ability to cover the real sexual identity of the male characters, but I disagree with Harretche with regards to Elena's intent. Harretche emphasizes that Elena helps the men to hide their true sexual orientation, and it is apparent that she believes that this character does so willingly and even maliciously. She portrays Elena as the scheming, deceitful female who acts as a shelter for cowering gay men who desire a façade. In a conversation between Man 3 and Elena, we see that she is like a caged bird who dreams of escaping because she feels smothered by his adoration (128). Elena shows that she feels trapped in the relationship with Man 3, and she desires to be set free. This woman does not want to continue as the mask for Man 3 and the director. I believe that Lorca portrays Elena as an unwilling accomplice to this heterosexual farce. She is shown as a character who is coerced into these fake relationships, and when she threatens to leave, she meets with resistance, and later, with violence. Julieta exposes the sexual relationship between the director and Man 3 when she exclaims:

> (Al Hombre 3.) ¡Vete con él! Y confiésame ya la verdad que me ocultas. No me importa que estuvieras borracho y que te quieras justificar, pero tú lo has besado y has dormido en la misma cama. (128)

> Go with him! And confess the truth that you hide from me. I do not care that you were drunk and that you want to justify yourself, but you have kissed him and slept in the same bed.

This incites a violent reaction in Man 3, who whips the director and accuses him of lying. Man 3 cannot face the reality of his sexuality; thus, he fiercely denies the relationship. By beating the director, Man 3 hopes to subdue and repress his own "unacceptable" feelings, thus, showing the public that he could not possibly care for someone he whips so mercilessly. Elena believes Julieta, despite Man 3's display of anger and denial. Man 3 furiously lashes out at Elena as well, but she will not change her mind (129). Rather than being portrayed as a woman who lies and shields the men, she is seen as a brave woman who, despite Man 3's ferocity, confronts him and essentially announces her belief that he is gay. He tries to make her recall her statement by using brute force, but this only makes her stronger in her resolution to see the truth.

The love triangle involving the director, Man 3, and Elena reveals an interesting phenomenon that is discussed by Eve Kosofsky Sedgwick:

> . . . patriarchal heterosexuality can best be discussed in terms of one or another form of the traffic in women: it is the use of women as exchangeable, perhaps symbolic, property for the primary purpose of cementing the bonds of men with men. (26)

According to Sedgwick, women are sometimes used as a social prop intended to cover the truth of men who desire to be in a sexual relationship. One could use the slang term "beard" to describe Elena who is used as an accessory to give the false appearance of a heterosexual relationship between the men and this female character.[19] Clearly, Elena fits into this description, and it is evident that the male characters do not see her as an independent woman with feelings of her own. She is immobile and looks like a Greek statue. Her very nature allows her to be treated as an object and employed as a pawn, although she protests. The director and Man 3 simply use Elena as a commodity in order to gain acceptance in a heterosexual society. They fight over the right to use her to disguise their identities, but their competition also cements the bond between them. If Elena appears to participate in the love triangle, this allows the men to have access to each other.

Elena and Juliet are the only two female characters in *El público*, and they both must endure male characters' attempts to manipulate them and use them as social props that disguise homoerotic desires. Thus, Sedgwick's theory can also be applied to the character Juliet. Juliet's interaction with the white horses, described earlier in this chapter, is another example of male characters attempting to use a female character as a mask. After being rebuffed by the director, the white horses pursue Juliet as the object of their desire. They vigorously and violently proclaim their masculinity by shaking their phallic walking sticks and announcing that they desire to sleep with Juliet. This masculine posturing and vocalization of their need of female companionship serves to cover the horses' gay tendencies expressed earlier when they beseeched the director to sleep with them. As is the case with Man 3, the horses' sexual frustration leads to their aggressive attitude toward

Juliet as they violently wave their black lacquered sticks at her. Although they attempt to use Juliet as a cover for their alternative sexuality, Juliet, like Elena, protests such treatment and declares that she will not be their servant (154). Juliet forcefully opposes being used as a "slave" who must follow the orders of the horses. It is no accident that the horses choose to pursue Juliet, a main character in the director's play, since she would act as a bridge to connect the horses to the director, their real love interest. Thus, Juliet forms part of the love triangle that Sedgwick describes since this female character is utilized as a commodity that allows the horses to both gain acceptance in a heterosexual world and bring them closer to the man they truly desire. Both Elena and Juliet are pulled into a volatile love triangle that actually creates a stronger link between the male characters.

THE MASK'S ULTIMATE REPRESSION

Although the director fights against showing his true nature, and even goes so far as to camouflage his sexual orientation by having a relationship with Elena, he eventually creates a theater beneath the sand. The proponents of the underground theater push the director behind a screen, and when he emerges on the other side; he has changed into a boy dressed in a white satin suit with a ruffled collar. The director's mental state is also changed, and he no longer represses his sexual desires. His world crashes down upon him when the audience rejects the true theater and forms an angry mob. In *Cuadro III* the director becomes frightened again and announces that he despises and scornfully discards the theater that reveals all. He is again terrified of the all-knowing mask of morality which will seek vengeance if it is ignored. Thus, if one mocks the mask and defies it, the mask will retaliate with swift, brutal, deadly force. The director recalls the horrifying image of the boy from America who was hanged for revealing his sexuality (156). In the same scene, Man 1 declares his love for the director, but the director vehemently rejects him, and again we see the repression of the director's true identity. Man 1 has succeeded in taking off the mask of conformity, and he feels free to display his true queer identity. He thinks he has torn this mask off the director, but the director admits that he is weak and denies any feelings for Man 1. The director physically fights Man 1 and even spits in face of the man he loves; therefore, he fiercely battles his own emotions to conform to society's expectations (157). In fear, the director has placed the mask back on, and in doing so, he represses his sexual identity even further.

At the end of the play, one can see that the director has retreated into the world of false appearances permanently since he has dedicated himself once again to the open-air theater. He distances himself from the theater beneath the sand and proclaims that the performance ended hours ago, and he does not hold himself accountable for the audience's response and subsequent destruction of the scene and violence toward the people involved in the production (187). The more he denies his involvement in the theater project, the more the temperature drops. It eventually starts to snow, and the air becomes frigid. The director must endure an intense cold, suggesting that the denial of his true self will eventually freeze and kill him.

In conclusion, *El público* dramatizes the confusion, embarrassment, sadness, and anger of characters who are thoroughly perplexed about whether they should unmask their genuine identity. Man 1 declares:

> Pero el ano es el castigo del hombre. El ano es el fracaso del hombre, es su vergüenza y su muerte. (141)
>
> But the anus is man's punishment. The anus is the failure of man, it is his shame and death.

Man 1 is frightened by the pull of his sexuality and, therefore, forcefully denounces it as shameful and unacceptable. A man's anus can bring about his downfall by releasing his id and tempting him to succumb to his most intimate sexual desires. The director dreads the pull of his libidinal impulses, and, therefore, he banishes the horses that represent the instinctual side of human behavior. He even tries to convince himself to fit into a conventional society that refuses to recognize a non-heteronormative sexuality as a legitimate sexual identity. Fear is expressed as violent rage when the masculine characters physically abuse each other in order to suppress and deny their feelings. We see the director's feelings of self-hatred, which eventually transform into an acceptance that facilitates the birth of the theater beneath the sand. Unfortunately, the director's acceptance of his gay identity is short-lived, and it quickly degenerates into self-loathing and resentment of his pure theatrical creation. *El público* might very well be a window into the tortured soul of Federico García Lorca, who, we know, struggled with his own sexuality and acceptance in society. In this theatrical work, Lorca travels to the core of the human psyche in order to reveal a dark truth about the suffocation of one's identity. The director's mask of conformity crumbles and reveals his gay identity, but in the end, he rebuilds his mask and hides behind its false security only to be asphyxiated by its unbearable pressure.

NOTES

1. Ian Gibson is a Hispanist who is very well known for his extensive biographical work on Federico García Lorca. He has written many groundbreaking and

painstakingly researched books on Lorca's work, relationships, and death including *Vida, pasión y muerte de Federico García Lorca (Life, Passion, and Death of Federico García Lorca)*, *Lorca-Dalí, el amor que no pudo ser (Lorca-Dalí, a Love that could Never Be)*, *La represión nacionalista de Granada en 1936 y la muerte de Federico García Lorca (The Nationalist Repression of Granada in 1936 and the Death of Federico García Lorca)*, and *Lorca y el mundo gay (Lorca and the Gay World)*. In this book, when I cite Gibson, I refer to his book *Federico García Lorca: A Life* unless otherwise specified.

2. Gibson explains "Another letter sent earlier that summer to Palencia leaves little doubt that the principal cause of Federico's depression was his feelings for Dalí. 'I haven't forgotten the Barcelona business,' Lorca had written. 'It's the only possibility I have of being able to see our friend Dalí this summer'" (153). In these letters, Lorca expresses his desire to see Dalí and his wish for a stable relationship.

3. See George, Harretche and Rubia Barcia for an in-depth study of the function of masks in *El público*.

4. For more information on cross-dressing in general, see Garber. See Monegal for an analysis of cross-dressing and the tragic elements of *El público*. In the article "Transvestism and Sexual Transgression in García Lorca's *The Public*," Jerez-Farrán explores the link between cross-dressing and sexuality.

5. In "'Una desorientación absoluta': Juliet and the Shifting Sands in García Lorca's *El público*," Anderson examines the main female character Juliet and delves into the symbolism that surrounds her. In Figure's article, he analyzes the female images in the play and the idea of love.

6. García and Jerez-Farrán both explore the topic of violence and sadomasochism as the consequence of homophobia in *El público*. Stewart's book is a general analysis of male masochistic relationships in life and literature.

7. Belamich, Feal, Menarini, Soufas, Hardison Londré, Millán, and Monleon have all written articles comparing *El público* to other literature by Lorca. Since *El público* is extremely different from Lorca's other works, critics find the comparison of his other literature to this play an especially rich topic. Gene, Newberry, Sanz Barajas, and Torner analyze the similarities and differences between *El público* and works by other authors. These critics find links between Lorca's writing style and the styles of other writers.

8. See Delgado, Dowling, Gómez Torres, Lacomba, Newton, and Sáenz for critical analyses of *El público*'s presentations and the reactions of audience members.

9. Anderson, DeLong-Tonelli, Gullón, and Millán give summaries of the history of *El público* and overviews of the most important symbolic elements of the play. Huelamo Kosma studies the influence of Freud in Lorca's works, and Jerez-Farrán uses Foucauldian theory to analyze an act of Lorca's play *El público*. Finke focuses on the origins and symbolism of the characters' names in *El público*. Kidd delves into the mysterious manuscript and style of *El público* and artfully translates it into English along with three of Lorca's most famous plays. In this book, I use my own translations of quotes from *El público*.

10. Emilio Aladrén Perojo (1906–1944) was a sculptor and student, along with Dalí and Lorca, at the School of Fine Arts. Lorca and Aladrén started a tumultuous

relationship in 1927 of which Lorca's friends disapproved since they highly disliked the sculptor and felt that he was a bad influence on Lorca. Not many details are known of their relationship (Gibson 209–212). In his book *Lorca y el mundo gay*, Gibson delves more deeply into Lorca's relationships and his emotional state when he wrote *El público* and other works.

11. Rafael Martínez Nadal describes the original manuscript of *El público* in detail (20–24).

12. For more information on Lorca's assassination, see Gibson's investigative book *La represión nacionalista de Granada en 1936 y la muerte de Federico García Lorca (The Nationalist Repression of Granada in 1936 and the Death of Federico García Lorca)* which was later published in English as *The Death of Lorca*. This book was banned in Spain during the Francoist dictatorship. In 2015, The Guardian news website announced that they had official documents that prove Franco-era officials assassinated Lorca because of his political beliefs and his sexual orientation. Before these documents became public, the regime denied that they specifically targeted Lorca for these reasons and claimed he was killed because he fraternized with the rebels.

13. Lorca ignores the Aristotelian rules of drama that require unity of time and action. According to Aristotle, there should be one coherent action or theme within a play, and this action should occur in the span of one day. The audience should focus on one action and should not have to follow many different unrelated stories within the drama. Lorca completely disregards these rules, producing a disjointed play with an erratic plot that Aristotle would not have considered a true tragedy. For more regarding Aristotelian rules, see Aristotle's *Poetics*.

14. In "La estética expresionista en *El público* de García Lorca," (Expressionist Aesthetics in García Lorca's *The Public*) Carlos Jerez-Farrán also refuses to categorize Lorca's play as a strictly surrealist work, and he thoroughly explains his reasoning in this article. He also discusses the expressionist elements in *El público*.

15. For more information on the symbolic value of horses in Lorca's other literary works, see Nadal 185–217.

16. And the Lord God took the man, and put him into the garden of Eden to dress it and to keep it. And the Lord God commanded the man, saying: "Of every tree of the garden thou mayest freely eat; but of the tree of the knowledge of good and evil, thou shalt not eat of it; for in the day that thou eatest thereof thou shalt surely die." (Gen. 2.15–17)

17. One can compare the director's motivation to create a conventional theatrical work to the motivation of Vélez de Guevara. The director yearns to be accepted by society, as does Vélez. Vélez wrote *Virtudes vencen señales* in such a way that it would be accepted by audiences of seventeenth-century Spain. He did not challenge established ideas about race in Spanish society. Because the audience was comfortable with the messages in Vélez's works, he was a successful playwright. Vélez could be seen as a proponent of the open-air theater. On the other hand, in his play *El retablo de las maravillas* Cervantes criticizes seventeenth-century Spanish society's obsession with *pureza de sangre*. The people of this period did not want to watch a theatrical work that would make them feel uncomfortable or criticize their

anti-Semitic attitudes, so *El retablo de las maravillas* was never performed in the seventeenth century. Therefore, *El retablo de las maravillas* represents the theater beneath the sand.

18. For more information on Helen of Troy, see Bell.

19. The Oxford English Dictionary defines the slang term "beard" as "A person who pretends to have a romantic or sexual relationship with someone else in order to conceal the other's true sexual orientation."

Chapter 4

Living Beyond the Binary

Questioning Socially Accepted Gender Roles in La llamada de Lauren

At times, society attempts to mold personal identities so that people conform to a heteronormative culture, but many people have questioned the identities that society imposes upon them. In modern society, differing gender and sexual identities are becoming more accepted, but there is still a struggle to define what is approved in our society. We often perform our gender, and many still subscribe to the gender binary system where if one is born male, he must adhere to the strict laws of masculine attire and sexual attraction toward women, and if one is born female, she will also follow the rules of femininity in society. At first glance, people will often unconsciously categorize others as either male or female. Society is learning to accept fluidity in gender and sexual identities, but this is still a controversial topic. In the play *El público*, we have seen how Federico García Lorca struggles with the idea of sexual identity and social conformity. He addresses the taboo subject of alternative sexuality which could never be tolerated by the ultra-conservative, Spanish Catholic society of the 1930s. In *El público*, the characters are torn between showing their true feelings and conforming to a society that accepts only heteronormative relationships. The play *La llamada de Lauren* by Paloma Pedrero also deals with the repression of a nonbinary identity and the desire to fit into society.[1] In this play, we follow the psychological journey of the character Pedro who, until now, has repressed his non-heteronormative desires to answer "Lauren's call," dress as a woman, and show the feminine side of his identity. We also see how Pedro's journey affects his wife's identity. Both Lorca's and Pedrero's plays address the theme of sexuality and gender identity and the struggle against conformity within a rigid society. The twentieth-century drama I analyze focuses more on non-heteronormative identity than on the questions of race and ethnicity that we have observed in the early modern period. Many people are reaching for acceptance of alternative sexuality, cross-dressing, and not adhering to a binary idea of gender identity with regard to gender expression. Therefore, issues of exploring the spectrum of sexuality and nonbinary gender identity are made the focus of contemporary theatrical works.[2]

Because of the metatheatrical aspects of this play, I use the theories of Lionel Abel and Richard Hornby. Abel's theory aids me in analyzing the characters of this play because they are aware of their own theatricality. Rosa and Pedro wear costumes and become actors in their own theatrical work. I use Hornby's performance theory to discuss the idea of role-play in Pedrero's work. Pedro and Rosa reinvent themselves as different characters, and they escape reality to explore the possibilities of other identities.

Since this play is set during the festivities of Carnival, I apply Mikhail Bakhtin's theory that Carnival can be used as a vehicle to liberate people from socially accepted roles. Pedro feels liberated because he is permitted to explore his feminine side and dress as a woman during the time of Carnival. Bakhtin's theory aids in understanding the actions of the characters during this celebration of role-play.

The playwright Paloma Pedrero Díaz-Caneja, born in Madrid in 1957, has been involved in almost every aspect surrounding the theater. She is an actress, a drama teacher, a producer, a director and, of course, a playwright. Paloma Pedrero became interested in drama while she was in grade school and acted in several school productions. From 1978 to 1981, Pedrero worked with the independent theater group called "Cachivache" as an actress and writer. In 1985, Pedrero began to receive attention as a playwright with her controversial and groundbreaking play *La llamada de Lauren* in which she played the main female character Rosa. She is an accomplished and innovative playwright who has written numerous plays that deal with current issues and identity. She founded the nonprofit organization "Caídos del Cielo" (Fallen from Heaven) which is dedicated to transforming lives of those at risk through their involvement in theater. Pedrero works with this organization to help people who are at risk of being ostracized by society by involving them in theatrical productions. Her most recent thought-provoking play, *Transformación* (Transformation), was performed in Madrid from October 2 through November 8, 2020, and it follows the inspiring evolution of three transgender people who confront society and embrace their true identity. Pedrero has a personal connection to the issue of gender identity and has gone through this journey of understanding, acceptance, and embracing transformation because her son is transgender and came out as male when he was eighteen years old.[3] Iride Lamartina-Lens comments on Pedrero's theatrical works:

> Her stark, realistic portrayal of a contemporary Spanish society in social and cultural transition reveals the angst, concerns, and complex realities of the

current generation. Throughout her work, the dramatist expresses a genuine concern for the psychological and spiritual development of the individual, and for his/her quest for self-realization and authenticity. (54)

Paloma Pedrero's dramatic works were written after Franco's regime had ended, and this gave the playwright freedom to write about certain controversial issues which could not be discussed during the time Franco was in power. In an interview by Eduardo Galan, Pedrero was asked about the theater of her generation. She responded:

> La gente de mi generación no ha sentido la censura y esto se nota en nuestras obras. Se cuentan las cosas con bastante claridad, sin metáforas ni alegorías. La gente de mi generación no se interesa por el teatro histórico. Al contrario, escribimos para contar las cosas que nos suceden y nos preocupan. Creo que caminamos por un teatro comprometido, claro y esperanzador. (13)

> People in my generation have not dealt with censorship, and that is evident in our work. Things are told with quite a lot of clarity and without metaphors or allegories. On the contrary, we write about things that happen to us and worry us. I think that we strive for theater that is committed, clear, and inspiring.

Paloma Pedrero's pen is a magnifying glass which she turns inward and uses to examine and explore the identity problems of her generation.

In Carolyn Harris's interview with Pedrero, the dramatist was asked about the prevalence of identity crises in our society, and she replied:

> A mí me parece que se debe a la crisis espiritual. Se ha perdido totalmente la conexión interior de las personas, y la gente vive hacia fuera. Busca afuera, critica lo de afuera, intenta cambiar lo de afuera, y no se atreve a ver qué pasa dentro de sí. Para mí, esa falta de mirada interior hace que exista una crisis de identidad. Uno acaba sin saber quién es. (32)

> It seems to me that it is due to spiritual crisis. Connection with one's inner self has been totally lost, and people focus on the outward appearance. People search and criticize the outside, try to change what is on the outside, and do not dare to explore their interior selves. For me, this lack of an inner gaze causes an identity crisis. You end up not knowing who you are.

Pedrero sees this obsession with outward appearances as the cause of identity crises, and, therefore, she is motivated to delve further into the psyche of her characters in order to peel away the false cover and reveal their true nature. In her play *La llamada de Lauren*, the main characters, Rosa and Pedro, must deal with Pedro's identity crisis by confronting his nonbinary gender identity and attraction to wearing clothing traditionally worn by women. Rosa then questions her own identity since her marital relationship serves to uphold her feminine identity. Her personal identity crumbles when Pedro expresses his confusion. I will analyze the issues of gender and sexual identity that surface in this play and that make the audience reevaluate the roles which society thrusts upon us.

PEDRO FLIRTS WITH CROSS-DRESSING

In this play, the character Pedro reveals his secret desire to defy the binary gender rules by dressing as Lauren Bacall, the immensely popular American actress from the 1940s. This alters his masculine identity. Normally, Pedro does not show his true nature because he hides his feminine gender identity, and now his instinct calls him to transform himself into a woman. Joan Torres-Pou comments on the title of the play that communicates the central theme to the audience:

> ... Pedrero titula la obra *La llamada de Lauren*, aludiendo posiblemente a la popular novela de Jack London *La llamada de la selva*. Pedro, al igual que los personajes de London, se siente llamado por una fuerza interior que lo impulsa a exteriorizar sus deseos más reprimidos. (26)

> ... Pedrero titled the work *Lauren's Call*, possibly referring to the popular Jack London novel *Call of the Wild*. Pedro, like the characters in London's work, feels called by an inner force that drives him to externalize his most repressed desires.

Torres-Pou also notes that Lauren is an icon who does not represent a real woman but rather an artificial or mythical figure immortalized by the big screen (27). In Pedrero's introduction to her theatrical work, "Palabras con el lector" (words with the reader), the writer describes Lauren Bacall as "una mujer hermosa, una estrella, un deseo" (19) ("A beautiful woman, a star, a wish"). Pedro tries to attain the impossible by becoming the iconic figure of Lauren Bacall who is formed by the collective masculine desire of society. In her article, "Intertextualidad y metateatro en la obra de Paloma Pedrero," Phyllis Zatlin explains the public's interpretation of fictional idols created by the movie industry:

> Las estrellas de cine de la gran época de Hollywood, estrellas conocidas hoy en día por películas presentadas en la televisión, se imponen como más reales que

la realidad misma. Los actores como seres humanos desaparecen para confundirse con los papeles que desempeñan. (15)

The movie stars of Hollywood's great era, today's stars known for television films, are more real than reality itself. Actors are no longer seen as human beings. They disappear and become the roles that they play.

For Pedro, transforming into Lauren Bacall will help him flee from the frustration and responsibility of his male heterosexual life.

In the beginning of Pedrero's play, we watch as the character Pedro transforms himself and dresses as a woman. This first scene causes dramatic tension since the audience is not exactly sure about what is taking place. Peter L. Podol comments on the appearance of the character Rosa:

> Rosa's entrance, her delighted reaction to her husband's appearance, and the revelation that it is Carnival all function to alleviate tension and reassure the audience that both Pedro and the circumstances of the play are "normal." (22)

At the beginning of the play, the couple's tastefully decorated apartment is described, and it is the very picture of normalcy, creating a clashing backdrop to the character Pedro. When Pedro enters the scene, he is wearing a robe. The audience knows that he will get dressed, and pants and a stylish shirt would be appropriate with the décor of the apartment. Instead of reaching for this predictable outfit, Pedro surprises the audience by pulling a woman's dress out of the closet. Pedro continues to shock the audience when he pulls sexy underwear out of a drawer and puts them on along with a bra which he stuffs with cotton in an attempt to achieve a feminine figure (26). It is obvious that Pedro is attempting to achieve the complete look of a woman and even goes as far as to wear risqué underwear and a stuffed bra. We see his complete transformation, and not one detail is excluded, from his wig down to his black high-heel shoes.

This transformation has the ability to make the audience feel very uncomfortable about the situation. In the prologue to this controversial play *La llamada de Lauren*, Patricia O'Connor comments on the public's reaction to the play:

> Polémica aparte, lo cierto es que nadie ha salido indiferente del espectáculo. El público se ha sentido sacudido y ansioso de cambiar ideas sobre la problemática de la obra. Esta reacción, a fin de cuentas, es una señal muy positiva para la obra . . . ya es hora de que nos sacudan la modorra inerte que nos hace aceptar sin rechistar el papel que nos asignan. (17)

Controversy aside, the truth is that nobody has left the show indifferent. The public has felt shaken and eager to change their opinion about the play's central problem. This reaction, after all, is a very positive sign for this theatrical work . . . it is time to shake the inert drowsiness that makes us accept without questioning the role assigned to us.

Like Lorca's play *El público*, the play *La llamada de Lauren* also possesses some qualities that Brecht assigns to modern theater even though it does not have the surreal qualities associated with Brecht's new theater. The reactions show that Pedrero's play has the power to shake us out of a comfortable complacency, and it also makes us ponder the fragility of the gender roles that we so easily accept. We see a man dress as a woman at the beginning of the play, and this starts the uncomfortable roller coaster ride of emotions for the public. Brecht describes his epic theater as one where "the human being is the object of the inquiry" (37) and the audience "is made to face something" (37) and forced to make decisions. The audience of Pedrero's play reacts in the manner of Brecht's descriptions, as it is made to face the idea of a shifting gender identity.

Upon entering the apartment, Rosa is frightened at first when she does not recognize the feminine figure as her husband Pedro. After realizing that the tall woman is actually her husband, she is delighted with his appearance. This defuses the strangeness of the situation, and the audience begins to see that Pedro's feminine attire is not as incongruous as it appears. Rosa is surprised that Pedro has used her makeup, her pantyhose, and even her underwear. She exclaims that Pedro will tear her new stockings by wearing them (27). Pedro does not have the womanly proportions of his wife, and Rosa's comment is the first sign that she has a problem with her husband's choice in wearing her own articles of clothing. Pedro could be seen as trying to usurp Rosa's role in their relationship by appropriating the parts of her wardrobe that are uniquely feminine. Another surprise for Rosa is that Pedro can walk perfectly in high heels. Since this is not something that would come easily for anyone inexperienced in walking in high heels, one assumes that Pedro might have had some practice before. It is clear that Pedro wants to seem as womanly as possible when he asks Rosa "¿Parezco una mujer o un travestí?" (28) ("Do I look like a woman or a transvestite?"). We see that Pedro does not merely want to wear a dress to parody women or make a comical statement. He really is concerned about having a realistic feminine appearance and would like others to believe that he is a woman. Pedro wants to seem completely transformed.

A short while later, it is made clear that it is Carnival time. During Carnival, one can dress in the wildest costumes and be accepted in society. A man can dress as a woman, and this is regarded as merely a disguise which hides one's real identity. Rosa makes remarks about the verisimilitude of his transformation:

> Yo desde luego si fuera un hombre te tiraría los tejos. Se te ven unos ojazos que no te los mereces. *(Observándole.)* ¡No te falta un detalle! (28)

> Of course, if I were a man, I would make a play for you. You don't deserve those big, beautiful eyes. (Watching him.) Not one detail is missing!

Here we see the beginning of the game of switching genders. Rosa imagines that if she were a man, she would be attracted to him. She obviously does not take his transformation seriously since it is in the context of Carnival, and she thinks that it is only temporary. The truth of the situation is that Pedro is using Carnival as an opportunity to live out his fantasy. During this festive time, Pedro has the freedom to explore his repressed femininity and sexual desires; therefore, he uses Carnival as an excuse to fulfill his desire to dress as a woman. Carnival allows people to pretend to be what they are not; thus, there is a temporary shift in social structure. In his book *Rabelais and His World*, Mikhail Bakhtin explains:

> One might say that carnival celebrated temporary liberation from the prevailing truth and from the established order; it marked the suspension of all hierarchical rank, privileges, norms, and prohibitions. (10)

Pedro is temporarily released from the confines of his masculine role and is free to explore the realm of femininity. His costume acts as a key to his happiness, and he looks forward to participating in the festivities. Pedro exclaims:

> Hoy quiero pasármelo muy bien. Reírme . . . , olvidarme de todo: de las facturas, de los albaranes, de los alumnos. . . . Quiero ir al carnaval así . . . contigo. (31)

> Today I want to have a great time. Laugh . . . , forget about everything: the bills, the delivery notes, the students. . . . I want to go to the carnival like this . . . with you.

Pedro's transformation and involvement in Carnival allows him to shed his responsibilities and forget his worries; he escapes from drudgery in order to taste exotic pleasures. Carnival allows him the freedom to become what is strictly taboo in a social environment where non-heteronormativity is unacceptable. Bakhtin states:

126   *Chapter 4*

>   This carnival spirit offers the chance to have a new outlook on the world, to realize the relative nature of all that exists, and to enter a completely new order of things. (34)

Pedro wants to see the world through feminine eyes, and he is allowed this opportunity through the magic of Carnival. Unfortunately for Pedro, Carnival is the opposite of what it is supposed to be. For him, everyday life is carnivalesque in that he dresses up to play his role as a male. During Carnival, Pedro can assume a new identity and express who he truly wishes to be. Pedro is free of the constraints of the conservative, traditional society, and he takes advantage of the topsy-turvy nature of the Carnival ambiance.

MARRIAGE AND METATHEATER

Metatheater, as described by Lionel Abel, is the lifting of the play-within-a-play concept from a mere device to a philosophical commentary on the theatricality of life:

>   Yet the plays I am pointing at do have a common character: all of them are theatre pieces about life seen as already theatricalized. By this I mean that the persons appearing on the stage in these plays are there not simply because they were caught by the playwright in dramatic postures as a camera might catch them, but because they themselves knew they were dramatic before the playwright took note of them . . . they are aware of their own theatricality. (60)

Rosa and Pedro are celebrating their third wedding anniversary during Carnival, and they reminisce about their wedding and honeymoon which also took place during the Carnival season. This fact brings one back to Abel's ideas:

>   I have defined metatheatre as resting on two basic postulates: (1) the world is a stage and (2) life is a dream. (105)

If the world is a stage, we are all just actors, and while we may think we are living, we are all just acting out imposed societal roles. We all wear masks and costumes in order to be socially acceptable. The fact that Rosa's marriage to Pedro took place during Carnival raises the question: was the wedding simply a performance complete with Carnival costumes? This might be the case for Pedro, who, judging from what we learn in the play, felt pressured into fulfilling the socially acceptable masculine role of husband and future father. In contrast, Rosa genuinely desires to be married to her husband, and therefore accepts the marriage as reality rather than performance. When Rosa and Pedro look back on their honeymoon, they talk about the fact that they were the only ones who did not wear costumes during the festivities:

Rosa: . . . Eran los carnavales, como ahora. Nuestro aniversario siempre va a ser en carnaval.
Pedro: No; sólo cuando coincida, tonta . . . ¡Qué pinta de pardillos llevábamos! ¿Te acuerdas? Todo el mundo iba disfrazado, menos nosotros. (30)

Rosa: . . . It was during carnival, like now. Our anniversary will always be during carnival time.
Pedro: No; only when it coincides, silly . . . We looked like such dummies! You remember? Everyone was dressed up, except us.

They were in fact donning the costumes that society handed to them instead of choosing a costume to fit in with the festive atmosphere of Carnival.

For Pedro, Carnival is a portal that leads into and out of metatheater. Three years prior to the beginning of the play, Pedro stepped through this portal on his wedding day and tried on the costume of the typical married male. He has lived in this ill-fitting disguise for three years, and this year, during Carnival, Pedro is ready to exit through the portal of Carnival and shed his costume in favor of a more natural skin. Pedro's life becomes less metatheatrical when he finally uses Carnival as a door through which he travels to find his true self.

We see that there are some elements of self-hatred when Pedro's feelings about Carnival come to light. He has never dressed up as a woman for Carnival and indicated that he would never do so. It is obvious that Pedro has previously lashed out against those who wear the costume he secretly covets because Rosa is incredibly surprised when Pedro, for this Carnival, decides to transform himself into a woman. She declares:

Pues la verdad es que no me lo esperaba de ti. Como siempre has dicho que los que hacían esto eran todos maricones . . . (31)

Well, the truth is that I didn't expect it from you. You have always said that those who did this were all faggots . . .

In the past, Pedro has not only denied his urges, but has also hurled ugly insults at those who dare to fulfill his personal desires. Before, Pedro despised men who defied gender roles during Carnival, but now he defies this emotion in order to fulfill a secret wish.

Rosa exclaims that she likes his new look and is happy with the transformation because she sees a joyful man instead of a man who leads a dreary existence and hates his job (31).

Even Rosa recognizes that Pedro wears a mask every day to fit in, and she finds this ordinary mask repulsive. Rosa is gleeful at the sight of this "new man" because of Pedro's new attitude and outlook on life. Rosa does not realize that Pedro has taken off his mask to reveal that his true face is much more feminine. Although Pedro made up his mind to reveal his hidden desires, he still feels the need to hide his intentions. When he rents his dress from a costume shop, he lies and says that the dress is for his wife. There is really no need for Pedro to lie about the use of the dress since it is an acceptable costume for Carnival, but he feels that he has not yet entered the realm of Carnival, and therefore cannot divulge his plan. When Pedro denies that the dress is for his own use, he reveals his guilt and shame about the act of cross-dressing, showing that this dress is not merely a costume.

Pedro's fantasy is not only about himself, but rather, it includes transforming his wife into a masculine figure who assumes the male role in the relationship. With Pedro's transformation of Rosa, we see the complete objectification of this woman. When Pedro surprises Rosa with a complete suit which is to become her Humphrey Bogart disguise for Carnival, he insists upon dressing her. At this time, Rosa relinquishes the power she has over her own body and becomes a life-size doll for Pedro to do with as he wishes. According to Cornelia Weege:

> ... Pedro la está convirtiendo de este modo en objeto, la está rebajando a la categoría de una envoltura vacía que ha de servir mera y exclusivamente para hacer realidad a sus propios deseos. (112)

> ... Pedro is making her into an object in this way, he is reducing her to the category of an empty wrapper that is to serve merely and exclusively to make his own desires a reality.

Pedro orders Rosa to take off her clothes, and as she sits in front of the mirror naked, she is stripped of the feminine costume that society has imposed upon her. Now Pedro will take this vulnerable woman and treat her as malleable clay which he will mold into a form that he finds pleasurable. Rosa has passed from the hands of society into the hands of a controlling husband. Pedro asks Rosa if she likes herself with her feminine attire removed. Rosa shows her insecurity when she responds to Pedro's question with her own question, "¿Te gusto a ti?" (Do you like me?) The power that Pedro exhibits over Rosa is apparent since she seems to measure her attractiveness by the response of her husband, and she does not feel desirable as a woman unless he finds her attractive. Thus, Pedro acts as Rosa's mirror.

Pedro announces that he will perform a difficult operation (33). Pedro defines Rosa's transformation as a surgical procedure because he is attempting to transplant her sexual identity with a different one. Pedro first wraps a bandage around his wife, flattening her breasts. At first Rosa refuses to comply with her husband and exclaims that she will be extremely uncomfortable and that binding her breasts would hurt her. Her reaction shows that she does not want to hide her breasts which are a symbol of her femininity. Rosa finally allows Pedro to wrap the bandage around her for the sake of her Carnival costume. Pedro's act of "removing" Rosa's breasts is an act of metaphorical castration as Pedro tries to forcefully amputate Rosa's sexual identity. In this dialogue, Pedro is tightening the bandage around Rosa in order to sculpt her into his personal object of desire:

Rosa: ¡Que no me aprietes tanto, que me las vas a dejar hechas polvo!
Pedro: Anda, no seas quejica. Tienes que parecer un hombre total.
Rosa: Eso es imposible.
Pedro: Imposible no hay nada. (*Atando los cabos de la venda.*) Ya está.
Rosa: Me siento mutilada.

Rosa: Don't squeeze me so much, you're going to crush them!
Pedro: Come on, don't be such a complainer. You have to look like a real man.
Rosa: That's impossible.
Pedro: Nothing is impossible. (Tying up the ends of the bandage.) All done.
Rosa: I feel mutilated.

Rosa is forced into assuming a masculine identity, and because she does not wish to change, she feels mutilated.

Rosa's bandaged body is wrapped in a complete masculine suit. Pedro now sets to work on her feminine face, and he uses her own makeup to draw on bigger eyebrows and sideburns. Again, Rosa begs for acceptance and panders to Pedro's desires when she asks, "¿Ya estoy a tu gusto?" (36) (Am I to your liking yet?). She laughs because she thinks that she is simply being dressed up to participate in Carnival. Little does she know how serious Pedro is about concealing her femininity. After creating new facial features, Pedro still finds Rosa's face too womanly, so he hides it behind a fake mustache.

Pedro is a perfectionist when it comes to his wife's conversion, and he is not happy with a mere masculine disguise. She must be taught to perform as a man, and he shows her how to assume a manly gait. Here, the characters' conversation exposes Pedro's need for Rosa's total metamorphosis:

Pedro: El hábito no hace al monje, cariño.
Rosa: ¡Ya! Y el cuerpo es el reflejo del alma ¿no?
Pedro: Exactamente. Eso es lo que quiero que modifiques . . . el alma. (37)

Pedro: Clothes don't make the man, darling.
Rosa: Come on! And the body is the reflection of the soul, isn't it?
Pedro: Exactly. That is what I want you to modify . . . the soul.

Pedro's request that Rosa change her soul suggests that Rosa make the ultimate sacrifice for her husband: She must bend the core of her being and cease existing as the woman known as Rosa.

In order to complete his creation, Pedro hands Rosa his anniversary gift: a fake phallus. This grotesque offering is the one thing that Rosa requires to become a whole man. Rosa is disgusted, and when Pedro suggests that she wear the phallus, she rejects the idea and openly shows her repulsion at what she feels is a perverse request. Candyce Leonard notes:

> She will not yield her own female sexual identity, and further, she rejects the masculine one that Pedro tries to impose on her . . . the phallus in this play does not empower Rosa; that is, attaching a phallus does not sexualize her. (249)

On the contrary, the phallus does sexualize Rosa in the eyes of her husband since he wants a new type of sexual stimulation from her. However, it has the opposite effect on Rosa, and the false body part imparts a sexuality that is not at all appealing to her. Pedro's strange present prompts Rosa to try to communicate with Pedro and talk about their relationship. Because of Pedro's odd behavior, Rosa senses that he is keeping secrets from her and that he is dissatisfied with his life with her. Pedro's hunger to transform her leads Rosa to believe that she does not excite her husband anymore. Pedro refuses to talk about the situation and, thus, pushes his wife away from him emotionally. Rosa's frustration about the huge lack of communication provokes sympathy from the audience, and we see her as a victim. Pedro is a victim of a powerful society that dictates what he must be, but Rosa is also a victim caught in an unusual relationship. Weege observes:

> Ella es la víctima de su marido en dos sentidos: Por un lado por la situación, completamente inesperada, con la que Pedro le confronta abruptamente; por otro lado, por la conducta que Pedro muestra a continuación. Él esquiva todos los intentos de Rosa de establecer una comunicación entre ambos, y se concentra exclusivamente en convertir a Rosa en un perfecto Bogart ocultándole los pechos y adosándole un pene artificial. Con ello le está imponiendo

violentamente una identidad sexual ajena, además de hacerle ahora sufrir a ella lo mismo que él ha estado sufriendo desde su infancia. (112)

She is the victim of her husband in two ways: On the one hand, because of the completely unexpected situation with which Pedro confronts her abruptly; on the other hand, for Pedro's subsequent behavior. He dodges all of Rosa's attempts to establish communication between them and concentrates exclusively on turning Rosa into a perfect Bogart by hiding her breasts and attaching an artificial penis. With this, he is violently imposing a foreign sexual identity on her, in addition to making her suffer the same as he has been suffering since childhood.

Society has forced Pedro to don the garb of a "normal" male, and now Pedro is acting as society has acted toward him: He is now forcing his wife to be something that she is not. She must assume a new masculine identity, and she does not feel comfortable with it. Rosa is a victim because Pedro's power over her causes her to suffer similar to the way that he has suffered under society.

A METATHEATRICAL GAME OF SEDUCTION

After Rosa tries to communicate with Pedro about their marriage, Pedro changes the subject and initiates the first game in which they assume different gender roles. When Pedro invites Rosa to seduce him, she must do so by playing the role of a man. Rosa reinvents herself as Carlos, and Pedro plays the part of the woman whom Carlos will seduce. Pedro performs as a hairdresser named Azucena. Thus, he chooses to be a woman whose profession allows her to transform people by altering their physical appearance. With the creation of new identities, the role-play game begins. According to Carolyn Harris:

> Para que sus personajes se vean obligados a analizar lo que pasa dentro de sí, Pedrero los coloca frecuentemente en un momento de crisis emocional y recurre al juego metateatral. (170)

> For her characters to be forced to analyze what is happening internally, Pedrero frequently places them in a moment of emotional crisis and turns to the metatheatrical game.

The audience observes a game that allows the characters to analyze their roles in society, reflect on their perception of reality, and ponder their feelings toward one another. According to Richard Hornby's examination of metadrama,

> Role playing within the role sets up a special acting situation that goes beyond the usual exploration of specific roles; it exposes the very nature of role itself. The theatrical efficacy of role playing within the role is the result of its reminding us that all human roles are relative, that identities are learned rather than innate. (72)

In Hornby's analysis, identity is not a fixed element that remains the same throughout one's life. Identity is not innate and does, in fact, shift depending on the roles we assume in different situations. We learn from our surroundings how we are supposed to act, and at times, these outside pressures cause an internal conflict with the identity we desire. Pedro has learned that a man who plays the role of a husband, a provider, and a father is regarded as a valuable part of society and rewarded with acceptance. For Pedro to dare to be gender nonconforming and leave the confines of this prescribed identity would mean risking his reputation. Therefore, he acts out his desires in a metatheatrical game that allows him to explore gender fluidity and his fantasy of assuming a feminine identity without risk.

When the game begins, Rosa approaches it as a learning tool for Pedro. Rosa does not want to be the man in the relationship; she merely is showing Pedro how she would like to be seduced. By contrast, Pedro is using the game to fulfill a secret desire. Pedro is very involved in acting out the role of Azucena, and he is lost in the fantasy of the character. In comparison, Rosa is using the character Carlos as a device to help open the lines of communication between her and her husband and regain the intimacy that they once had.

When Rosa initiates sexual contact, Pedro protests and insists that Rosa continue to play her part as Carlos. At this point, when Rosa steps out of character, she wants to end the game and regain her own identity. Pedro is angry because while he wants to continue to live in his imaginary, gender nonconforming world, she has broken the enchantment of the role-play game. In this dialogue, Rosa, again assuming the role of Carlos, begins to explain that this character is a very busy man who works too much and does not have the time or energy for his partner (44). Rosa echoes her husband's life as she talks about Carlos' background, using the character as a vehicle to voice her complaints about Pedro's treatment of her. In turn, Pedro angrily lashes out at his wife because he recognizes this as a criticism. He does not want reality to enter this drama which he is determined to control. The reason Pedro is playing this game is to escape from a heteronormative reality, not to evaluate the state of their marriage.

The typical game of seduction is too close to reality for Pedro, and in order to escape their real-life problems, he must invent a game that removes them further from the real world. We delve deeper into metadrama as a new game begins. Pedro urges Rosa to play the role of Humphrey Bogart, and as Pedro and Rosa step into the characters of Bacall and Bogart, the audience is reminded of another dramatic work, and, therefore, the play refers to literature in the real world. Hornby comments on this metatheatrical aspect of the play:

> The imaginary world of the main play is disrupted by a reminder of its relation, as a literary construct, to another literary work or works. (88)

Therefore, the audience is better able to understand the actions of the characters and accept the play as a reflection of part of popular culture because of references to the film *To Have and Have Not* (1944) with actors Humphrey Bogart and Lauren Bacall. Before Rosa starts portraying Bogart, we know from cinematographic works that this character is a cisgender, masculine, hardened, romantic man.

While trying to seduce her husband, Rosa tries to talk as Bogart and describes the world in very poetic terms. Harris explains:

> El mundo fantástico que crea Rosa en esta improvisación es uno que está cerca de la naturaleza y lejos de los adornos y la ilusión de la vida diaria. (172)

> The fantastic world that Rosa creates in this improvisation is one that is close to nature and far from the decorations and illusion of daily life.

Rosa talks of a faraway island where purity reigns, and in this environment, she will encounter

> Sirenas que emerjan del agua sin los collares puestos, sin las uñas pintadas, sin olor a perfume barato, sino a algas saladas . . . (48)

> Mermaids emerging from the water without necklaces on, without painted nails, and instead of smelling of cheap perfume, they smell of salty seaweed . . .

Although Rosa is acting out the part of a fictional character, she is really expressing her own desires. She yearns for a pure, uncomplicated life where no one has the necessity to hide behind created masks and gaudy accessories. Rosa's Bogart does not want a painted lady, and Pedro in drag represents this type of false beauty. His appearance prompts us to contemplate two types of deception. It is socially accepted for women to apply makeup in order to mask imperfections and add bright color to the skin, thus creating an enhanced reality. In a world where one must stick to binary norms of gender identity, men who apply women's makeup are seen as trying to create the illusion of femininity, and, therefore, attempting to mask masculinity. Makeup becomes a masking agent and beauty tool for both sexes, but Pedro uses makeup to go against gender norms and as a device to show gender fluidity. Rosa speaks out against layers of deception and all false beauty since she desires the absence of makeup even in the feminine figures or the "sirenas."

Instead of listening to her words, Pedro sees Rosa only as a desirable masculine figure. Torres-Pou clarifies this dramatic scene:

> ... éste ignora sus palabras y, prestando atención tan sólo al disfraz y a la actitud activa de Rosa, va forjando sus propias fantasías eróticas. La objetualización de Rosa es total. Esa noche Pedro le ha infundido los atributos de galán duro y tierno de película y no importa lo que ella diga. No es Rosa para Pedro sino una fantasía. (28)

> ... he ignores Rosa's words and, paying attention only to her disguise and active attitude, forges his own erotic fantasies. Rosa is completely objectified. That night Pedro has infused her with the attributes of a tough, yet loving movie star hunk, and it does not matter what she says. It is not Rosa for Pedro, but rather a fantasy.

Rosa does not understand that she is being used as a vehicle for Pedro's sexual fantasies, and when she attempts to shed her Bogart persona and become Rosa again, she is met with protests as Pedro demands, "No rompas el encanto." (49) ("Don't break the spell.") Rosa believes that the role-play game will end when they become intimate, but Pedro's intention is to remain in costume and experience sex as a woman. Pedro is obviously very excited about this idea, and he exclaims, "Te deseo, mi amor. Te deseo más que nunca." (49) ("I desire you, my love, I desire you more than ever.") Before, Pedro did not seem to have much interest in Rosa sexually, but when Rosa is dressed as a man, he is suddenly very attracted. He insists that Rosa touch his false breasts, but Rosa is extremely uncomfortable with the situation and struggles to emerge from her suit. She is suffocating in her masculine attire, and she longs to reassume her cisgender feminine identity.

The violent climax occurs when Pedro practically drags Rosa to the bed, places her on top of him, and hands her the fake phallus. Pedro bellows, "No me llames Pedro... Penétrame, por favor... Penétrame." (51) ("Don't call me Pedro... Penetrate me, please... Penetrate me.") Rosa is utterly repulsed by this, and she shouts, "¡Se acabó el juego!" (51) ("The game is over!") Here Karla Zepeda interprets the phallic symbol:

A dildo is simply an object. It becomes encoded with meaning in the private exchange between Pedro and Rosa. For Pedro, the object represents desire. For Rosa, the object represents aberrancy. (12)

Pedro ignores his own penis as a sexual organ and instead thrusts the phallus upon Rosa who vehemently refuses to adopt it and penetrate her partner. The game has gone too far for Rosa, and from Rosa's point of view, Pedro has completely assumed the female gender role which leaves her confused and in a state of limbo. The lines between fantasy and reality have now been blurred. Performance becomes reality as soon as Rosa sees Pedro's true desire to bend gender roles and live beyond the binary.

Rosa has never seen this side of her husband and asks for an explanation of Pedro's unusual behavior because she is unable to interpret it. At first, she thinks that he no longer loves her and puts the blame on herself for not being attractive enough to her spouse. When he assures her that this is not the case, she immediately jumps to the conclusion that there is another woman in his life. In truth, the only other woman in Pedro's life is the one that he has buried deep within himself.

The audience can see a secret side to Pedro when he explains his feelings to his wife:

Pedro: . . . A veces es tan duro ser una persona normal. Quiero decir que a veces uno tiene sensaciones o necesidades . . . inadmisibles.
Rosa: ¿Inadmisibles? ¿Qué tipo de necesidades?
Pedro: No, no son cosas concretas. Es como si lo que esperan de ti estuviera en contradicción con . . . , o sea, rompiera tu lógica . . . tu lógica interna. (55)

Pedro: . . . Sometimes it's so hard to be a normal person. I mean, that sometimes one has feelings or needs . . . that are inadmissible.
Rosa: Inadmissible? What kind of needs?
Pedro: They are not concrete things. It's as if what is expected of you is in contradiction with . . . that is, it breaks your logic . . . your internal logic.

In this revealing conversation, Pedro admits that his personal identity does not mesh with the cisgender, heteronormative role he must play in society. Before, Pedro did everything that society wanted of him, but he cannot pretend to fit into that mold anymore. He must acknowledge who he really is, but doing so is difficult since Pedro is not really sure himself. One thing is certain—he is incapable of repressing his desires any longer.

Pedro feels the need for gender fluidity and to be a woman at times, and he has felt this longing ever since he was a boy and could naturally walk better than his sister in high heels. Since then, he has always felt that he has had to compensate for his secret feelings and prove his masculinity to himself and to others. Therefore, when he participated in fights as a boy, he would swallow his fear:

Pedro: Para vencerlo gritaba y me reía más que ninguno. Siempre me ponía en primera línea, frente al bando enemigo, y desafiaba las piedras. Entonces sentía cómo crecía ante los demás. . . . Buscaba sus miradas que me decían: ¡Eres un valiente! ¡Un machote! (56)

Pedro: To overcome it, I screamed and laughed more than anyone. I always put myself on the front line, facing the enemy side, and I dared to face the stones. Then I felt how I grew up before others . . . I looked for their gazes that told me: You are brave! A real tough guy!

Pedro hides behind a macho persona as a reaction to his own inclinations so that he can get reassurance from others that he is "normal."

When Pedro lets his guard down in front of his sister, he cracks the hard, protective shell of masculinity that society prompts and encourages him to grow. He describes the day that his father catches him without this shell:

Un día mi padre me pegó una hostia, ¿sabes? Estaba cantando para mi hermana Piluca, disfrazado de Marisol. Nos lo estábamos pasando estupendamente. Llegó él y me dio una bofetada. Lo que más me jodió es que le pegara también a ella. Le dijo: "Vas a hacer de tu hermano un maricón." (57)

One day my father beat the hell out of me, you know? I was singing for my sister Piluca, dressed up as Marisol. We were having an amazing time. He arrived and slapped me hard. What pissed me off the most is that he hit her too. He said: "You are going to make your brother a fag."

His father violently rejects Pedro's transgressive behavior that defies heteronormativity and partly blames his sister for it. Pedro's father believes that outside influences, such as Pedro's sister, are able to influence Pedro's sexual orientation and gender identity. In fact, his sister does not change Pedro; she embraces her brother for who he is and facilitates Pedro in revealing his true self. After Pedro's father viciously punishes his son for dressing as the famous child actress and singer Marisol, Pedro vows that he will show the world that he is "más hombre que nadie" (57) ("More man than anyone"), and he withdraws into his cisgender-conforming shell until he allows himself to re-emerge during Carnival. Joan Torres-Pou examines Pedro's actions:

Desde ese día fue de "machote" por la vida, sin comprender que tanto ir de Marisol como ir de "machote" no era, en definitiva, más que asumir ficciones y mitos. Así, sin darse cuenta, se dejó llevar por lo que la moral en el poder consideraba masculino y femenino, aniquilando paulatinamente su verdadera identidad. (27)

From that day on, it was "the macho guy" for life, without understanding that both playing the role of Marisol and the role of "the macho guy" was, in short, nothing more than assuming fictions and myths. Thus, without realizing it, he let himself be controlled by what morals in power considered male and female, gradually annihilating his true identity.

Because of societal pressure, Pedro is relegated to wearing a masculine costume. Although Pedro is only wearing a costume when he plays the role of Marisol, he is exploring his personal identity in a way that lifts the boundaries off binary gender distinction. When the door of exploration is shut and Pedro can no longer search for his true self, his masculine disguise acts to construct a dam to inhibit gender fluidity and build rather than break down the walls between masculine and feminine.

Although Rosa tries to understand Pedro's dilemma, she is unable to comprehend the mental anguish of her husband. Rosa tries to rationalize all of Pedro's actions, and when Pedro describes his childhood fights and his need to prove his masculinity to the other boys, Rosa responds that all little boys act this way. When Pedro comments about playing with his sister and dressing up as a girl, Rosa replies, "¿Qué niño no se ha puesto los vestidos de su hermana?" (57) ("What boy hasn't worn his sister's dresses?"). Rosa seems to have an explanation for all of Pedro's past actions, and she does not see them as problematic or different from the norm. Pedro is unable to communicate his thoughts, and although Rosa is trying to understand, she does not see the true nature of Pedro's identity problems. Pedro is immensely frustrated with his wife because she does not comply with his demands and because she cannot grasp the meaning of his stories from the past. Pedro then wrongly accuses her of judging him just like his father has done. Torres-Pou expounds upon this idea:

Acusa a Rosa de no ser capaz de comprenderlo, cuando no ha buscado en ella comprensión sino la sumisión y la aceptación de una geisha. (28)

He accuses Rosa of not being capable of understanding him, when he has not sought in her understanding, but rather the submission and acceptance of a geisha.

When Rosa makes an effort to understand and is met with hostility from her husband, she loses control, throws herself at him and violently grasps at his dress in an attempt to undress him, and screams, "¡Quítate eso! ¡Quítate toda esa mierda! ¡Pareces un maricón! ¡Maricón! (59)" ("Take that off! Take off all that shit! You look like a fag! Faggot!"). Rosa's emotions overwhelm her, and she cannot deal with Pedro's altered appearance, defensive attitude, and controlling behavior. Because she is so confused and hurt, she responds with an eruption of anger which represents a shift from her emotions so far. Podol comments:

> Rosa's response is credible in its multiplicity . . . before and after that outburst, she demonstrates real sympathy and love as well as a genuine desire to help him. (22–23)

Rosa feels that she is on shaky ground since the stability of her whole marriage is called into question. Therefore, her insult reflects her insecurity that Pedro does not love her anymore.

CROSS-DRESSING AND SEXUAL ORIENTATION

Rosa does not know how to separate Pedro's desire to cross-dress from his sexual identity. In her mind, she jumps to the conclusion that he is a "maricón" ("fag") because she cannot absorb Pedro's motivation for wanting to wear women's clothing. Pedro attempts to bend the rules of heteronormativity and experiments with gender expression and the gender nonbinary idea that men can wear women's clothing. The fact that Pedro is a person who cross-dresses does not mean that he is gay. In fact, he proclaims his love for his wife. Marjorie Garber acknowledges the confusion between cross-dressing and sexuality:

> In mainstream culture it thus appears just as unlikely that a gay man will be pictured in non-transvestite terms as it is that a transvestite man will be pictured in non-gay terms. It is as though the hegemonic cultural imaginary is saying to itself: if there is a difference (between gay and straight), we want to be able to *see* it, and if we see a difference (a man in women's clothes), we want to be able to *interpret* it. In both cases, the conflation is fueled by a desire to tell the *difference,* to guard against a difference that might otherwise put the identity of one's own position in question. (130)

Gender identity and sexuality are two separate issues. In the future, Pedro could identify as transgender and still be attracted only to women since one's gender identity is different than one's sexual orientation. It is evident that the ambiguity of the situation bothers Rosa. She is confused and unable to interpret her husband's gender identity and sexuality. She cannot place him in a category, and her perception of Pedro is completely changed. She knows that his behavior is not socially acceptable in society where gender is a binary construct and the rules of masculine and feminine gender expression are strict, but she does not know how it will affect her. Rosa questions her own identity and wonders if she is still attractive to Pedro. Pedro tries to explain that his gender nonconforming identity is different from the accepted heteronormative paradigm, but this does not change the way he feels about Rosa. Virtudes Serrano clarifies Pedro's motives for cross-dressing:

> Él ha decidido romper con un pasado que lo obliga a adoptar un papel canónicamente varonil con el que no se siente identificado. Pero Pedro no es un homosexual, ahí reside precisamente el gran acierto de la construcción del personaje, es un hombre en conflicto consigo mismo que busca el camino de su verdad. (63)

> He has decided to break with a past that forces him to adopt a canonically manly role with which he does not identify. But Pedro is not gay; that is precisely the great success of the character's construction. He is a man in conflict with himself who seeks the path of his truth.

Ever since Pedro was a little boy, he has denied himself the right to explore his own identity. Pedro's situation is very confusing and difficult to explain to his wife because he wants to explore nonbinary and feminine gender roles, but he does not express any desire to leave his wife. Now the question of his identity cannot be denied any longer. Pedro feels a burning need to explain his desires to the woman that he loves because he feels that she should know everything about him even though it could ruin their marriage.

At Rosa's command, Pedro quickly removes his feminine costume and replaces it with another: the disguise of the model cisgender male citizen. When Pedro is dressed to fit into mainstream society, Rosa can look at him and talk to him again. The stage directions describe Rosa as being a bit startled after seeing Pedro in his usual clothes again, and it is if she has been awakened from a nightmare (60). Pedro even reacts as if it has all been a bad dream. Rosa is very sympathetic and asks Pedro again if he would like to talk about his problems. Pedro denies the importance of their discussion, and when Rosa tries to coax him to talk, he interrupts her and says, "No te preocupes, si en realidad lo que te estaba contando era una tontería" (60) ("Don't worry, what I was telling you was nonsense"). Pedro's demeanor fits in with his normal clothes, and he is back to acting like the cisgender, hard-working, non-communicative husband who hides his feelings. He has retreated into his shell once more, and he tries to avoid Rosa's questions. Pedro would like his wife to forget the whole event ever happened, and then he blames everything on the fact that he works too hard and needs time for a vacation.

Pedro also shows that he has stepped back into the role of the macho male when he denies Rosa the opportunity of working. He would rather continue to be miserable working too many hours than to allow his wife to get a job. Carolyn Harris comments on this situation:

> ... Rosa ... quiere seguir en su rol femenino de esposa, pero a la vez desea algo más. Menciona la posibilidad de salir a trabajar, idea que Pedro rechaza por sentirse menos hombre si no mantiene a su esposa. (173)

> ... Rosa ... wants to continue in her feminine role as the wife, but at the same time she wants something else. She mentions the possibility of going to work, an idea that Pedro rejects because he feels like less of a man if he does not financially support his wife.

Pedro feels he must follow the traditional male role in society that upholds binary gender roles, and his pride would be hurt if Rosa helped to earn money. It would damage the masculine image that he has worked so hard to protect.

Rosa feels that she needs to fill a void in her life, and she then suggests that they have a child together. Pedro denies her the right of motherhood because he feels that he is incapable of providing what he believes the child needs (65). Leonard analyzes Pedro's resistance to becoming a father:

> While Pedro's argument superficially might suggest his economic insecurity, his unwillingness to have a child is deep-seated in his unwillingness to impose traditional gender expectations on his male offspring. (248)

Pedro's response to Rosa's desire to have a child can be interpreted on an even deeper level. It is not just that he is unwilling to teach his child about gender roles, but also that he does not have the ability since he himself cannot follow traditional binary gender expectations. Pedro does not believe that he could give their child what he or she needs emotionally. He thinks that he would never be a good role model for a child since he does not fit into the traditional male-dominated society. He is not sure of his own identity, and he does not want to be responsible for the formation of his offspring's identity. Therefore, although Pedro is now the picture of normalcy, he cannot offer Rosa the emotionally fulfilling life that she craves.

Rosa is exhausted, and she decides to go to bed, leaving Pedro to work on his lesson plans for the classes he will teach the following week. Pedro cannot concentrate on his work, and his mind focuses on the dress and other accessories strewn across the floor. Lauren's call and the call of the Carnival festivities are too much to bear, and Pedro knows that Carnival can serve as the escape portal that leads to the exploration of his identity. He checks to make sure that Rosa is truly asleep, and then he timidly applies bright red lipstick. When he thinks that he hears Rosa awaken, he hastily wipes off the lipstick with his shirtsleeve. He then decides to leave the apartment and packs a bag full of feminine garb. As Pedro tries to sneak out of the house, Rosa wakes up and asks him where he is going. Pedro does not lie, and he tells her that he will participate in the Carnival parties. In an infinitely sympathetic and understanding gesture, Rosa fixes Pedro's smeared lipstick, hands him a rose and wishes him a happy Carnival. After Pedro leaves, Rosa realizes the importance of her husband's actions, and as she contemplates the situation, a strange chill goes through her, and she begins to tremble (69). Rosa can feel the change in her bones, but she does her best to put herself in Pedro's position in order to better understand him. She puts on the Humphrey Bogart hat and begins to play the role of a man seducing a woman, but she cannot endure the charade for long. Rosa's confusion and sadness grip her as she embraces the bed and attempts to stifle her sobs. In the end, Rosa does not understand Pedro's ambiguous gender identity and sexuality, and she cries because she is unsure of her future with him.

Rosa is also unsure of her own identity, and this causes her great distress. According to Harris:

> Rosa se siente incompleta y cree que necesita sobre todo una relación auténtica con su marido para poder definirse y saber quién es. (173)

> Rosa feels incomplete and believes that she needs, above all, an authentic relationship with her husband in order to define herself and know who she is.

She feels bewildered and lost since her marital relationship is based on the façade that her husband has built to protect himself. She has watched the façade crumble, and this terrifies her, but at least the truth is out in the open. In Galan's interview, the playwright comments on the ambiguous nature of her play:

> En *La llamada de Lauren* hay un final abierto; además vemos a un hombre que descubre su identidad y se atreve a afrontarla, y eso es hermoso; no me parece pesimista, sino esperanzador. (12)

> In *Lauren's call* there is an open ending; also, we see a man who discovers his identity and dares to face it, and that is beautiful; I don't think it's pessimistic, but hopeful.

Pedrero sees hope in the fact that Pedro has broken through his shell, and he is on the right path to finding his authentic self. There is also some hope that Pedro and Rosa's marriage will survive this crisis because Rosa demonstrates a desire to comprehend and perhaps accept Pedro's non-gender nonconforming identity and desire to cross-dress. On the other hand, we do not know if their relationship is strong enough to continue after Pedro's huge revelation. We do know that Pedro is exploring gender expression and has embarked on a brave, new journey in search of himself.

PUBLIC REACTION

In this play, we are confronted with shocking images which force us to think about socially constructed gender roles. The public divides certain actions into socially acceptable and deviant behaviors. According to the mores of Spanish society, a cisgender, heterosexual male should not want to dress and act as a female. This is considered a deviant behavior that threatens a male dominated, gender binary society.

It is not surprising that some critics reacted strongly against the play *La llamada de Lauren*. The sexual subject matter made some people uncomfortable, especially since such a subject would never have been discussed in the theater during the years in which Franco was in power. Older men especially disliked the questioning of gender identity by a young female playwright. According to Pedrero in her interview with Harris:

La llamada de Lauren . . . fue otra cosa, es una obra muy especial. Además, se estrenó en el 85 con un montaje muy duro y dio lugar a polémica. Desde luego, con las mujeres no he tenido ningún problema . . . El problema lo he tenido alguna vez con cierto tipo de hombres que parecen sentirse heridos en su dignidad . . . algunos hombres, mayores sobre todo se indignaban con lo que veían. (34)

Lauren's call . . . was something else, it's a very special theatrical work. In addition, it was released in '85, was difficult to stage, and it gave rise to controversy. Of course, I have not had any problem with women . . . I have had problems, sometimes, with a certain type of man, who seems to feel that his dignity is wounded . . . some men, mainly older men, were outraged with what they saw.

Pedrero suspected that the men who had a problem with her play saw something of themselves reflected in the drama, and since they did not like what they saw, they completely rejected Pedrero's work. Francisco Alvaro is one critic who offered a harsh review:

La llamada de Lauren . . . diálogo dramático-sexual, de la autora-actriz Paloma Pedrero, compartido en la interpretación con Jesús Ruymán, carece de interés y aburre. El tema de un marica reprimido y una mujer tontorrona que se presta al juego erótico, entre la extravagancia y la obscenidad para incitarle de forma grosera y violenta, se le va, a la autora e intérpretes, de las manos. Vimos una representación en Valladolid con tristeza y cierta perplejidad, y no nos explicamos por qué se estrenan estas cosas. (216)

Lauren's call . . . a dramatic, sexual dialogue by author-actress Paloma Pedrero, along with actor Jesús Ruymán, is boring and uninteresting. This play is about a repressed fag and a dimwitted woman who gets involved with an erotic game. The action alternates between extravagance and obscenity in order to stimulate and excite in a vulgar and violent way. The author and performers completely lose control of this dramatic work. We saw a performance in Valladolid which only made us sad and confused. We don't understand why these types of things are performed.

This critic trivializes the important identity issues in the play and obviously does not take Pedrero's work seriously. Alvaro seems to want to feel secure in the "normal" gender roles that society has assigned to men and women, and he cannot accept a man who does not fit the typical macho mold without referring to him in vulgar, insulting terms. According to Patricia O'Connor:

Los hombres mayores de espíritu—críticos incluidos—se asustaron de que una mujer tocara temas tan sagrados y ocultos para ellos. Tampoco eran capaces de reconocer que un hombre puede tener conflictos de identidad aparente sin ser, automáticamente, homosexual. (16)

The men who were stuck in old ways of thinking—critics included—were frightened that a woman dealt with such themes, that for them, were sacred and hidden. Nor were they able to recognize that a man can have apparent identity conflicts without being automatically gay.

Critics could not understand why anyone, let alone a woman playwright, would want to explore this taboo subject, and, therefore, they could not accept her work.

Society imposes constraints that require many people to hide their true identities. In many societies, it is considered socially unacceptable to express one's identity if that identity is judged to be a deviant one from the heteronormative paradigm. In order to escape punishment for breaking the social norms, people repress their genuine desires and relegate themselves to a life within the constructed moral binary boundaries. In *La llamada de Lauren*, Pedro is forced to confront his own identity and must accept that the majority will not approve of this. The public's opinion controls Pedro's life, and he feels that he is a puppet whose strings are being pulled constantly by a vigilant and judgmental cisgender society that only accepts heteronormativity. Pedro attempts to explain himself to his wife, but his frustration and anger erupts when he shouts:

> ¡Que estoy harto! ¿Eso lo entiendes? Que estoy hasta los cojones de que me digan lo que tengo que hacer, cuándo lo tengo que hacer, con quién lo tengo que hacer, cómo lo tengo que hacer . . . siempre tengo que estar demostrando a alguien que sé tirar piedras. (58)

> I'm fed up! Do you understand that? That I have fucking had it with being told what I have to do, when I have to do it, who I have to do it with, how I have to do it . . . I always have to show someone that I know how to throw stones.

Ever since he was a boy, Pedro has felt the need to gain the respect of his male peers by making a show of his strength, fearlessness, and masculinity, but now he is sick of maintaining this false veneer. He is sick of trying to prove that he belongs on the ultra-macho side of the "binary divide" of masculinity and femininity. Pedro has accepted that he is different, and he knows that there is a part of himself that he has externally denied for a long time. He desires to be "normal," but the temptation to explore his urges and leave the house while playing a feminine role proves too great to resist. Pedro must embark upon a psychological journey in order to deal with his true identity.

Pedro is not the only victim in this play. Rosa also is a victim when Pedro thrusts her into a situation which leaves her lost and perplexed about her own identity. Unfortunately, Rosa evaluates herself based on her husband's reaction to her. Leonard explains:

> When Pedro rejects Rosa's female sexuality in substitution for male sexuality, she is no longer woman, but a monster unable to recognize herself. (249)

Rosa does not feel that she is a desirable woman because she cannot fulfill her husband's sexual needs. Rosa needs to fill a void in her life, so she struggles to gain autonomy by suggesting to Pedro that she find a job or have a child. Both would make her less emotionally dependent on Pedro, but he denies Rosa any opportunity to free herself from him. Therefore, Rosa feels trapped in Pedro's world of ambiguous gender identities. Both Pedro and Rosa are suspended in their own spheres of loneliness where they yearn to know themselves.

After one watches or reads this dramatic work, it is harder to blindly accept traditional, binary gender roles without pondering their validity. Is gender simply a social construct? Why must there be barriers separating masculine from feminine, and why are we unable to invent our own fluid identities instead of limiting ourselves to the relegated, heteronormative ones? We start with an innate identity, but, at times, we feel the pressure to manipulate and mold our personal identities according to our surroundings. As Richard Hornby states, "Identity, then, is something that human beings have to learn, and the learning is an inherently painful process" (70). We see that it is even more painful when one goes against the accepted social mores. The theater allows us to experience different identities and see through the eyes of others. Harris explains:

> Junto con los actores, los espectadores se prueban nuevas identidades y analizan qué significa en una sociedad ser un hombre, una mujer, un trabajador, o un padre. El teatro funciona como un laboratorio en el que se examina la identidad. (171)

> Together with the actors, the spectators test new identities and analyze what it means to be a man, a woman, a worker, or a father in society. The theater functions as a laboratory in which identity is examined.

A close examination of identity issues in this play exposes the absurdity in rejecting any identity that does not mesh with society's heteronormative expectations and fit into the masculine/feminine binary box. In *La llamada de Lauren*, performance and reality blend, and gender identity is called into question as the character Pedro becomes the woman he had never allowed himself to be.

NOTES

1. For more information on other plays by Paloma Pedrero, see Bigelow, Fagundo, Rodríguez López-Vázquez, and Zatlin. Zepeda discusses her innovative ideas and activities for teaching *La llamada de Lauren* to students in advanced Spanish courses of second language acquisition. On photography of Pedrero's theatrical works, see Hodge. On psychoanalysis and Pedrero's play *La llamada de Lauren*, see Sullivan. For an interview with Pedrero, see Villán.
2. On cross-dressing, see Docter and Ackroyd.
3. For more information on the theatrical work *Transformación* and in-depth interviews with Pedrero about this play and her experience as a mother whose child came out as transgender, see Ródenas and Díaz.

Conclusion

Shifting Identities in Four Spanish Plays and Parallels in Modern Popular Culture

In this book, I study gender, sexuality, race, and ethnicity as portrayed in two twentieth-century plays and two seventeenth-century plays from Spain. The seventeenth-century theatrical works *El retablo de las maravillas* and *Virtudes vencen señales* deal with ethnic and racial identity, respectively. In the two plays from the twentieth century, *El público* and *La llamada de Lauren*, the playwrights broach the subjects of non-heteronormative sexual and gender identities. The four plays in this book are linked in that they all deal with a different issue of identity. They are similar in that the protagonists in all plays struggle with shifting identities and must decide whether to conform to social precepts in terms of disguising or rejecting their differences. In *Virtudes vencen señales*, the main character, Filipo, is unable to cover up the racial identity that marks him as different; thus, he constantly verbally rejects his blackness in an attempt to mask it. His physical difference is impossible to disguise, and he finds it difficult to fit into a white society. On the other hand, in *El retablo de las maravillas*, *El público*, and *La llamada de Lauren*, which are the plays concerning ethnicity, sexuality and gender, the characters are able to mask their differences more easily since their outward appearances do not call attention to their inner differences.

In Cervantes' play *El retablo de las maravillas*, three swindlers come to a small town in Spain to show their "puppet show," which actually does not exist. The tricksters explain that only those who have absolutely no Jewish blood will be able to see the show. Hijinks ensue, and the silly villagers react outrageously to the nonexistent show. The characters are aware of their own theatricality; hence one can apply Abel's theory because of the metatheatrical nature of this play. An admission by any character that he cannot view the actions of the "puppet show" is taken as a confession of Jewish heritage; therefore, the rustic characters must participate in the illusion to avoid being exiled and labeled as Jews. As Gilman suggests, the characters show feelings of self-hatred because of their imagined Jewish identity. Cervantes, believed to be of Jewish heritage himself, uses his play to criticize seventeenth-century Spanish society's anti-Semitism and obsession with "blood purity." This play is the more subversive of the two seventeenth-century theatrical works since the playwright challenges society's rules on identity and comments on the foolish nature of judgment based on *pureza de sangre*.

Although *Virtudes vencen señales* deals with the issue of racial identity, it too is linked to the idea of ethnicity and *pureza de sangre* because the playwright Vélez de Guevara seems to be obsessed with his own lineage. Unlike Cervantes, who uses his satirical writing to parody society's obsession with blood purity, Vélez's writing does not harshly criticize or make fun of Spanish society's fixation on difference and identity. Vélez is determined to be accepted by Spanish society, despite his *converso* origin. He changes his name from "Santander" to "Vélez" in hopes of masking his Jewish heritage and making himself more acceptable in a society where blood purity is important. It seems that the playwright uses his theatrical work as a vehicle to announce his message that one can be virtuous and noble in spite of one's difference.

In *Virtudes vencen señales*, Vélez tells the story of a Black prince born to the white king and queen of Albania. Although unlikable because of his extremely boastful and overconfident attitude, the Black prince Filipo demonstrates that his virtue overcomes his portentous appearance because he believes that his soul is white and noble even though his appearance is seen by society as Black and ignoble. Like the characters around him who constantly refer to his appearance as "monstrous," Filipo rejects his own black identity, and like the playwright who created him, he wishes to discard his difference in favor of a more acceptable identity. Gilman's theories of self-hatred and difference aid in analyzing the protagonist's behavior. Filipo constantly refers to his white, royal Albanian soul as a reflection of his true self, thereby rejecting his racial difference.

Like Vélez de Guevara, Federico García Lorca struggles with his own identity issues. Non-heteronormative sexuality was not accepted in the conservative Catholic Spanish society of the 1930s. By using surrealistic, highly symbolic images and characters in *El público*, Lorca displays his own tormented soul and expresses his need to deal with his alternative sexuality. Brecht's theories of theater work well to aid in analyzing this surrealistic style of writing. The main character, the director, is similar to Lorca in that he too must choose between showing his true sexual identity and masking it in order to be accepted in society. In the end, the director chooses to suppress and disguise his true identity, but the mask of conformism slowly kills him as he symbolically grows cold and freezes at the end of the play. Freud's theories help to examine the complex psychological aspects of this theatrical work. Lorca's characters reflect his own battle with self-acceptance in terms of his sexuality.

The playwright Paloma Pedrero also deals with the taboo subject of sexuality and gender identity in *La llamada de Lauren*. As in *El público*, repression of sexual difference and desire for acceptance are the main themes in this theatrical work. The play is set during the time of Carnival, and the character Pedro reveals his hidden desire to dress as a woman. Bakhtin suggests that Carnival is a liberating festival that allows for the exploration of identity. Pedro's wife Rosa must deal with his difference and confront her fear of rejection. Unlike the characters in the other plays who reject their differences in favor of acceptance in society, Pedro does not seem to give in to the pressure to conform at the end of the play. He leaves his home dressed as the woman he longs to be, and it is possible that he will no longer suppress his desires to cross-dress and escape a binary, heteronormative gender identity. It is unclear if Pedro identifies as transgender, but that is a possibility in this open-ended theatrical work. Rosa is devastated since now her relationship with Pedro is in limbo, and the audience is left wondering about their marriage. Pedro risks his relationship and acceptance in society by deciding to embrace his difference and wear women's clothing, although we do not know if he will follow his urges in the future outside of the realm of Carnival. The theories of Abel and Hornby assist in discussing metatheater and examining the idea of role-play as shown in Pedrero's play.

Pedrero's theatrical work reflects the atmosphere of a Spanish society recently liberated from Franco's regime and the uncertainty surrounding acceptance of a nontraditional gender identity. If Lorca's *El público* reflects a repressed society on the brink of succumbing to dictatorial rule, then *La llamada de Lauren* shows what happens after the suffocating veil of oppression is lifted, and people are once again allowed to express their differences. Even though there is more tolerance of non-heteronormative sexual and gender identities later in the twentieth century and currently, it is still a struggle to gain societal acceptance of these differences in a heterosexual paradigm.

This study of identity in four Spanish plays is an interpretation of highly provocative literature, and we examine four extremely different theatrical works that share the common theme of identity. The seventeenth-century plays focus on race and ethnicity, while the twentieth-century works shift the emphasis to gender and sexual identity. Each play offers a snapshot of Spanish society in the period each was written. The theatrical works function as a portal into different time periods, and we are able to gain insight and, therefore, strive to understand the struggles and motivations of people in Spanish society of the seventeenth and twentieth centuries. The important historical background provided for each play permits a detailed analysis of the theatrical works and gives a distinct perspective on the literature.

THE ENDURING LEGACY OF IDENTITY POLITICS

The topic of identity is as provocative and controversial now as it was in the seventeenth and twentieth centuries. Although I discuss literature of the past, this is timely and relevant to modern society because humanity still constantly struggles with accepting people who have identities that are different from the perceived majority. People are still labeled as "other," excluded from the dominant reference group, and are sometimes met with horrific violence and abuse just because they are deemed different. The issue of identity is a much-deliberated subject as evidenced by our current societal problems with systemic racism and racist policies, increased visibility of emboldened white supremacist groups, homophobia, transphobia, and anti-Semitism.

One would like to think that the world is different now. One would like to think that those racist and anti-Semitic policies of past societies would have disappeared long ago to evolve into an enlightened civilization where all people are treated equally. Unfortunately, that is not the case, and we must fight against the bigotry, intolerance, and xenophobia deemed acceptable in society today. There seems to be but a thin veneer of tolerance of the Other in society, and when this veneer is stripped, we see the prejudice that lurks underneath the shiny facade that we believe is acceptance of difference. In his book *How to Be an Antiracist*, Ibram Kendi compares racism to a cancer that could be lethal to humanity (238). According to the author, we must strive to be antiracist, and here he defines the terms "racism" and "antiracism":

> Racism is a powerful collection of racist policies that lead to racial inequity and are substantiated by racist ideas. Antiracism is a powerful collection of antiracist policies that lead to racial equity and are substantiated by antiracist ideas. (20)

Racist ideas are the centerpiece of the theatrical work *Virtudes vencen señales*, and the blatant racism throughout the play serves to shock most modern-day readers who would deny that these persistent ideas exist today. This denial of racism is problematic in that we then do not confront the idea that systemic racism and racial inequity are alive and well. It is a denial of a poisonous cancer that is growing in humanity. In his article, "Is This the Beginning of the End of American Racism," Kendi masterfully analyzes the impact that President Donald Trump has had on our society:

He has held up a mirror to American society, and it has reflected back a grotesque image that many people had until now refused to see: an image not just of the racism still coursing through the country, but also of the reflex to deny that reality. Though it was hardly his intention, no president has caused more Americans to stop denying the existence of racism than Donald Trump.

The mirror is a powerful symbol of the truth, and one must confront reality when gazing in the mirror. The character Filipo peers into the water to see his own reflection, and instead of embracing his identity, he rejects his appearance. Here, Filipo realizes that he is a black man, but he is full of self-hatred and espouses the racism that is accepted in seventeenth century Spanish society. The ugly truth of racism and anti-Semitism in seventeenth-century Spain is reflected in the plot of this theatrical work. Today, we must not look away from the grotesque, racist image that Trump has revealed in the heart of American society. We must not deny that racism exists, but rather, we must confront the fact that racism is still very much alive. By acknowledging it and seeing that it thrives among us, we can take action and fight against this cancer of humanity, striving to eliminate racist policy.[1]

El retablo de las maravillas also acts as a mirror that reveals and criticizes anti-Semitism and discrimination in seventeenth-century Spanish society. We must confront the fact that anti-Semitism did not die off with the fall of Nazi Germany. White supremacist groups scapegoat the Jewish people and still tout the anti-Semitic idea that they are to blame for society's problems. Intolerance appears in the mirror and rears its ugly head in society, and the danger is that some are more than willing to join the intolerant crowd. Just as the problem of bigotry persists, contemporary forms of entertainment continue to deal with prejudice in a variety of forms. Sacha Baron Cohen, a popular Jewish comedian from England, boldly confronts issues concerning ethnicity, gender, sexuality, and race. Through his alter egos, he manages to touch upon various stereotypes concerning identity. Baron Cohen's *Showtime* show from the summer of 2018, "Who Is America" caused a stir when he donned many outlandish disguises and duped many politicians who, after much encouragement by Baron Cohen, revealed ridiculous prejudiced ideas and beliefs in stereotypes. His hit HBO comedy show, "Da Ali G Show," features Borat Sagdiyev, an anti-Semitic, misogynistic reporter from Kazakhstan; Bruno, a gay fashion show presenter; and Ali G, a hip-hop journalist. Baron Cohen humorously portrays all these characters, and some deem him a comic genius. In 2019, Sacha Baron Cohen was the recipient of the Anti-Defamation League's (ADL) International Leadership Award and delivered the keynote address at the ADL's Never Is Now summit on Anti-Semitism and hate. During this speech, he discussed his famous characters:

> When Borat was able to get an entire bar in Arizona to sing "Throw the Jew down the well," it did reveal people's indifference to anti-Semitism. When—as Bruno, the gay fashion reporter from Austria—I started kissing a man in a cage fight in Arkansas, nearly starting a riot, it showed the violent potential of homophobia. And when—disguised as an ultra-woke developer—I proposed building a mosque in one rural community, prompting a resident to proudly admit, "I am racist, against Muslims"—it showed the acceptance of Islamophobia.... Today around the world, demagogues appeal to our worst instincts.

While in character, Sacha Baron Cohen possesses the ability to reveal a despicable aspect of the people with which he interacts, and he fears that those in power make hateful discrimination acceptable.

Baron Cohen's character Borat is his most popular character. In 2006, Cohen helped to create and starred in a film entitled *Borat! Cultural Learnings of America for Make Benefit Glorious Nation of Kazakhstan* where the character interviews many people who are completely unaware that Borat is not a real correspondent from Kazakhstan. The sequel of this film entitled *Borat Subsequent Moviefilm: Delivery of Prodigious Bribe to American Regime for Make Benefit Once Glorious Nation of Kazakhstan* was released on October 23, 2020. This latest film is filled with more of Borat's wild antics which expose people's xenophobia and deep prejudice against Jews. In one scene, Borat goes to a bakery to buy a chocolate cake and asks the cake decorator to write the white supremacist slogan, "Jews will not replace us," along with smiley faces in blue icing on his cake, and she does so without any hesitation, thus showing herself as a willing participant in dangerous hate speech. Many times, throughout this film and other past performances, Cohen reveals the anti-Semitic, misogynistic, racist, and homophobic beliefs of the people with whom he interacts. Of course, some are offended by his brand of humor, but Quentin Schaffer, a spokesperson for HBO, says that these people are missing the point of Cohen's comedy, and he defends the comedian by stating:

> Through his alter-egos, he delivers an obvious satire that exposes people's ignorance and prejudice in much the same way *All in the Family* did years ago. (*The Jewish Week*)

There is the fear that people will not understand that this is a parody and not see the real message, but rather imitate this behavior and believe that it is truly acceptable to be anti-Semitic. Obviously, Cohen uses his character as a tool to critique anti-Semitism and unacceptable ideas in society.

The comedian Cohen embraces his Jewish heritage and is the grandson of a holocaust survivor. Cohen conceals his true identity and goes undercover, disguised as Borat, the Kazakhstani reporter, and sings an anti-Semitic song in a country-western bar in Tucson, Arizona in an episode of *"Da Ali G Show."* In much the same way Cervantes approaches the issue of *pureza de sangre* in *El retablo de las maravillas,* Cohen performs his own *retablo* in hopes of provoking a reaction that reflects the audience members' prejudices towards Jews. In Cervantes' comical play, three trickster characters provoke gullible villagers to react outrageously and, thus, reveal their hatred towards Jews. Like Chirinos' and Chanfalla's audience in the short play by Cervantes, it appears that the people in Cohen's audience are not Jewish and probably do not even know anyone who is Jewish. As his character Borat, Cohen steps onto the stage at the bar wearing a western-style jacket and a cowboy hat. The audience applauds this foreigner who seems eager to perform his country song. The song starts innocently enough, and people start to clap along. Cohen warms up the audience by singing about his frustration with the innocuous problems of his country, such as slow public transportation. The song then abruptly changes, and the singer blames all Kazakhstan's problems on the Jewish people. As the character Borat, Cohen belts out lyrics accusing Jews of taking money from others and never returning it, thus evoking the dangerous stereotype of the miserly, thieving, and controlling Jew. He even evokes the ridiculous anti-Semitic image of Jews having horns. Eventually, Borat leads almost everyone in the bar to join him by boisterously and enthusiastically singing the rowdy chorus:

Throw the Jew down the well,
So my country can be free.
 (Baron Cohen)

Cohen uses several Jewish stereotypes in the lyrics, and instead of receiving a reaction of rejection, anger, and horror at a song that portrays Jews stereotypically and advocates for violence against them, this modern American audience reacts in much the same way a seventeenth-century Spanish audience would react, thus showing the universality of anti-Semitism that exists across centuries and countries. The audience enthusiastically claps, hoots and hollers, and joins Borat in a raucous, rousing rendition of "Throw the Jew Down the Well," and only a couple of people seem vaguely uncomfortable. In his play, Cervantes is making fun of the buffoonish characters who reflect the anti-Semitic attitude of seventeenth-century Spanish society. Cohen is also poking fun at his ignorant, gullible audience. Therefore, Cohen performs his own "puppet show" in hopes of provoking a reaction that reflects the twenty-first-century audience members' prejudices toward Jews and indifference to anti-Semitism.

Sacha Baron Cohen's comedy demonstrates that some attitudes have not changed that much since the seventeenth century in terms of intolerance. In a Rolling Stone interview, Baron explains:

> When I was in university, there was this major historian of the Third Reich, Ian Kershaw, who said, "The path to Auschwitz was paved with indifference." I know it's not very funny being a comedian talking about the Holocaust, but it's an interesting idea that not everyone in Germany had to be a raving anti-Semite. They just had to be apathetic."[23]

Baron Cohen is not sure if all the members of the audience in that Arizona bar are anti-Semitic, but he is sure of one thing. The unknowing participants of this social experiment *retablo* are indifferent to anti-Semitism, and this indifference is poison. Sacha Baron Cohen's comedy and *El retablo de las maravillas* both serve to emphasize and criticize the injustice of bigotry in society.

Unfortunately, amongst some people it is still acceptable to discriminate, based on race and ethnicity, as well as sexual orientation and gender identification. It is not deemed normal in a cis-normative, gender binary system for a man to dress as a woman, as Pedro does in *La llamada de Lauren*. The man who engages in such behavior suffers the consequences in our society since it is not always considered acceptable. Transgender and gender non-binary people are more visible today and may feel free to express themselves in more liberal communities, but they still face much discrimination and must fight for their rights to live as their true selves. Lorca made sexual orientation the main dilemma in *El público*, and although now it is more accepted to be gay in our society, as compared to Spain in the 1930s, there are still many problems because some people consider same-sex relationships wrong. Their ignorance and misunderstanding of non-heteronormative identities lead them to think that people can choose to be straight or gay, and they justify discrimination and even violence against gay people because they believe that it is an evil lifestyle that has been chosen. Therefore, many people of alternative sexual and gender identities decide to hide their identities because of their fear of being rejected by society and even being violently attacked. They are forever stifled by the mask of conformity. However, people are fighting against this stifling mask, and we see people who proudly identify themselves as non-heteronormative represented in pop culture. Currently, there are many examples of such characters in popular television shows and movies from around the world. The films of internationally renowned Spanish filmmaker Pedro Almodóvar include many complex transgender and LGBTQ+ characters. The shows *Queer Eye* (formerly *Queer Eye for the Straight Guy*), *Modern Family, Will and Grace, Transparent, Orange Is the New Black, Big*

Mouth, and *Schitt's Creek,* to name a few, have been tremendously successful and celebrate and embrace non-heteronormative identities. In the popular Canadian sitcom *Schitt's Creek,* the character David Rose is one of the first pansexual characters depicted in a television series. David's sexual orientation is not an issue in the ideal world of *Schitt's Creek* where everyone is accepted, and homophobia is nonexistent. In fact, David does not identify as gay or straight when he explains his sexuality to his best friend and one-time female lover Stevie. In the episode *Honeymoon,* David ingeniously describes his pansexual identity by using metaphorical language, and he exclaims, "I like the wine and not the label. Does that make sense?" It is the essence of a person that is attractive to David, no matter the gender identity.

In her famous song, "Born this Way," Lady Gaga, a cisgender popstar who is a strong ally of all those with non-heteronormative identities, urges people to practice self-love and to reject the mask of conformity when she sings:

Don't hide yourself in regret
Just love yourself and you're set

Lady Gaga's uplifting anthem is one of acceptance, positivity, and the importance of showing one's true identity. The main characters of *El público* and *La llamada de Lauren* want to hide themselves and wrap themselves in a heteronormative cisgender disguise, but the singer fiercely protests this idea and states how important it is for them to love themselves the way they were created. Her song also emphasizes that non-heteronormativity is not a choice since people are simply "born this way."

An individual's identity is like an intricate puzzle piece in the complicated jigsaw puzzle that is society, and through the study of four Spanish plays of the seventeenth and twentieth centuries, we can discuss how the characters strive to make themselves fit into the puzzle and form part of society. Sometimes the characters feel they must cram themselves into the puzzle and make themselves fit, even if they are shoved into a space that is too small, thereby cramping their individual identity and making them uncomfortable. Although uncomfortable, they gain acceptance in the big picture that is society by sacrificing their differences. The plights of the characters struggling with identities that differ from the accepted norm raise an unsettling question about ourselves: Are we willing to jam our piece of the puzzle into an ill-fitting space and mask our differences in order to fit into society's tight restrictions? In the future, I hope that instead of trying to squeeze into a restrictive space as a piece of the puzzle that is society, people will be able to openly embrace their true identities and form part of a beautiful mosaic where every intricate, unique piece is appreciated for its individuality.

NOTE

1. In her book *So You Want to Talk about Race*, Ijeoma Oluo examines the issue of race and helps readers better understand the many facets of modern-day racism. Oluo discusses navigating difficult discussions about race, and her book serves to enlighten readers and facilitate conversations concerning the difficult truths about racism in today's society.

Works Cited

Abel, Lionel. *Metatheatre*. New York: Hill and Wang, 1964.
Ackroyd, Peter. *Dressing Up. Transvestism and Drag: The History of an Obsession*. New York: Simon and Schuster, 1979.
Allen, Zel, and Reuben Allen. *Onion Aficionados Weep, Vegetarians in Paradise*, December, 2001. https://www.vegparadise.com/highestperch312.html/.
Alvaro, Francisco, ed. *El espectador y la crítica. El teatro en España en 1985*. Valladolid: Edición del autor, 1986.
Andersen, Hans Christian. *The Emperor's New Clothes*. Translated by Naomi Lewis. Cambridge: Candlewick, 1997.
Anderson, Andrew A. "'Un dificilísimo juego poético': Theme and Symbol in Lorca's El público." *Romance Quarterly* 39, no. 3 (1992): 331–346.
———. "'Una desorientación absoluta': Juliet and the Shifting Sands in García Lorca's El público." *Revista Hispánica Moderna* 50, no. 1 (1997): 67–85.
Arboleda, Carlos Arturo. *Teoría y formas del metateatro en Cervantes*. Salamanca: Universidad de Salamanca, 1991.
Aristotle. *Poetics*. Translated by S. H. Butcher. New York: Hill and Wang, 1961.
Artigas, María del Carmen. "Un breve comentario sobre el converso en El licenciado vidriera." *Romance Notes* 43, no. 1 (2002): 37–41.
Bakhtin, Mikhail. *Rabelais and His World*. Translated by Hélene Iswolsky. Bloomington: Indiana University Press, 1984.
Barajas, Sanz Jorge. "José Bergamín y El público." *Boletín de la Fundación Federico García Lorca* 17 (1995): 41–48.
Barcia Rubia, José. "El público, Naked and Unmasked." In *"Cuando yo me muera...": Essays in Memory of Federico García Lorca*, edited by C. Brian Morris, 233–257. Lanham: University Press of America, 1988.
Baron Cohen, Sacha. *Da Ali G.Show*. HBO. *Peace*, 2004.
———. "Sacha Baron Cohen's Keynote Address at ADL's 2019 Never Is Now Summit on Anti-Semitism and Hate." *Anti-Defamation League*, November 21, 2019.

Bauer, Carlos Introduction. *The Public and Play Without a Title*. Edited by Federico García Lorca. Translated by Carlos Bauer. New York: New Directions, 1983.

Belamich, André. "El público y La casa de Bernarda Alba, polos opuestos en la dramaturgia de Lorca." In *La casa de Bernarda Alba y el teatro de García Lorca*, edited by Ricardo Domenech, 77–92. Madrid: Cátedra, 1985.

Bell, Robert E. *Women of Classical Mythology*. Santa Barbara: ABC-CLIO, 1991.

Bigelow, Gary. "Identidad y desencuentro en dos obras de Paloma Pedrero." In *Selected Proceedings of the Pennsylvania Foreign Language Conference*, edited by Gregorio C. Martin, 41–55. Pittsburgh: Duquesne University Press, 1988.

Bravo, A. María Dolores. *Los entremeses Cervantinos, valores sociales y risa crítica: El retablo de las maravillas." Dramaturgia española y novohispana: siglos XVI–XVII*. Edited by Serafín González García and Lillian Walde. Mexico City: Universidad Autónoma Metropolitana, Unidad Iztapalapa, 1993.

Brecht, Bertolt. *Brecht on Theatre: The Development of an Aesthetic*. London: Eyre Methuen, 1974.

Breton, André. *What is Surrealism?* Translated by David Gascoyne. New York: Haskell House, 1974.

Brioso Santos, Héctor. "*Cervantes frente a la comedia nueva: El retablo de las maravillas y las maravillas del nuevo teatro.*" *eHumanista: Journal of Iberian Studies* 38 (2018): 723–745.

Brown, Kenneth. "El Retablo de las maravillas, sus contextos mosaicos y el chiste del judío retajado." *eHumanista/Cervantes* 2 (2013): 283–296.

Butler, Judith. *Bodies That Matter: On the Discursive Limits of "Sex."* New York: Routledge, 1993.

———. *Gender Trouble: Feminism and the Subversion of Identity*. New York: Routledge, 1999.

Byron, William. *Cervantes: A Biography*. New York: Doubleday, 1978.

Canavaggio, Jean. *Cervantes: En busca del perfil perdido*. Madrid: Espasa-Calpe, 1992.

Carlson, Marvin. *Theories of the Theatre: A Historical and Critical Survey, from the Greeks to the Present*. Ithaca: Cornell University Press, 1984.

Cartagena-Calderón, José R. "El retablo de las maravillas y la construcción cultural de la masculinidad en la España de Miguel de Cervantes." *Gestos: Teoría y Práctica del Teatro Hispánico* 14, no. 27 (1999): 25–41.

Casalduero, Joaquín. *Sentido y forma del teatro de Cervantes*. Madrid: Gredos, 1966.

Castillón, Verónica Azcue. "La disputa del baciyelmo y El retablo de las maravillas: sobre el carácter dramático de los capítulos 44 y 45 de la primera parte de Don Quijote." *Cervantes* 22, no. 1 (2002): 71–81.

Castro, Américo. *De la edad conflictiva: el drama de la honra en España y en su literatura*. Madrid: Taurus, 1961.

———. *Los Españoles: cómo llegaron a serlo*. Madrid: Taurus, 1965.

Cervantes Saavedra, Miguel de. *El retablo de las maravillas*. Edited by Nicholas Spadaccini. Madrid: Cátedra, 1615.

———. *Don Quijote de La Mancha*. Edited by Martín Riquer. Barcelona: Juventud, 1995.

Charles, Larry. *Borat: Cultural Learnings of America for Make Benefit Glorious Nation of Kazakhstan*. Comedy. 20th Century Fox Home Entertainment, 2007.
Chevalier, Maxime. "El embuste del llovista (Cervantes, El retablo de las maravillas)." *Bulletin Hispanique* 78 (1976): 97–98.
Coogan, Michael D., ed. *The New Oxford Annotated Bible: New Revised Standard Version with the Apocrypha*. New York: Oxford University Press, 2001.
Córdoba, Ibn Hazm. *El collar de la paloma: Tratado sobre el amor y los amantes*. Translated by Emilio García Gómez. Madrid: Alianza, 1971.
Cotarelo, Emilio. "Luis Vélez de Guevara y sus obras dramáticas." *Boletín de la Real Academia Española* 3, no. 3 (1916): 621–652.
Davies, Gareth A. "Luis Vélez de Guevara and Court Life." In *Antigüedad y Actualidad de Luis Vélez de Guevara*, edited by C. George Peale, 20–38. Amsterdam: John Benjamins, 1983.
Delgado, María, and Gwynne Edwards. "From Madrid to Stratford East: The Public in Performance." *Estreno* 16, no. 2 (1990): 11–17.
DeLong-Tonelli, Beverly J. "The Trials and Tribulations of Lorca's El Público." *García Lorca Review* 9, no. 2 (1981): 153–168.
Díaz, Sergio. "La Capacidad Transformadora De Paloma Pedrero." *Revista Godot*, October 8, 2020. http://www.revistagodot.com/la-capacidad-transformadora-de-paloma-pedrero/.
Docter, Richard. *Transvestites and Transsexuals: Toward a Theory of Cross-Gender Behavior*. New York: Plenum Press, 1988.
Dowling, John. "La 'bestia fiera' de Federico García Lorca: El autor dramático y su público." *Estreno* 12, no. 2 (1986): 16–20.
Egginton, William. "The Baroque as a Problem of Thought." *PMLA* 124, no. 1 (2009): 143–149.
Egginton, William, and David R. Castillo. "The Rules of Chanfalla's Game." *Romance Languages Annual* 6 (1994): 444–449.
Evers, Michelle Lee. "Staging the Nations: Performing Identity in Post-Franco Spain." Dissertation, University of Kansas, 2002.
Fagundo, Ana M. *La mujer en el teatro de Paloma Pedrero. La nueva mujer en la escritura de autoras hispánicas*. Edited by Juana A. Arancibia and Yolanda Rosas. Montevideo: Instituto Literario y Cultural Hispánico, 1995.
Fanon, Frantz. *Black Skin, White Masks*. Translated by Charles Lam Markmann. New York: Grove Press Inc, 1967.
Feal, Carlos. "El Lorca Postumo: El público y Comedia sin título." *Anales de la Literatura Española Contemporanea* 6 (1981): 43–62.
"Federico García Lorca Was Killed on Official Orders, Say 1960s Police Files." *The Guardian, Guardian News and Media*, April 23, 2015.
Figure, Paul. "The Mystification of Love and Lorca's Female Image in El Público." *Cincinnati Romance Review* 2 (1983): 26–32.
Finke, Wayne. "Naming Practice in Federico García Lorca's Newly Discovered Plays." *Literary Onomastics Studies* 14 (1987): 139–150.
Forastieri-Braschi, Eduardo. "Entre retablos cervantinos." *Ideologies and Literature* 4, no. 1 (1989): 345–353.

Foucault, Michel. *Power/Knowledge: Selected Interviews and Other Writings 1972–1977*. Edited by Colin Gordon. Translated by Colin Gordon. New York: Pantheon, 1980.

Fra-Molinero, Baltasar. *La imagen de los negros en el teatro del Siglo de Oro*. Madrid: Siglo Veintiuno, 1995.

———. "The Play of Race and Gender in Vélez de Guevara's Virtudes vencen señales." *Bulletin of the Comediantes* 49, no. 2 (1997): 337–355.

Freud, Sigmund. *The Standard Edition of the Complete Psychological Works of Sigmund Freud*. Edited by James Strachey. Vol. 23. London: Hogarth, 1974.

Friedman, Edward H. "Dramatic Structure in Cervantes and Lope: The Two 'Pedro de Urdemalas' Plays." *Hispania* 60, no. 3 (1977): 486–497.

Gaga, Lady. "Lyrics to "Born This Way." *Genius*, 2011.

Galan, Eduardo. "Paloma Pedrero, una joven dramaturga que necesita expresar sus vivencias." *Estreno* 16, no. 1 (1990): 11–13.

Garber, Marjorie. *Vested Interests: Cross-Dressing and Cultural Anxiety*. New York: Harper Perennial, 1992.

García, Kay. "Violence in Two Plays by Federico García Lorca." In *Violence in Drama*, edited by James Redmond, 203–213. Cambridge: Cambridge University Press, 1991.

García Lorca, Federico. *El público*. Edited by María Clementa Millán. Madrid: Cátedra, 1995.

———. *Four Key Plays: The Audience, Blood Wedding, Yerma, The House of Bernarda Alba*. Translated by Michael Kidd. Hackett Publishing Company, Inc, 2019.

Gene, Juan Carlos. "Misterio y desafio." *Primer Acto* 241 (1991): 121–125.

Genesis, Ch. 2. *Pentateuch and Haftorahs*. Edited by J. H. Hertz, 2nd ed. London: Soncino, 1978.

George, David. "Commedia Dell'arte and the Mask in Lorca." In *Lorca: Poet and Playwright*, edited by Robert Havard. New York: St. Martin's, 1992.

Gerber, Jane S. *The Jews of Spain: A History of the Sephardic Experience*. New York: The Free Press, 1992.

Gerli, E. Michael. "El retablo de las maravillas: Cervantes' arte nuevo de deshacer comedias." *Hispanic Review* 57, no. 4 (1989): 477–492.

Gibson, Ian. *La represión nacionalista de Granada en 1936 y la muerte de Federico García Lorca*. Ruedo Ibirico, 1971.

———. *The Death of Lorca*. W.H. Allen, 1973.

———. *Federico García Lorca: A Life*. New York: Pantheon, 1989.

———. *Lorca y el mundo gay*. Barcelona: Ediciones B, 2016a.

———. *Pasion y Muerte De Federico Garcia Lorca*. Debolsillo, 2016b.

Gilman, Sander L. *Difference and Pathology: Stereotypes of Sexuality, Race, and Madness*. Ithaca: Cornell University Press, 1985.

———. *Jewish Self-Hatred: Anti-Semitism and the Hidden Language of the Jews*. Baltimore: Johns Hopkins University Press, 1992.

Goff, Robert. *The Essential Salvador Dalí*. New York: The Wonderland, 1998.

Gómez Torres, Ana María. "Historia de una recepción teatral: Los estrenos de El público de Federico García Lorca." *Revista de Literatura* 59, no. 118 (1997): 505–519.

González, Aníbal. "Ética y teatralidad: El retablo de las maravillas de Cervantes y El arpa y la sombra de Alejo Carpentier." *La Torre* 7, no. 27–28 (1993): 485–502.

Guillén, Gracia Diego. "Chirino en El retablo de las maravillas." *Papeles de Son Armadans* 92 (1979): 9–27.

Gullón, Ricardo. *Radiografía de El público. Estudios en homenaje a Enrique Ruiz-Fornells.* Edited by Juan Fernandez Jimenez. Erie: ALDEEU, 1990.

Gutwirth, Eleazar. "From Jewish to Converso Humour in Fifteenth-Century Spain." *Bulletin of Hispanic Studies* 67, no. 3 (1990): 223–233.

Hardison Londré, Felicia. "Lorca in Metamorphosis: His Posthumous Plays." *Theatre Journal* 35, no. 1 (1983): 102–108.

Harretche, María Estela. "Máscara, transformación y sentido en el teatro desnudo de Federico García Lorca." In *Actas del X Congreso de la Asociación de Hispanistas*, edited by Antonio Vilanova, 1815–1823. Barcelona: Promociones y Pubs. Universitarias Barcelona, 1992.

Harris, Carolyn J. "Concha Romero y Paloma Pedrero hablan de sus obras." *Estreno* 19, no. 1 (1993): 29–35.

———. *Juego y metateatro en la obra de Paloma Pedrero. De lo particular a lo universal: El teatro español del siglo XX y su contexto.* Edited by John P. Gabriele. Frankfurt-Madrid: Vervuert-Iboamericana, 1994.

Hauer, Mary G. *Luis Vélez de Guevara: A Critical Bibliography.* Chapel Hill: University of North Carolina Press, 1975.

Heliodorus. *Ethiopian Story.* Translated by Walter Lamb. *Everyman's Library 276.* London: J.M. Dent & Sons Ltd, 1961.

Hodge, Polly J. "Photography of Theater: Reading between the Spanish Scenes." *Gestos* 11, no. 22 (1996): 35–58.

Hornby, Richard. *Drama, Metadrama, and Perception.* Cranbury, NJ: Associated University Press, 1986.

Huelamo Kosma, Julio. "La influencia de Freud en el teatro de García Lorca." *Boletín de la Fundación Federico García Lorca* 3, no. 6 (1989): 59–83.

Huet, Marie-Helene. "Living Images: Monstrosity and Representation." *Representations* 4 (1983): 73–87.

Jerez-Farrán, Carlos. "La estética expresionista en El público de García Lorca." *Anales de la Literatura Española Contemporanea* 11 (1986): 1–2.

———. "El sadomasoquismo homoerótico como expresión de homofobia internalizada en el cuadro 2 de El público de García Lorca." *Modern Philology* 93, no. 4 (1996): 468–497.

———. "Towards a Foucauldian Exegesis of Act V of García Lorca's El Público." *Modern Language Review* 95, no. 3 (2000): 728–743.

———. "Transvestism and Sexual Transgression in García Lorca's the Public." *Modern Drama* 44, no. 2 (2001): 188–213.

Kamen, Henry. *A Concise History of Spain.* London: Thames and Hudson, 1973.

———. *Inquisition and Society in Spain in the Sixteenth and Seventeenth Centuries.* Bloomington: Indiana University Press, 1985.

Kendi, Ibram X. *How to Be an Antiracist.* New York: One World, 2019.

———. *Is This the Beginning of the End of American Racism? The Atlantic*. Atlantic Media Company, 2020.

Kidd, Michael. "The Fairest of Them All: Racial and Sexual Signification in Vélez de Guevara's Virtudes Vencen Señales." In *A Society on Stage: Essays on Spanish Golden Age Drama*, edited by Edward H. Friedman, 117–132. New Orleans: University Press of the South, 1998.

———. *Stages of Desire: The Mythological Tradition in Classical and Contemporary Spanish Theater*. University Park: Pennsylvania State University Press, 1999.

Kirk, Charles Frederick. *A Critical Edition, with Introduction and Notes, of Vélez de Guevara's Virtudes Vencen Señales*. Dissertation, Ohio State University, 1957.

Kirschner, Teresa. "El retablo de las maravillas, de Cervantes, o la dramatización del miedo." In *Cervantes, su obra y su mundo: actas del I Congreso Internacional sobre Cervantes*, edited by Manuel Criado Val, 819–827. Madrid: EDI-6, 1981.

La barrentina, 2004. web.archive.org/web/20040302190319/, //www.somiserem.org/barretina.htm.

Lacomba, José. "El público de García Lorca: Estreno mundial." *Sin Nombre* 9, no. 1 (1978): 77–90.

Lamartina-Lens, Iride. "Paloma Pedrero: A Profile." *Western European Stages* 9, no. 1 (1997): 53–54.

Larson, Catherine. "The Visible and the Hidden: Speech Act Theory and Cervantes's El Retablo de Las Maravillas." In *El Arte Nuevo de Estudiar Comedias: Literary Theory and Spanish Golden Age Drama*, edited by Barbara Simerka, 52–65. New Jersey: Bucknell UP-Associated University Press, 1996.

Leibovitz, Liel. "Did Ali G Go Too Far?" *The Jewish Week*, August 13, 2004. http://www.thejewishweek.com/news/newscontent.php3?artid=9732.

Leonard, Candyce. "Body, Sex, Woman: The Struggle for Autonomy in Paloma Pedrero's Theater." In *La Chispa '97: Selected Proceedings*, edited by Claire J. Paolini, 245–254. New Orleans: Tulane University, 1997.

Lexico Dictionaries|English. "Beard: Definition of Beard by Oxford Dictionary on Lexico.com Also Meaning of Beard." *Lexico Dictionaries*. Accessed January 15, 2021. https://www.lexico.com/en/definition/beard.

Lipski, John M. "Golden Age 'Black Spanish': Existence and Coexistence." *Afro-Hispanic Review* 5, no. 1–3 (1986): 7–12.

Llosa Sanz, Álvaro. "La figura del alcalde en el Retablo de las maravillas de Miguel de Cervantes." *Espéculo* 18 (2001): 1–15.

Lokos, Ellen. "The Politics of Identity and the Enigma of Cervantine Genealogy." In *Cervantes and His Postmodern Constituencies*, edited by Anne J. Cruz and Carroll B. Johnson, 116–133. New York: Garland, 1999.

MacEoin, Gary. *Cervantes*. Milwaukee: The Bruce Publishing Company, 1950.

Manuel, Juan. *El conde Lucanor*. Edited by Antonio Martínez-Menchén. Madrid: Editora, 1978.

Martínez López, Enrique. "Mezclar berzas con capachos: armonía y guerra de castas en el Entremés del retablo de las maravillas de Cervantes." *Boletín de la Real Academia Española* 72, no. 255 (1992): 67–171.

Martínez Nadal, Rafael. *Federico García Lorca and The Public: A Study of an Unfinished Play and of Love and Death in Lorca's Work*. New York: Schocken, 1974.
McCrory, Donald P. *No Ordinary Man: The Life and Times of Miguel de Cervantes*. London: Peter Owen, 2002.
McGaha, Michael D. Entre el 'noble moor' y el 'negro perro moro': Otelo y Las misas de San Vicente Ferrer." *Vidas Paralelas: el teatro español y el teatro isabelino 1580–1680*. Edited by Anita K. Stoll. Madrid: Támesis S.L, 1993.
McKendrick, Melveena. *Cervantes*. Boston: Little, Brown and Company, 1980.
Menarini, Piero. "El público y Comedia sin título: Dos enmiendas posibles y un reportaje olvidado." *Salina* 9 (1995): 67–74.
Millán, María C. "El público, de García Lorca: Obra de hoy." *Cuadernos Hispanoamericanos* 433–434 (1986a): 399–407.
———. "Poeta en Nueva York y El público, dos obras afines." *Insula: Revista de Letras y Ciencias Humanas* 41, no. 476–477 (1986b): 9–10.
———. "Introduction." In *El público*. By Federico García Lorca. Madrid: Cátedra, 1995.
Molho, Mauricio. *Cervantes: Raíces Folklóricas*. Madrid: Gredos, 1976.
Monegal, Antonio. "Un-Masking the Maskuline: Transvestism and Tragedy in García Lorca's El público." *MLN* 109, no. 2 (1994): 204–216.
Moner, Michel. *Las maravillosas figuras de El retablo de las maravillas. Cervantes, su obra y su mundo: actas del I Congreso Internacional sobre Cervantes*. Edited by Manuel Criado Val. Madrid: EDI-6, 1981.
Monleon, José. "Tres heterodoxos en el teatro español del siglo XX." *Primer Acto* 261 (1995): 5–17.
Mujica, Barbara. "Cervantes' Use of Skepticism in El retablo de las maravillas." In *Looking at the "Comedia" in the Year of the Quincentennial*, edited by Barbara Mujica and Sharon D. Voros, 149–157. Maryland: University Press of America, 1993.
Newberry, Wilma. "Aesthetic Distance in García Lorca's El público: Pirandello and Ortega." *Hispanic Review* 37 (1969): 276–296.
Newton, Candelas. "El público en El público de García Lorca." *Estreno* 21, no. 2 (1995): 49–55.
O'Connor, Patricia, and W. Prologue. *La llamada de Lauren de Paloma Pedrero*. Madrid: Antonio Machado, 1987.
Oliva, Cesar. "De El retablo de las maravillas de Cervantes al de Lauro Olmo." In *Estudios literarios dedicados al profesor Mariano Baquero Goyanes*, edited by Victorino Polo García, 367–373. Murcia: Universidad de Murcia, 1974.
Oluo, Ijeoma. *So You Want to Talk About Race*. New York: Seal Press, 2019.
Oppenheimer, Paul. *Till Eulenspiegel: His Adventures*. London: Routledge, 2002.
Parker, Alexander A. "Segismundo's Tower: A Calderonian Myth." *Bulletin of Hispanic Studies* 59 (1982): 247–256.
Patterson, Charles. "Blood Purity in Recent Productions of El Retablo De Las Maravillas." *Comedia Performance* 13, no. 1 (2016): 145–168.

Paulson, Michael G., and Tamara Alvarez-Detrell. *Lepanto: Fact, Fiction and Fantasy, with a Critical Edition of Luis Vélez de Guevara's El Águila Del Agua, a Play in Three Acts*. Lanham: University Press of America, 1986.

Pedrero, Paloma. *La llamada de Lauren*. Madrid: Antonio Machado, 1987.

Pellegrini, Ann. *Performance Anxieties: Staging Psychoanalysis, Staging Race*. New York: Routledge, 1997.

Podol, Peter L. "Sexuality and Marital Relationships in Paloma Pedrero's La llamada de Lauren and María Manuela Reina's La cinta dorada." *Estreno* 17, no. 1 (1991): 22–25.

Profeti, Maria Grazia. "Emisor y receptores: Luis Vélez de Guevara y el enfoque crítico." In *Antigüedad y Actualidad de Luis Vélez de Guevara*, edited by C. George Peale, 1–19. Amsterdam: John Benjamins, 1983.

Ramos de Castro, Epifanio. "El retablo de Cervantes y Prevert." *Anales Cervantinos* 10 (1971): 169–190.

Reed, Cory A. "Dirty Dancing: Salome, Herodias and El retablo de las maravillas." *Bulletin of the Comediantes* 44 (1992): 7–17.

———. *The Novelist as Playwright: Cervantes and the Entremés Nuevo*. New York: Peter Lang Publishing, Inc, 1993.

Ródenas, Daniel. "Paloma Pedrero: 'Ninguna persona trans tiene que esconder lo que es.'" *Shangay*, March 31, 2020. https://shangay.com/2020/03/31/paloma-pedrero-trans-teatro-transformacion-obra-entrevista/.

Rodríguez López-Vázquez, Alfredo. "La mujer en el teatro español del siglo XX: De María Martínez Sierra a Paloma Pedrero." In *Estudios sobre mujer, lengua y literatura*, edited by Aurora Marco, 121–136. Santiago de Compostela: US Compostela, 1996.

Ruano de la Haza, José María. "Introduction." In *Virtudes vencen señales by Luis Vélez de Guevara*. Delaware: Juan de la Cuesta-Hispanic Monographs, 2010.

Sáenz, María Ascensión. "Rebelión en la escena: El público contra la audiencia." *Romance Languages Annual* 9 (1997): 681–684.

Schevill, Rudolph. "Virtudes vencen señales and La vida es sueño." *Hispanic Review* 1, no. 3 (1933): 181–195.

Schitt's Creek. "Honeymoon." *Netflix* video, 21:52. March 10, 2015.

Seator, Lynette H. "A Study of the Plays of Alfonso Sastre: Man's Struggle for Identity in a Hostile World." Dissertation, University of Illinois, 1973.

Sedgwick, Eve Kosofsky. *Between Men: English Literature and Male Homosocial Desire*. New York: Columbia University Press, 1992.

Serrano, Virtudes. "La personal dramaturgia de Paloma Pedrero." *Primer Acto* 258 (1995): 62–66.

Sloane, Robert A. *Character and Role: The Problem of Identity in Four Plays by Pedro Calderón de La Barca*. Dissertation, Johns Hopkins University Press, 1973.

Smith, Colin. *Collins Spanish-English/English-Spanish Dictionary*. Glasgow: HarperCollins, 1992.

Smith, Dawn L. "Cervantes and His Audience: Aspects of Reception Theory in El Retablo de Las Maravillas." In *The Golden Age Comedia: Text, Theory, and*

Performance, edited by Charles Ganelin and Howard Mancing, 249–261. Indiana: Purdue University Press, 1994.

Smith, Paul Julian. *The Body Hispanic: Gender and Sexuality in Spanish and Spanish American Literature*. Oxford: Clarendon Press, 1989.

Smith, Shawn O. "Pedro de Urdemalas: Contesting the Spanish Hapsburg Discourse of Blood." *Vanderbilt e-Journal of Luso-Hispanic Studies* 2 (2005): N. Pag." Online. Internet, February 23, 2006. http://ejournals.library.vanderbilt.edu/lusohispanic/viewarticle.php?id=10&layout=html.

Soufas, C. Christopher, Jr. "Bodas de sangre and the Problematics of Representation." *Revista de Estudios Hispanicos* 21, no. 1 (1987): 29–48.

Spadaccini, Nicholas Cervantes, ed. *Spain 1469–1714: A Society of Conflict*. New York: Longman, 1983.

———. *1615*. Madrid: Cátedra, 1989.

Spencer, Forrest Eugene, and Rudolph Schevill. "The Dramatic Works of Luis Vélez de Guevara: Their Plots, Sources, and Bibliography." *University of California Publications in Modern Philology* 19 (1937).

Stewart, Suzanne R. *Sublime Surrender: Male Masochism at the Fin-De-Siecle*. Ithaca: Cornell University Press, 1998.

Stoll, Anita. "Do Clothes Make the Man? Gender and Identity Fluidity in Tirso's Plays." *Romance Languages Annual* 10, no. 2 (1998): 832–835.

Strauss, Neil. "Sacha Baron Cohen: The Man Behind the Mustache." *Rolling Stone*, June 25, 2018. https://www.rollingstone.com/movies/movie-news/sacha-baron-cohen-the-man-behind-the-mustache-249539/.

Sullivan, Mary Lee. "The Theatrics of Transference in Federico García Lorca's La Casa de Bernarda Alba and Paloma Pedrero's La Llamada de Lauren." *Hispanic Journal* 16, no. 1 (1995): 169–176.

Terracini, Lore. "Burladors entre paños y retablos: invariantes y variables." In *Crítica semiológica de textos literarios hispánicos*, edited by Miguel Ángel Garrido Gallardo, 43–51. Madrid: Consejo Superior de Investigaciones Científicas, 1986.

Thacker, Jonathan. *Role-Play and the World as Stage in the Comedia*. Liverpool: Liverpool University Press, 2002.

Torner, Enrique. "El público de Lorca como contrarreplica de Seis personajes en busca de autor, de Pirandello." *Revista de Estudios Hispanicos* 21 (1994): 25–33.

Torres-Pau, Joan. "El elemento paródico en La llamada de Lauren de Paloma Pedrero." *Estreno* 19, no. 1 (1993): 26–28.

Vega, Lope de. *El arte nuevo de hacer comedias en este tiempo*. Edited by Juana José Prades. Madrid: Clásicos Hispanicos, 1971.

"Vegetarians in Paradise 3.12 (2001): n. pag." Online. Internet, January 17, 2006. http://www.vegparadise.com/highestperch312.html.

Vélez de Guevara, Luis. *Virtudes vencen señales*. Edited by M. G. Profeti. Pisa: Istituto di Letteratura Spagnola e Ispano-Americana, 1965.

———. *Virtudes vencen señales*. Edited by William R. Manson and C. George Peale. Delaware: Juan de la Cuesta-Hispanic Monographs, 2010.

Vigil, Mariló. *La vida de las mujeres en los siglos XVI y XVII*. Madrid: Siglo XXI de España Editores, 1986.

Villán, Javier. "Con Paloma Pedrero." *Primer Acto* 258 (1995): 59–61.
Volpe, Germana. "Note su El retablo de las maravillas di Miguel de Cervantes Saavedra." *Annali Istituto Universitario Orientale, Napoli, Sezione Romanza* 44, no. 2 (2002): 703–714.
Wardropper, Bruce W. "The Butt of the Satire in El Retablo de Las Maravillas." *Cervantes* 4, no. 1 (1984): 25–33.
Weber de Kurlat, Frida. "Sobre el negro como tipo cómico en el teatro español del siglo XVI." *Romance Philology* 17 (1963): 380–391.
———. "El tipo del negro en el teatro de Lope de Vega: tradición y creación." *Nueva Revista de Filología Hispánica* 19, no. 2 (1970): 337–359.
Weege, Cornelia. *El discurso femenino en la obra de Paloma Pedrero. Teatro contemporáneo español posfranquista: Autores y tendencias.* Edited by Herbert Fritz and Klaus Portl. Berlin: Edition Tranvía, 2000.
Wilkins, Constance. "Subversion Through Comedy? Two Plays by Sor Juana Inés de La Cruz and María de Zayas." In *The Perception of Women in Spanish Theater of the Golden Age*, edited by Anita K. Stoll, 102–120. Lewisburg: Bucknell University Press, 1991.
Wilson, Edward M., and Duncan Moir. *A Literary History of Spain: The Golden Age Drama 1492–1700*. London: Ernest Benn Limited, 1971.
Woliner, Jason. *Borat Subsequent Moviefilm*. Comedy, 2020.
Zahareas, Anthony N., and Reyes Coll Tellechea. "Cervantes, Shakespeare and Calderón: Theater and Society." In *Selected Proceedings: Louisiana Conference on Hispanic Languages and Literatures*, edited by Joseph V. Ricapito, 225–240. Baton Rouge: Louisiana State University Press, 1994.
Zatlin, Phyllis. "Paloma Pedrero and the Search for Identity." *Estreno* 16, no. 1 (1990): 6–10.
———. "Intertextualidad y metateatro en la obra de Paloma Pedrero." *Letras Femeninas* 19, no. 1–2 (1993): 14–20.
———. "From Night Games to Postmodern Satire: The Theater of Paloma Pedrero." *Hispania* 84, no. 2 (2001): 193–204.
Zepeda, Karla P. "Identity and Performance in Paloma Pedrero's La llamada de Lauren." In *Contextos: Estudios de humanidades y ciencias* 45 (2019): 1–17.
Zimic, Stanislav. "El retablo de las maravillas, parábola de la mentira." *Anales Cervantinos* 20 (1982): 153–172.
———. *El teatro de Cervantes*. Madrid: Castalia, 1992.
Zugasti, Miguel. "Luis Vélez De Guevara y La Comedia Palatina." *Criticón*, no. 129 (2017): 41–68. https://doi.org/10.4000/criticon.3303.

Index

Abel, Lionel, 4–6, 18–19, 46–49, 120, 126, 147
Acquaviva, Giulio, 12
ADL. *See* Anti-Defamation League
adultery, 63
African heritage, 66, 84
Africanity, 57
Aladrén Perojo, Emilio, 115n10
alienation effect, 5, 95–96
Almodóvar, Pedro, 154–55
alternative identities: expression of, 3; treatment of people with, 5
Alvaro, Francisco, 142–43
Andersen, Hans Christian, 15
Anti-Defamation League (ADL), 151–52
antiquity, philosophy of, 62
antiracism, 150–51
anti-Semitism, 17, 34; in *Borat!*, 154; confronting, 151; increased visibility of, 150; in Spanish society, 148; speaking out against, 54
Arboleda, Carlos Arturo, 47
aristocracy, 49
Aristotle, 45, 52n18, 94
arrogance, 43
El arte nuevo de hacer comedias (*The New Art of Writing Plays*) (Lope de Vega), 44–45, 52n18

Auclair, Marcelle, 89
audience: consciousness of, 95; fear of, 95; hypocritical nature of, 41; as shocked, 107
The Audience (*El público*) (García Lorca), 1
authoritarianism, 3

Bakhtin, Mikhail, 4, 6, 120, 125
Baron Cohen, Sacha, 7, 151–54
baroque philosophy, 52n14
Bible, 34–35, 42, 51n12
bigotry, 56, 150
black horse, 103–5
Black identity, 57; rejection of, 56; self-hatred and, 69
Blackness, 66–68, 72, 85–86
blood purity. *See pureza de sangre*
Borat! (film), 7, 152–54
Borat Subsequent Moviefilm (film), 152
bourgeoisie, 49
bravery, 56
Brecht, Bertolt, 4–5, 92–95, 106, 124
Breton, André, 96–97

Calderón de la Barca, Pedro, 58, 87n6, 87n8
Carnival, 6, 120; costumes during, 127; cross-dressing during, 124–25;

freedom allowed during, 125–26; sexual identity exploration during, 140–41
Castro, Américo, 83, 86n3
censorship, 2, 90; Franco imposing, 3; freedom from, 3; generation of, 121
Cervantes Saavedra, Miguel de, 30, 153; as *converso*, 12–13; *Don Quijote de la Mancha* by, 13, 44–45; Jewish heritage of, 148; *El licenciado vidriera* by, 50n3; Lope de Vega disapproved of by, 44–46; *Ocho comedias, y ocho entremeses nuevos, nunca representados* by, 13; parodies by, 57; stereotypes depicted by, 24–27. See also *El retablo de las maravillas*
Christianity, 11, 38
classical theory, 52n18
Code of Hammurabi, 73
El collar de la paloma (Hazm de Córdoba), 63
communication, within marriage, 130–31
complacency, 124
A Concise History of Spain (Kamen), 2–3
confidence, 56
conformity, 1; gender identity and, 132; masks of, 113–14, 148–49, 154; sexual identity and, 90, 119; struggle against, 9
conscience, 22
conversos (converts), 10n4; Cervantes Saavedra, 12–13; *cristianos nuevos* and, 84; heritage of, 18–21; labeling, 26–27; oppression of, 11; power given to, 64; *pureza de sangre* and, 88n16; self-worth of, 83; Vélez de Guevara, 54
Cotarelo, Emilio, 55, 86n3
cowardice, 26–27, 61, 108
cristianos nuevos (New Christians), 11, 83, 86n3; *conversos* and, 84; as virtuous, 83

cristianos viejos (Old Christians), 11, 24–25, 55
cross-dressing, 115n4; acceptance for, 119–20; during Carnival, 124–25; in *La llamada de Lauren*, 122–37; sexual orientation and, 9, 138–42

Dalí, Salvador, 90, 93
Davies, Gareth A., 54, 86n3
Dead Sea, 105
death, black horse embodying, 103–5
deceit, symbols of, 34–35
defense mechanisms, 32
depression, of García Lorca, 89–90
El diablo cojuelo (*The Limping Devil*) (Vélez de Guevara), 87n7
Difference and Pathology (Gilman), 5, 58, 61
Don Quijote de la Mancha (Cervantes Saavedra), 13, 44–45
Drama, Metadrama, and Perception (Hornby), 5–6, 106

ecclesiastical ideology, 88n15
Eight Comedies, and Eight New Interludes, Never Performed (*Ocho comedias, y ocho entremeses nuevos, nunca representados*) (Cervantes Saavedra), 13
The Emperor's New Clothes (Andersen), 15
ethnic identity, 2; new, 17; in *El retablo de las maravillas*, 147
ethnicity, 1–2; *pureza de sangre* and, 148; race and, 149
ethnic prejudices, 7, 50
expressionism, 116n14

Fanon, Franz, 67
fantasy: in *La llamada de Lauren*, 128; reality and, 29, 46–48
Feal, Carlos, 107–8
fear: of audience, 95; doubt, hopelessness and, 32; of gender

roles, 136; of Jewish identity, 49; of lineage, 27; of Other, 5
Federico García Lorca (Gibson), 89
feminine mask, 110–13
femininity, 119, 144; in clothing, 124; repressed, 125; symbols of, 129
Filipo (fictional character), 148; becomes king, 75–77; conception of, 62–64; condemnation of, 65; dichotomy, 65–72; existence of, 61–62; leadership for, 74–75; narcissism of, 70, 76–77, 86; noble actions of, 72–75; racial identity of, 57–59; reality confronted by, 151; rebellion against, 78–82; self-identification of, 65–69; transformational journey of, 56; Vélez de Guevara connection with, 82–86
fluid identity, 2
Forastieri-Braschi, Eduardo, 43, 48
Foucault, Michel, 115n9
Fra-Molinero, Baltasar, 57, 59, 76, 82
Franco, Francisco, 3, 121, 142
freedom, 1; artistic, 97; Carnival allowing, 125–26; from censorship, 3; as dangerous, 91
Freud, Sigmund, 4–5, 69, 92, 97, 115n9; on horses, 100–103; theories of, 148–49

Galan, Eduardo, 121, 141
Garber, Marjorie, 9, 138
García Lorca, Federico, 1–2, 5; assassination of, 116n12; audience shocked by, 107; depression of, 89–90; horses as symbolic for, 97–100; innermost feelings on homosexuality, 92–93; innovative techniques of, 94–96; knowledge of theory, 94–95; romantic relationships of, 115n10; self-hatred of, 114; sexual orientation of, 89–90; surrealism and, 96–97; talents of, 89; works by, 114n1. *See also El público*
Garden of Eden, 105

gender, 1; as binary, 138–39; issues of, 58; race, sexuality and, 4; as social construct, 9n2, 144–45; superiority of, 79
gender binary system, 119
gender fluidity, 132–36
gender identity, 2, 9, 149; acceptance of nonconforming, 142; ambiguous, 141; binary norms of, 134; conformity and, 132; journey of, 120–21; in *La llamada de Lauren*, 147, 149; nonbinary, 122; normalcy and, 140–41; performance, reality and, 145; sexuality and, 119–20, 138–39; shifting, 124; trivializing, 143
gender roles: assuming, 134; defying, 127–28; fear of, 136; fragility of, 124; in marriage, 138–40; nonbinary, 139–40; normalcy of, 131; public reaction to deviance surrounding, 142–45; validity of, 144–45
Gerber, Jane S., 12, 18
Gerli, E. Michael, 46
Gibson, Ian, 89–93, 114nn1–2
Gilman, Sander, 18–19, 72; *Difference and Pathology* by, 5, 58, 61; on Jewish self-hatred, 33, 58–59, 148; *Jewish Self-Hatred* by, 4
Golden Age of Spain, 2–3
Guillén, Gracia Diego, 19

Hardison Londré, Felicia, 95, 110
Harretche, María Estela, 109–11
Harris, Carolyn, 121, 131, 133, 140, 145
Hauer, Mary G., 54–55, 86n3
Haza, Ruano de la, 57
Hazm de Córdoba, Ibn, 63
Helen of Troy, 110
heraldry, symbols of, 36–37
Herodias (fictional character), 37–41
heteronormativity, 8–9; bending rules of, 138; in *La llamada de Lauren*, 135–36; rebellion against, 1; society vigilance of, 144

hoax (*mistificación*), 15; reality of, 29; victims to, 35
holy rain, in *El retablo de las maravillas*, 26, 35–36, 47–48
homophobia, 105; consequence of, 115n6; increased visibility of, 150; in *Schitt's Creek*, 155
homosexuality, 89, 92–93, 108, 138
Hornby, Richard, 4–6, 106, 120; on identity, 145; on *La llamada de Lauren*, 133; on metadrama, 132
horses, 116n15; black horse, 103–5; Freudian aspect of, 100–103; in *El público*, 97–105
How to Be an Antiracist (Kendi), 150–51

identity: construction of, 4; false, 1–2; fragility of, 32; Hornby on, 145; impure, 41, 47; lineage, illegitimacy and, 16; motivation and, 4, 17; provocative and controversial topic of, 150; self-doubt about real, 41; society-imposed, 119. See also specific topics
identity crisis, 6, 9; in *La llamada de Lauren*, 121–22; of Vélez de Guevara, 54–55
identity politics, legacy of, 150–55
illegitimate children, identity, lineage and, 16
illusion: creation of, 32; of Jewish identity, 18; reality and, 4–6
imagination, 29
improvisation, 133
individuality, 3, 106, 155
insanity, 29–30
integrity, 26
intelligence: cowardice and, 26–27; Jewish heritage and, 26
internal identity, 2
isolation, of Spain, 60

Jesus Christ, 30–31, 38
Jewish heritage, 3, 40, 147–48; of Cervantes Saavedra, 148; confession of, 30; intelligence and, 26; lineage and, 35; in *El retablo de las maravillas*, 24; spread of, 10n4
Jewish identity: disguising, 47; fear of, 49; illusion of, 18; self-doubt of, 32
Jewish Self-Hatred (Gilman), 4
John the Baptist, 37–38, 52n15
Judaism: symbols of, 34–35; theme of, in *El retablo de las maravillas*, 38–39

Kamen, Henry, 2–3, 10n3
Kendi, Ibram, 150–51
Kidd, Michael, 58–64, 79, 82
Kirschner, Teresa, 40–41, 49

Lamartina-Lens, Iride, 120–21
language: in *El retablo de las maravillas*, 51n7; Spanish, 67; transcending barriers of, 89; of *Virtudes vencen señales*, 86n5
Larson, Catherine, 51n7
Lauren's Call. See *La llamada de Lauren*
The Lawyer of Glass (*El licenciado vidriera*) (Cervantes Saavedra), 50n3
legitimacy, 34–35, 78
Leonard, Candyce, 130, 140, 144
limpieza de sangre laws. See *pureza de sangre* laws
The Limping Devil (*El diablo cojuelo*) (Vélez de Guevara), 87n7
lineage, 84; disguising, 55; fear of, 27; identity, illegitimacy and, 16; Jewish heritage and, 35; obsession with, 13, 18, 30, 37, 42–43, 148; in *El retablo de las maravillas*, 49–50; symbols of, 34–35
Lipski, John, 66
La llamada de Lauren (*Lauren's Call*) (Pedrero Díaz-Caneja), 1–2, 90; controversial, groundbreaking, 120; cross-dressing in, 122–37; fantasy in, 128; gender identity in, 147, 149; heteronormativity in, 135–36;

Hornby on, 133; identity crisis in, 121–22; illusion and reality in, 4–6; overview of, 8–9; "play within a play" aspect of, 4, 126; prologue for, 123–24; role-playing in, 131; self-hatred in, 127–28; sexual identity in, 8–9; transformation of characters in, 124–28
Lokos, Ellen, 12–13
Lope de Vega, 44–46, 50, 52n18, 53, 88n14
love, 90–91, 96; acceptable, 106; self, 69; transcendental power of, 99

The Manifesto of Surrealism (Breton), 96
manipulation, 22, 38, 79
Manson, William R., 57
marginalized groups, 2, 3, 57
Marrast, Robert, 37
marriage: communication within, 130–31; gender roles in, 138–40; intimacy in, 132–33; masculinity in, 126–27; metatheater and, 126–31
Martínez López, Enrique, 24–27, 51n11
Martínez Nadal, Rafael, 90–100, 103–5, 116n11
The Marvelous Puppet Show. *See El retablo de las maravillas*
masculitity, 144; in marriage, 126–27; proving, 136–37; threatened, 36; violent claims of, 112–13
masks: of conformity, 113–14, 148–49, 154; feminine, 110–13; oppression and, 109; sexual identity obscured by, 105–10; symbolic role of, 91
Mesopotamia, 73
metadrama, 5–6; Hornby on, 132; reality within, 132–33
metatheater, 4–6, 18–19; Abel on, 126; marriage and, 126–31; in *El retablo de las maravillas*, 46–50; seduction and, 131–38
mice, in *El retablo de las maravillas*, 32–37, 42–45

Middle Ages, 57
Millán, María Celementa, 105–6
mistificación. *See* hoax
Molho, Mauricio, 15, 36
Moner, Michel, 35–37
morality, 56, 75, 107; defending, 98; sexuality and, 90
mortality, 105
motivation, identity and, 4, 17

narcissism, of Filipo, 70, 76–77, 86
Narcissus, 68–69
narrow-mindedness, 2
Nazi Germany, 151
New Christians. *See cristianos nuevos*
New Testament, 30–31, 35, 37
Noah's ark, 37, 42
noble heritage, 55
nonheteronormativity, 125–26; from birth, 155; tolerance of, 149
normalcy, 1, 131, 140–41

Ocho comedias, y ocho entremeses nuevos, nunca representados (*Eight Comedies, and Eight New Interludes, Never Performed*) (Cervantes Saavedra), 13
O'Connor, Patricia, 123–24, 143
Old Christians. *See cristianos viejos*
Old Testament, 35
oppression, 2; of *conversos*, 11; overcoming, 3; as suffocating, 149
optimism, 3
Other, 4, 51n13; fear of, 5; labeling, 17, 150; power given to, 60; psychology of, 58; resisting classification of, 33; symbolism of, 64

Palencia, Benjamín, 90
pansexual identity, 155
paranoia, 50
Paulson, Michael G., 53
Peale, George C., 57
Pedrero Díaz-Caneja, Paloma, 1–2, 4–6; career of, 121–22; experiences

of, 145n3; hope of, 141–42; outrage expressed toward, 142; role-playing and, 120. *See also La llamada de Lauren*
performance: gender identity, reality and, 145; psychoanalysis, race and, 9n2; reality and, 6
performance theory, 6, 9n2
phallocentrism, 51n7
Philip II, 3
Philip III, 3
Philip IV, 3
"play within a play" aspect: of *La llamada de Lauren*, 4, 126; of *El retablo de las maravillas*, 4
Podol, Peter L., 123, 138
Pope Nicholas V, 11–12
popular culture, 133
Primo de Rivera, Miguel, 3, 90
psychoanalysis, performance, race and, 9n2
psychological pressures, 17
El público (The Audience) (García Lorca), 1–2; background on, 92–93; comparisons with, 115n7; critical approaches to, 91–92; horses depicted in, 97–105; innovative techniques used in, 94–96; main dilemma in, 90–91; overview of, 8–9; sexual identity in, 5, 8, 147; sexual orientation in, 154; symbolism in, 148–49; violence in, 111–12; women characters in, 112
public reaction, to deviance surrounding gender roles, 142–45
pureza de sangre (blood purity), 3, 6, 10n3; absurdity of, 37; *conversos* and, 88n16; ethnicity and, 148; high value placed on, 83; legitimacy of, 23–24; losing, 32; obsession with, 41, 45, 49–50; proving, 21–22; value of, 19; in *Virtudes vencen señales*, 84
pureza de sangre laws, 11–13

purity, 133

Rabelais and His World (Bakhtin), 6, 125
race, 1; ethnicity and, 149; gender, sexuality and, 4; issues of, 58; nobility and, 76; performance, psychoanalysis and, 9n2
racial discrimination: instruments of, 35; in *El retablo de las maravillas*, 151; in *Virtudes vencen señales*, 71–72
racial equality, 8, 56
racial identity, 2; acceptance of, 56; denying, 8; of Filipo, 57–59; in *Virtudes vencen señales*, 147–48
racism: definition of, 150; modern-day, 156n1; during Renaissance, 71, 81; systemic, 150; in *Virtudes vencen señales*, 55–56, 87n8, 150
Ramos de Castro, Epifanio, 20, 28
reality: fantasy and, 29, 46–48; Filipo confronting, 151; gender identity, performance and, 145; illusion and, 4–6; imagined, 6; within metadrama, 132–33; performance and, 6
reception theory, 51n7
Reed, Corey, 14, 31, 37–39
Renaissance, 62, 71, 81
reputation, 20
El retablo de las maravillas (The Marvelous Puppet Show) (Cervantes Saavedra), 1–2, 116n17; characters in, 19–22, 51n8; critical approaches to, 18–19; discrimination criticized in, 151; ethnic identity in, 147; holy rain in, 26, 35–36; Jewish heritage in, 24; Judaism as theme in, 38–39; language in, 51n7; lineage in, 49–50; metatheatre in, 46–50; mice in, 32–37, 42–45; overview of, 6–7; "play within a play" aspect of, 4; roots of, 13–15; self-hatred in, 18; stereotypes and rustic characters in, 24–28; symbolism in, 34–37; tricksters in, 14–21, 31, 46–50
role-playing, 5–6; in *La llamada de Lauren*, 131; Pedrero Díaz-Caneja and, 120
Rubia Barcia, José, 98, 103

sadomasochism, 115n6
Sáenz, María Ascensión, 94, 99–100
Salome (fictional character), 37–41
scapegoats, 28–32
Schaffer, Quentin, 152
Schitt's Creek, 155
Second Republic, 3
Sedgwick, Eve Kosofsky, 112
self-acceptance, 149
self-definition, 2
self-doubt: of Jewish identity, 32; projection of, 30; about real identities, 41
self-hatred: Black identity and, 69; as deep-rooted, 86; definition of, 4; of García Lorca, 114; Gilman on Jewish, 33, 58–59, 148; Jewish, 32–34; in *La llamada de Lauren*, 127–28; in *El retablo de las maravillas*, 18; in *Virtudes vencen señales*, 7, 58
self-identification, of Filipo, 65–69
self-importance, 20, 43
Sephardic Jews of Spain, 11
Serrano, Virtudes, 139
sexual acts, indecent, 110
sexual gratification, 105
sexual identity, 2, 149; conformity and, 90, 119; disturbing images used to convey messages about, 94; exploration of, during Carnival, 140–41; gender and, 122; in *La llamada de Lauren*, 8–9; masks obscuring, 105–10; in *El público*, 5, 8, 147; punishment for showing, 109; repression of, 113–14; revealing, 91; struggle with, 106; transformation of, 129–30
sexuality: audience pondering questions of, 96; exploration of, 109–10; gender identity and, 138–39; of horses, 102–3; morality and, 90; race, gender and, 4; symbols of, 34–35
sexual orientation, 1, 110; cross-dressing and, 9, 138–42; of García Lorca, 89–90; influence on, 136–37; political beliefs and, 116n12; in *El público*, 154
Sigura, Antonio de, 12
skepticism, 30, 51n7
slavery, 57
slaves, 57, 113
Smith, Paul Julian, 104
social change, 95
social norms, 60
sodomy, 36
Spadaccini, Nicholas Cervantes, 35
Spain, isolation of, 60
Spanish Civil War, 93
Spanish Inquisition, 2–3, 11, 50n1, 55; murders by, 55; repercussions of, 3
Spanish language, 67
speech-act theory, 51
Spencer, Forrest Eugene, 53–54
spiritual crisis, 121
stereotypes, 57; Cervantes Saavedra depicting, 24–27; of Jewish people, 26, 153; realities confused for, 4; in *El retablo de las maravillas*, 24–28; validity of, 28
surrealism: definition of, 96–97; García Lorca and, 96–97
surrealist manifestos, 5
surrealist movement, 97
symbolism: of femininity, 129; of masks, 91, 105–10; of mice, 42–43; of Other, 64; in *El público*, 148–49; in *El retablo de las maravillas*, 34–37

temptation, 105
theater: Brecht on modern, 124; as identity laboratory, 106; open-air, 98, 105–10; as vehicle for social change, 95
theatricality: characters awareness of, 48; of tricksters, 147–48
theatrical techniques, 94–96
To Have and Have Not (film), 133
Torres-Pou, Joan, 122, 134, 136–38

tragedy, rules of, 94
transphobia, 150
treachery, 34–35, 38
tricksters: in *El retablo de las maravillas*, 14–21, 31, 46–50; theatricality of, 147–48
Trump, Donald, 150–51

Vélez de Guevara, Luis, 1–2, 5–8, 116n17; *El diablo cojuelo* by, 87n7; Filipo connection with, 82–86; insecurity of, 55; overview of, 53; popularity of, 58, 87n7; on women, 80. *See also Virtudes vencen señales*
Vested Interests (Garber), 9
La vida es sueño (Calderón de la Barca), 58, 87n6, 87n8
violence, 3; in *El público*, 111–12; sadomasochism and, 115n6; between workers and employers, 90
virility, symbols of, 36–37
Virtudes vencen señales (*Virtues overcome Signs*) (Vélez de Guevara), 1–2, 5; conception story in, 62–63; critical approaches to, 55–59; identity issues in, 57; language and style of, 86n5; overview of, 7–8; *pureza de sangre* in, 84; racial discrimination in, 71–72; racial identity in, 147–48; racism in, 55–56, 87n8, 150; xenophobia in, 59–60, 75, 81. *See also* Filipo
vulgarity, 45–46
vulnerability, 50

Wardropper, Bruce W., 29–30, 35–38
Weege, Cornelia, 128
What Is Surrealism (Breton), 96–97
whiteness, 59
white supremacy, 150–51
Wilson, Edward M., 53
women: attitudes about, 88n15; characters, in *El público*, 112; condition of, 85; as emotional, 80; sexual attraction toward, 119; as social prop, 112

xenophobia: fighting against, 150; in *Virtudes vencen señales*, 59–60, 75, 81

Zatlin, Phyllis, 122
Zepeda, Karla, 134–35

About the Author

Beth Bernstein is a senior lecturer of Spanish in the Department of World Languages and Literatures at Texas State University. She is originally from Wisconsin and completed her PhD in Spanish literature at the University of New Mexico. Her specialty is seventeenth-century, twentieth-century, and modern peninsular theater and poetry, and she is especially interested in issues of identity. Beth enjoys teaching Spanish language courses, as well as innovating curricula exploring issues of identity in Spanish literature. She also created and organizes the *Intercambio*, a Spanish-language event which is an opportunity for students from Spanish-speaking countries to meet with Spanish language learners and share in a cultural dialogue. Beth lives in Austin, Texas with her husband, two children, and her pet cockatiel.

www.ingramcontent.com/pod-product-compliance
Lightning Source LLC
Chambersburg PA
CBHW020122010526
44115CB00008B/939